Tu Fu is, by universal consent, the greatest poet of the Chinese tradition. In the epochal An Lu-shan rebellion, he alone of his contemporaries consistently recorded in poetry the great events and pervasive sufferings of the time. For a millennium now, his poetry has been accepted as epitomizing the Chinese moral conscience at its highest, and as such his work has been placed almost beyond the reach of criticism. Indeed, objectivity about Tu Fu is often viewed as criticism of him.

In *Reconsidering Tu Fu*, Eva Shan Chou proposes that these thorny problems be met by separating his legacy into two distinct but related aspects: as cultural monument and as a great and original poet. Examining Tu Fu as cultural icon, she investigates the evolution and nature of his reputation and shows its continuing effect upon interpretations of his poetry. In her discussions of the poetic legacy, she introduces concepts relating to subject matter, style, genre, structure, theme, and voice, in order to provide for a fruitful reconsideration of his poetry. Many poems are discussed and translated, both well known and less familiar. Dr. Chou's analyses are original in their formulation and also considerate of the many fine readings of traditional commentators.

James R. Hightower's foreword introduces the book.

RECONSIDERING TU FU

Other books in the series

William T. Graham, Jr. "The Lament for the South": Yü Hsin's *Ai Chiang-Nan Fu*

Michael Godley The Mandarin-Capitalists from Nanyang: Overseas Chinese Enterprise in the Modernisation of China, 1893–1911

Charles Backus The Nan-chao Kingdom and T'ang China's Southwestern Frontier

A. R. Davis T'ao Yüan-ming: His Works and Their Meaning

Victor H. Mair Tunhuang Popular Narratives

Ira E. Kasoff The Thought of Chang Tsai

Robert Hymes Statesmen and Gentlemen: The Elite of Fu-chou, Chang-hsi, in Northern and Southern Sung

D. L. McMullen State and Scholars in T'ang China

Tim Wright Coal Mining in China's Economy and Society, 1895–1937

Chih-P'ing Chou Yüan Hung-tao and the Kung-an School

Arthur Waldron The Great Wall of China: From History to Myth

Hugh R. Clark Community, Trade, and Networks: Southern Fujian Province from the Third to the Thirteenth Centuries

Jo-Shui Chen Liu Tsung-yüan and Intellectual Change in T'ang China, 773–819

Brian E. McKnight Law and Order in Sung China

J. D. Schmidt Stone Lake: The Poetry of Fan Chengda

Denis Twitchett The Writing of Official History Under the T'ang

David Pong Shen Pao-chen and China's Modernization in the Nineteenth Century

J. D. Schmidt Within the Human Realm: The Poetry of Huang Zunxian, 1848–1905

Eva Shan Chou Reconsidering Tu Fu: Literary Greatness and Cultural Context

Reconsidering Tu Fu

Literary greatness and cultural context

Eva Shan Chou

CAMBRIDGE
UNIVERSITY PRESS

Published by the Press Syndicate of the University of Cambridge
The Pitt Building, Trumpington Street, Cambridge CB2 1RP
40 West 20th Street, New York, NY 10011-4211, USA
10 Stamford Road, Oakleigh, Melbourne 3166, Australia

© Cambridge University Press 1995

First published 1995

Printed in the United States of America

Library of Congress Cataloging-in-Publication Data
Chou, Eva Shan
Reconsidering Tu Fu: literary greatness and cultural context/Eva Shan Chou
p.   cm. – (Cambridge studies in Chinese history, literature, and institutions)
Includes bibliographical references and index.
ISBN 0-521-44039-4
1. Tu Fu, 712-770 – Criticism and interpretation.   I. Chou, E.
Shan (Eva Shan)   II. Tu Fu, 712-770.   Poems.   Selections.   1995.
III. Series.
PL2675.R43   1995   895.1'13 – dc20
94-25029
CIP

A catalog record for this book is available from the British Library.

ISBN   0-521-44039-4 Hardback

Contents

Foreword

Even the most casual acquaintance with Chinese poetry will have made the name of Tu Fu a familiar one, as the poet acknowledged throughout history by his countrymen to be China's greatest. And it is not only the poetry that is admired; the poet himself inspires respect, veneration even, as a good man. Though separated from us by a gap of thirteen centuries and an unfamiliar culture, we feel we know him, because the 1,400-odd poems reliably ascribed to him constitute a record of his life and his times that has earned him the epithet of poet-historian. There are poets of whom we know very little whose poetry is highly esteemed – Homer or Shakespeare, for example – and others of whom what we know does not enhance our appreciation of their poetry. In the case of Tu Fu, the identification of poet with the poetry is complete, to the point where it is possible to wonder how much of the esteem for the poetry is a product of admiration of the poet: how would we read "Journey to the North" if we thought it had been written by the lively Li Po? And conversely, how much do we like a poet who is continually telling us what a good man he is?

These are awkward questions that do not usually get asked. Professor Chou faces such problems and suggests solutions with far-ranging implications for future scholarship. By examining the part played in the judgment of Tu Fu's poetry by his status as a cultural icon created by the Confucian orientation of traditional critics, she is able to separate the "poetic and cultural factors in the legacy of Tu Fu," as she puts it, and to take a fresh look at the poetry. In the process she introduces a number of analytic concepts that significantly enhance our understanding of his work. Principal among these is an abrupt change of topic and tone that seems to break a poem into two unrelated parts, apparently fracturing its unity. She argues persuasively that this structural disjunction can be seen as a functional part of a poem that reinforces its effect by referring us back to the poet himself.

Professor Chou's criticism of poetry inspires respect. Her analysis is of great subtlety and originality, clearly presented and mercifully eschewing fashionable literary-critical jargon. Scholars already familiar with the poems she cites will recognize the aptness of her observations and will find their appreciation of the poems increased. This has certainly been my experience. On the other hand, those who come to Tu Fu from outside the tradition or whose access is limited to translations will be afforded a real grasp of the poetic achievement of the original Chinese versification and a glimpse of its dazzling dexterity. This is literary criticism of high order, focused on the poetry and not constrained by theory or dogma.

Despite the profoundly novel ideas advanced, this is not a debunking, revisionist study. Professor Chou raises questions ignored, glossed over, or rationalized by traditional Chinese critics, and she arrives at readings that make it possible to appreciate the poetry at its real value. Tu Fu emerges with his work newly illuminated and his reputation intact, both as a poet and as a good man.

James R. Hightower
Victor S. Thomas Professor of Chinese Literature, Emeritus
Harvard University

Preface

The study of a monument is not easy to write. For ten centuries, scholars and appreciative readers have devoted themselves to the examination of Tu Fu's every word and action. Erudition and personal attachment together produced a body of work on this poet that is formidable not only in volume but in dedication. Indeed the intense personal devotion which Tu Fu has always been able to inspire secured for both his poetry and the responses to it a certain immunity from objective evaluation. Today, when the personal patterns of the cultivated past cannot be convincingly reproduced, a critic venturing upon the study of Tu Fu cannot presume to the roles of either learned scholar or passionate reader in the old mold. Other available roles for the modern critic seem limited to the false promise of revisionism or the naïveté of a fresh Western approach. It is hoped that the present work has avoided these tendencies by undertaking to examine Tu Fu in terms of his two distinct but related legacies, as a cultural monument and as a figure of great poetic achievements. In approaching Tu Fu anew, my intentions were also to reformulate and answer some questions that are often asked about Tu Fu and to pose questions that I have not found asked elsewhere.

A formal occasion for the expression of gratitude brings on reflectiveness and a certain somberness. Life engenders debts of gratitude of many kinds, and in an academic life, where intellectual and personal debts are often intermingled, it is difficult adequately to express all that is due.

My first thanks are owed to Professor James R. Hightower of Harvard University and Professor Ronald C. Egan, now of the University of California, Santa Barbara. Not the least of their importance to the present work is chronological. Professors Hightower and Egan had earlier supervised my Ph.D. thesis, which concerned a group of Tu Fu's late poems and their employment of allusion. When, upon its completion, I decided to put it aside and to make an entirely new start, this time analyzing Tu Fu's poetry as a whole, they demurred at the practical consequences but were steadily encouraging in their confidence that such a project was possible. Each has generously read the chapters of this work in more than one version and made many improvements and corrections. Professor Hightower's sensitive appreciation for poetry has been a constant source of inspiration to me, especially in today's academia, where poetry is so often treated only as a "text." Moreover, his unerring sense for weak or trite arguments has saved me from many missteps. I am honored that he has written a Foreword here. Professor Egan has been both teacher and friend, invariably generous in sharing his insights and his extensive knowledge. In particular, the general argument of the section "Tu Fu and the Tradition of Tu Fu" in Chapter 1 was developed over the course of several months of enlightening conversations with Professor Egan. I am most grateful for his constant encouragement over the years.

To many others I owe much for advice and help on a range of matters. I thank Professors Denis C. Twitchett and Kao Yu-kung, both of Princeton University, for their support. Professor Kang-i Sun Chang of Yale University came to my aid, both practically and with moral support, at a difficult time. I would like also to thank Professors Donald Holzman of Institut des Hautes Études Chinoises, David Knechtges of the University of Washington, Patrick D. Hanan of Harvard University, Morris Rossabi of CUNY and Columbia University, Arthur N. Waldron of the U.S. Naval War College and Brown University, and Dore Levy of Brown University. Dr. Grace Chüan-ying Yen of Academia Sinica, Taipei, made comments about early versions of the manuscript that were both sensitive and rigorous. Two anonymous referees for Cambridge University Press offered valuable suggestions which improved the order of presentation of material in Chapter 1. The members of the Chinese Study Group, with whom I enjoyed nearly five years of monthly meetings in New York City, were a source of friendly intellectual stimulation; they included Cheng P'ei-k'ai, Wang Hao, Wu Wei-yuan and Hsieh Shih-min, Li Yao-tsung, Yü Kuang, and Hung Ming-shui. I also thank Christie Lerch, Camilla Palmer, and Elizabeth Neal at Cambridge University Press for their expert assistance.

A fellowship from the National Endowment for the Humanities provided me with a year in which to work through the basic issues underlying Chapters 3 and 4. A travel grant from the American Council of Learned Societies enabled me to present a paper at a conference at the University of Durham, England, that resulted in some parts of Chapter 1. I am grateful as well to the Bunting Institute, Radcliffe College, and to its director, Dr. Florence Ladd, for a fellowship year that provided intellectual stimulation and collegial friendships. A subvention from the Chiang Ching-kuo Foundation defrayed some of the costs of publication, for which I owe thanks. Chapter 2 has appeared in a somewhat different form in the *Harvard Journal of Asiatic Studies*; this chapter benefited from the meticulous attention of the journal's editor, Dr. Joanna Handlin Smith.

I cannot end without acknowledging the friends and family who supported my work without questioning its practicality: my mother, Jun-mei Chang Chou, and my sisters May, Ida, and Ana; Christie and Chris Wilbur, Carol Munroe and Andraś Riedlmayer, Andrew Klein, Elizabeth Perry, Marsha Collins, Dennis Grafflin, Wendy Zeldin, Ginny Mayer. My daughter, Heather, has helped put books in library return slots since she could lift books and stand on tiptoe. My husband, Richard G. McCarrick, has by his unfailing support and interest provided the secure and appreciative haven that so sorrowfully eluded the subject of this volume.

1
The legacy of Tu Fu

Tu Fu is, by universal consent, the greatest poet of the Chinese tradition. In Chinese culture, his works have been virtually canonized because, as the expression of the Chinese mind and moral being in their highest form, their supremacy in literature has been placed beyond merely literary considerations. He himself has been viewed as the embodiment of public-minded dedication and unceasing loyalty, a man who sought all his life, with great constancy, to serve his sovereign and his state. In the literary matters of innovative technique and the establishment of many new subgenres, Tu Fu is also seen as without peer: his precedent was influential equally in setting a poetic rule and in breaking it. In the allusive, imitation-based tradition of classical poetry, his work constituted an endless source of quotation and precedent, the lines studied and imitated, the imagery echoed, the subgenres enlarged.

When the history of T'ang poetry came to be constructed during the Sung dynasty, admiration for Tu Fu's technical brilliance and for the moral excellence of his character combined to raise him from relative obscurity to the apex of T'ang poetry. His work, and that of his contemporary Li Po, defined the boundaries of the High T'ang period, and this period in turn came to be identified with the extraordinary flourishing of culture and political power seen in the middle decades of the eighth century. Although in truth the culture of the elite was to evolve to a higher, more sophisticated, and more subtle level in later dynasties, the literati of those centuries looked back to the T'ang era for their foundation and inspiration. In the manner of Confucius, they preferred to regard their innovations as transmissions or revivals of past achievements. In Tu Fu's work, they found a poet who was able to satisfy all the levels – aesthetic, moral, and human – on which the traditional scholar-official defined himself. The editions, commentaries, anthologies, selections, and remarks (*shih-hua*) produced by traditional connoisseurship and scholarship proliferated. Already by the end of the fourteenth century, works on Tu Fu far outnumbered works on any other poet and they further multiplied with each succeeding century.[1] Even under the much altered conditions of today, Tu Fu is still routinely acknowledged to be the greatest Chinese poet. Now, as then, his reputation has been taken under government patronage. The sponsorship of monuments to Tu Fu, a tradition that dates to the Sung dynasty, is continued today by an elaborate complex of temples, halls, and gateways in Szechuan built on the putative site of his Thatched Hut, a mecca for visitors, both domestic and foreign.

Historical background and biography

The poetry of Tu Fu was written entirely out of his own experiences and the events he witnessed, but he lived in a fateful time, and so they gave him large themes. The crucial event in Tu Fu's life and work, and also in the history of the T'ang dynasty, occurred in the eleventh month of 755, when a brilliant era of prosperity and expansionism under Emperor Hsuan-tsung (r. 712–56) was brought to an abrupt end with the An Lu-shan rebellion. Fiscal, administrative, and military reforms during the first decades of Hsuan-tsung's reign had renewed the fortunes of the empire. By the 750s, the extent of its domain and the prosperity of its inhabitants invited comparisons, which were indeed frequently made, with the greatest moments of earlier Chinese empires. The onset of the rebellion revealed the interdependence and instability of the forces which held that empire together. Tu Fu's poetry, reflecting many of the shifting and dramatic events of the time, can be read on one level as a record of the devastation and decline of empire set in motion by that rebellion.

The rebellion, known in history after its instigator, An Lu-shan, was brought to an inconclusive end in 763, eight years after its beginning, but its repercussions lasted throughout the century and a half remaining to the dynasty. In the initial months, the rebellion was a clear-cut affair. Despite the many dramatic turns of fortune in those months, there were only two main actors (the imperial forces and the rebel forces under An Lu-shan), and the action followed a certain military and geographic logic. The rebels' choice of a line of advance and of targets, and the loyalists' choice of places at which to make a defensive stand, both followed the logic of a struggle for the control of the empire. The rebels began by making a rapid advance from their base in Yu-chou (modern

1. See the encyclopedic compilation *Tu chi shu lu*, by Chou Ts'ai-ch'üan, which provides a bibliographic description of every known edition of Tu Fu's works, including editions of selected poems and editions no longer extant.

Peking) down the Central Plains that lay on either side of the Yellow
River. Within a month their forces had captured the secondary capital of
Loyang. Six months later the main capital of Ch'ang-an fell to the rebel
forces. Initially Ch'ang-an had been ably defended from the rebels in the
Central Plains by the impregnable T'ung Pass, but the army guarding
the pass was ordered, against military wisdom, to move out onto the
plains to give battle, rather than merely holding their defensive positions. With the capitals lost, the choice on the imperial side was between
striking at the rebel base in Yu-chou or attempting to recover the two
capitals. The latter, more politically symbolic, course was taken, and in
the next year (757) first Ch'ang-an and then Lo-yang were retaken by
the imperial forces, with the help of Uighur mercenaries. Hereafter,
however, the initial simplicity of allegiances and goals disappeared. The
imperial victory was limited to the recovery of the capitals, whereas the
rebel forces not only were unsubdued but now presented a more complex challenge. The leadership of the rebels passed by patricide to An
Lu-shan's son, and at the same time Shih Ssu-ming rose from among An
Lu-shan's generals to take command of a separate, nominally allied,
rebel force. The division of rebel command coincided with the loss of
logistical imperative on the rebels' part. Their forces, already occupying
the Central Plains and unable to retake the capitals, lacked an obvious
military goal and found themselves drawn into defensive campaigns to
retain territories they had previously captured and to defend their line
of supply from Yu-chou.

The fragmentation of command in the rebel ranks was matched by
confused strategy on the imperial side. Control was difficult to assert,
since opportunistic secondary rebellions flared in many parts of the
empire. The imperial side faced the need for internal reorganization just
at a time when the rebel situation had become more complex. Emperor
Hsuan-tsung had abdicated to Su-tsung after the fall of Ch'ang-an, and
Hsuan-tsung's unpopular chief minister, Yang Kuo-chung, had been
executed to retain the loyalty of the troops. The subsequent reapportion-
ment of power took place at a time when the quantity of power had
suddenly increased. Generals defending the throne emerged among the
chief beneficiaries, for power devolved upon individual generals for long
periods of time, in civil as well as military matters. The power of the court
was weakened rather than strengthened by the massive arming of its
subjects, for the court's own generals became potential rebels. Concerted military action became more difficult to undertake at precisely
the time when the military situation was more difficult to control. A
prolonged stalemate resulted between imperial and rebel forces. The
campaigns which interrupted this stalemate at intervals – most notably a

3

great assault on the rebel stronghold of Hsiang-chou (near Lo-yang) in 759, carried out by a combined force of nine imperial armies[2] – did not alter it markedly, and it was not until 763, eight years after the rebellion began, that all sides had been sufficiently weakened to agree to a settlement. This came down to accepting the existing division of territorial control, modified by the language of sovereignty: a nominal end to the rebellion was obtained by the surrender of the rebel generals, while the emperor in turn confirmed them in their commands.

The An-Shih rebellion permanently weakened the T'ang dynasty, for imperial control was never fully recovered in the remaining century and a half of T'ang rule. Control of the armies was essentially ceded to generals whose allegiance the court was too weak to compel. The revenues and policies of the provinces lying in the Yellow River plains to the northeast (modern Hopei, Shansi, and Shantung) were never successfully brought under the court's command. More immediately relevant to Tu Fu, the uneasy peace obtained in the Central Plains had little effect in Szechuan and along the Yangtze River, where Tu Fu lived from 759 onward. All up and down the Yangtze and its Hsiang River tributary, local rebellions continued to flare up. In addition, raids and incursions by Tibetans upon a weak Szechuan were frequent. Tu Fu himself never saw the end of warfare, and to the end of his life his poetry reflected the displacements and devastations of wartime.

When the An Lu-shan rebellion began, Tu Fu was forty-four, and almost all his great poetry still lay ahead of him. Tu Fu said of himself that he had written copiously since childhood, but very little has survived that dates from before the onset of the rebellion in 755: only about 130 of some 1,400 extant poems. Although this early period did produce some notable poems, the major themes and the tragic vision were still to come. In a sense, the rebellion gave him his subject: the crucial event in his life and poetry centered on the crucial event of the T'ang dynasty.

Tu Fu was in many ways an unlikely candidate for this exemplary role. His life, whether before or after 755, when recounted without the poetry, makes a record of indifferent achievement and gives little hint of the esteem in which he was to be held by posterity.[3] Tu Fu was born in

2. In Tu Fu's poems, the aftermath of this assault is famously the setting for "Three Officials," 53/3/9–11, and "Three Partings," 54/3/12–14.

3. Brief official biographical accounts are given in *Chiu T'ang shu* 190C.5054–7 and *Hsin T'ang shu* 201.5736–8. Accounts more detailed than these depend largely on information gleaned from the poems. William Hung, in *Tu Fu: China's Greatest Poet*, translates 374 poems of biographical and poetic importance and joins them with a biographical narrative. See also A. R. Davis, *Tu Fu*, which gives a clear overview. Political events and

712 into a family of the official class whose distant ancestry he was proud to trace to the famous third-century general and *Tso chuan* commentator Tu Yü (222–84). In a more recent generation, Tu Fu's grandfather Tu Shen-yen was a middle-rank official, sufficiently notable as a poet to receive a biographical account in the "Garden of Letters" section in both of the T'ang histories.[4] Little, however, is known of Tu Fu's father, aside from some of his official positions.[5]

Tu Fu's life, like that of any member of the official class, had as its inevitable punctuation the record of his attempts to gain office and their results. Tu Fu at first sought to take the examination route to office. He probably first took the examinations in the mid-730s, when he was twenty-three or twenty-four.[6] Though he was perhaps a candidate from the capital prefecture, the prestigious provenance proved to be of no avail. He was unsuccessful, perhaps (following a hint in a later poem) the only one from the capital prefecture to fail that year.[7] The question of why he failed has consumed much ink because the candidate is Tu Fu, later to be so esteemed for his literary achievements. It may be, however, that one need look no farther for a cause than his having omitted to cultivate his connections in the capital.[8] Tu Fu next took the examinations some ten years later, in 747, again unsuccessfully. This time the cause is known to have been the chief minister Li Lin-fu, who, notorious

biographical information, copiously supported by quotations from the poems, are listed year by year in *Tu Fu nien-p'u*. This work also lists under its annual headings the poems known to have been written in that year or judged by the editors to be consistent with composition in that year.

4. Tu Shen-yen's biographies are in *Chiu T'ang shu* 190A.4999–5000 and *Hsin T'ang shu* 201.5735–6. *Chiu T'ang shu* places Tu Shen-yen and Tu Fu in separate chapters, whereas *Hsin T'ang shu* places Tu Fu's biography after his grandfather's. For a summary of the scholarship concerning the ancestry and family of Tu Fu, see Hung, *Tu Fu*, pp. 16–20, and his *Notes*, pp. 13–22.

5. Many issues connected with Tu Fu's life are much controverted, but they are only briefly mentioned in this summary of his life. For a careful reconsideration of such issues as the composition of Tu Fu's family, the dates of his examinations, and the dates of the rhapsodies offered to the emperor, see Ch'en Wen-hua, *Tu Fu chuan-chi T'ang Sung tzu-liao k'ao-pien* (hereafter *T'ang Sung tzu-liao k'ao*), pp. 1–120.

6. The exact date of Tu Fu's first attempt to pass the examinations is not known, four dates having been suggested by commentators (734, 735, 736, and 737). Hung argues for 736 (*Tu Fu*, p. 27, and *Notes*, p. 25), whereas Ch'en Wen-hua prefers 735 (*T'ang Sung tzu-liao k'ao*, pp. 55–66).

7. William Hung quotes the line "Alone I went to make my farewells" from "Wanderings of My Prime" and suggests that "alone" means that the other prefectural candidates had all passed (*Tu Fu*, p. 28). He also speculates that Tu Fu entered as a candidate from Ch'ang-an rather than Lo-yang, the prefecture to which his home village of Yen-shih belonged.

8. See, for example, the sensible discussion in Li Ju-lun, "Lo-ti-shih yü Tu Fu lo-ti" 落第詩 與杜甫落第, in his *Tu shih lun kao*, pp. 89–94.

already for the small number of men passed during his years, this time passed no one at all.[9] It was Tu Fu's second and last attempt.

Four years later, in 751, Tu Fu made an attempt to obtain a post by applying directly, so to speak, to the emperor. He presented a set of rhapsodies (*fu*) through an extra-examination avenue whereby if a submission caught the imperial attention a literary office might follow.[10] For a brief moment, "the emperor marveled at his talent,"[11] but after the initial flurry of hope, this too came to nothing. A second attempt to gain the notice of the throne in 754 and a third, possibly in the following year, were received with complete silence. It was not until the very eve of the rebellion that Tu Fu succeeded in obtaining a position, a low-ranking sinecure in the heir apparent's establishment. Before taking up this position, Tu Fu made a journey to Feng-hsien County, some miles northeast of Ch'ang-an, where he had recently settled his family. It was while he was at Feng-hsien that events overtook him. An Lu-shan began his revolt, and the rapid advance of the rebel forces meant that Tu Fu never took up this first post that had been won after such a length of time.

The nature of his struggle for a livelihood changed with the onset of the rebellion, and with the passage of years it grew more desperate. But this was to become apparent only gradually. Initially Tu Fu did well out of the rebellion, for, a few months after it began, a demonstration of loyalty brought him the office at the emperor's court that he had so ardently sought. Shortly after the onset of the rebellion, apparently with his family now resettled in another village, Tu Fu had set out with the intention of joining the emperor in exile. His next poems show him to be in rebel-held Ch'ang-an, but when he was able to slip away from there, he made his way to the emperor's court in exile rather than going back to his family. For this act of loyalty in a perilous time, Tu Fu was rewarded with the first position he actually held, Commissioner of the Right.[12] It was in this office that he witnessed the imperial recovery of Ch'ang-an half a year later (in the ninth month of 757), and it was this office that he held for some months at the court of a recovered Ch'ang-an. Thus in its first year and a half, the rebellion produced for Tu Fu a post in the

9. This according to Yuan Chieh's testimony. Yuan Chieh too was failed in this round. He memorably explained Li Lin-fu's manipulation of the examination results in his "An Account for a Friend" 喻友, *Ch'üan T'ang wen, chüan* 383.
10. The system is described in *Chiu T'ang shu* 43.414; *Hsin T'ang shu* 47.2; translated, des Rotours, *Examens*, pp. 143–6. See also Hung, *Tu Fu*, p. 67, and McMullen, *State and Scholars in T'ang China*, p. 138.
11. 帝奇之. So said *Chiu T'ang shu* 190C.5054 and *Hsin T'ang shu* 201.5763. Tu Fu gives his own account in "Wanderings of My Prime," lines 57–8, and in "Don't Doubt Me," lines 3–7.
12. *Yu-shih-yi* 右拾遺; see des Rotours, *Fonctionnaires*, 1:187.

central bureaucracy and also a chance personally to witness dramatic and historic events from a central vantage point. A natural expectation of a quick victory and a return to normalcy seem to have guided Tu Fu's actions, and indeed initially events seemed to bear out such hopes.

This possibly heady tenure at court did not last long. Tu Fu seems to have been unsuited for the rigors of political life. Early in 758, as the result of a larger political quarrel at court, he was exiled to a provincial post at Hua-chou, a town which lay between Ch'ang-an and the T'ung Pass. After about a year in Hua-chou, Tu Fu seems to have decided to take his family out of the Central Plains, where battles still raged. We do know that in 759 he and his family left the Central Plains for Ch'in-chou in the far west, and that from there they went on to Szechuan Province in the southwest. It was, in the event, a permanent departure. Although in the eleven years remaining to him Tu Fu never ceased to make plans to return to the capital area, he was to die on a tributary of the Yangtze River.

From the time of his departure from the Central Plains, Tu Fu's fortunes gradually but steadily declined. He was in Szechuan Province for five years, the latter part of his stay apparently prolonged by the patronage of a younger friend, Yen Wu, governor of Szechuan, whom he had first met at court in Ch'ang-an. Yen was a dependable patron, it seems,[13] for the Szechuan years – the Thatched Hut years – were relatively serene. Tu Fu left Szechuan, however, about the time of Yen Wu's death in 766, for reasons he does not mention in his surviving poems. The remaining four years of his life were spent in the river towns of the Yangtze, moving by stages downriver, in increasingly poor health. His longest stay was in K'uei-chou (766–8), where he purchased a farm with the help of another patron and where two years of a settled life produced the great poems of his last years. Then Tu Fu left K'uei-chou, again for reasons not stated or hinted at in his poems. The movements of his final two years seemed to be dictated by the search for a patron, a search that became quite desperate as ill luck dogged his tracks. One patron he sought at Heng-chou, on the Hsiang tributary of the Yangtze, had just

13. So one must suppose. There is much speculation concerning the relationship between Tu Fu and Yen Wu. A number of strange anecdotes about it are reported in Yen Wu's biographies (*Chiu T'ang shu* 117.3395–6 and *Hsin T'ang shu* 129.4484) as well as in Tu Fu's biographies. For example, Tu Fu is said to have sat on the end of Yen Wu's bed and taunted him; Yen Wu is said to have tried to kill Tu Fu and in fact to have killed one of his own father's wives. Plausible explanations of these episodes have been difficult to compose. The numerous suggestions that have been hazarded are discussed in Hung, *Notes*, pp. 93–5, and in Ch'en Wen-hua, *T'ang Sung tzu-liao k'ao*, pp. 147–74 . One must suppose that some complex relationship existed between the two men that could not be conveyed by the usual biographical anecdotes; hence the inexplicable stories.

been transferred to T'an-chou downriver, where in any case he soon died. At the same time, a local rebellion broke out in T'an-chou, and so Tu Fu wavered, adrift between Heng-chou and T'an-chou, with no reliable news and no prospects. Finally he made plans to go on with his family to Pin-chou, where an uncle was an official. This turned out to be the last journey Tu Fu undertook. Heavy rains turned him back and, at T'an-chou once again, Tu Fu died.

With Tu Fu's death, the record, which is derived entirely from references in his poetry, ends. One wonders about the fate of the family left in such straits upon the death of its head, about his wife and children, who had, as he repeatedly wrote, followed him about in their refugee life. Fan Huang, who collected 290 poems of Tu Fu's for an edition shortly after Tu Fu's death, mentions that two sons, Tsung-wen and Tsung-wu, were then living in the Chiang-ling area (near Tung-t'ing Lake). Some years later, a son, probably Tsung-wen, was employed in a prefectural office in Kuei-lin. A grandson reappears in history, still in Chiang-ling, with a request to Yuan Chen (779–831) for a grave inscription for Tu Fu. His request, made in 813, is the last historical trace of Tu Fu's descendents. Self-proclaimed descendants continued to surface periodically. In the twelfth century, the grandson of one Tu Hsin-lao produced a family genealogy that showed him to be a thirteenth-generation descendant of Tu Fu's. In the twentieth century, scholars in the adventurous early years of archaeological and anthropological fieldwork met villagers near Lo-yang who claimed descent from the poet.[14]

Recounted in this way, Tu Fu's life makes sorry reading. Exuberance, however, and even gaiety thread through his life. A simple change of focus to the periods between the failed examinations and the frequent moves uncovers some extended periods of contentment. Tu Fu's peregrinations have defined the periods into which his life falls, and his poetry has supplied the phrases that sum up the pleasures of each of the periods of contentment. The poet's characterizations have guided commentators in their understanding of his life and are used in the account that follows.

14. For the information about the sons, see Fan Huang's "Preface to *Tu kung-pu hsiao-chi*," in *Tu Fu chüan*, 1:7. For the son employed near Kuei-lin, see Hung, *Tu Fu*, p. 282, and *Notes*, pp. 115. Yuan Chen's grave inscription for Tu Fu is in *Tu Fu chüan*, 1:14–15. On the twelfth-century claims to descent from Tu Fu, see Wang Li-ch'i, "Chi Tu Fu yu hou yü Chiang-ching" in *Ts'ao-t'ang* 2,2 (1981), 62–4. This article by Wang is in part a compliment to an old school friend, surnamed Tu, of the author's, and the author accepts the claim of descent out of regional loyalty. For the villagers near Lo-yang who claimed in 1931 their descent from the poet, see Cheng Te-k'un's account of a field trip in *Yenching Journal of Chinese Studies*, Suppl. No. 1 (1932), 89–90.

In later life, Tu Fu often recalled the past, especially his youth, with great fondness and pride. We learn that in the years before his first attempt at the examinations, Tu Fu traveled in the region around the lower Yangtze. The memory of his itinerary was still fresh twenty years later, when he wrote "Wanderings of My Prime," lovingly recalling the many historical sites he had visited (lines 15–34). One may guess that his travels are an extension of the progress of the promising and confident youth that he portrayed himself to have been. After his first unsuccessful try at the examinations came four more years of traveling (736–40), still quite carefree in spirits. This time he traveled in the northeast ("I roamed about in Ch'i and Chao / Fine furs and spirited horses"). When in old age he took a spill from a horse, he good-humoredly compared it to his sure horsemanship as a young man, saying drink had made him forget the passage of years.[15] The travels in Ch'i and Chao were followed by four years in and about Lo-yang, during which time he also played a role in clan affairs in his home village of Yen-shih. A happy time for Tu Fu ("Eight or nine years in lively freedom"),[16] this is now best known as the period during which he met the poet Li Po (744) and undertook several excursions with him and Kao Shih. With his failure at the examinations of 747, supervised by Li Lin-fu, Tu Fu began a decade of living in Ch'ang-an. His prospects became increasingly dismal as the years passed ("Grey-haired, doltishly offering toasts").[17] Nonetheless, in later years Tu Fu always recalled the brilliance of the capital in those years and the brio of the company he kept.

The next interludes of peacefulness came after the rebellion or, more exactly, after Tu Fu had left the Central Plains. Five years in Szechuan (760–5) and two years in the river town of K'uei-chou in the Yangtze Gorges (766–8) offered some long periods of respite from war. In the comparative safety of the self-sufficient region of Szechuan, near the city of Ch'eng-tu, Tu Fu built, with the help of generous local officials, a thatched hut, and around this dwelling he planted a veritable woods – more than one hundred peach saplings, special bamboo from Mount Tzu-yen, specimens of the local shade trees, pine saplings, numerous types of fruit trees, and later a plot of medicinal plants.[18] Backed by a stream, within view of mountains, the Thatched Hut provided a comparatively peaceful three years out of the five Tu Fu lived in Szechuan Province. (It is at its putative site that the complex of grounds and

15. "Drunk, I fell from horseback; some friends came to see me, bringing wine," 215/14/2.
16. "Wanderings of My Prime" (169/12/7), lines 51. "Lively freedom" is Hung's inspired translation (p. 181) of *k'uai-yi* 快意.
17. Ibid., line 62.
18. See *Tu Fu nien-p'u*, p. 125.

9

buildings known as Tu Fu's Thatched Hut now receives tourists.) In K'uei-chou, on the Yangtze, where Tu Fu next lived, he was able after a year to reproduce some of the circumstances of the Thatched Hut: with money from a patron he acquired two farms, one of which had forty *mu* of orange groves, and hired some help with the farm work. He planted vegetables and crops, raised chickens, tended the orchard, and led a quiet life of directing farm chores and going into town for light socializing. Here, as in Ch'eng-tu, a briefly held office in the city proved only occasionally onerous.

In the Troubles,[19] Tu Fu's role was by and large passive, that of an average person (of the educated class) for whom mere survival required much planning, especially in wartime. Before 755, he was unlucky in his search for an official position, and afterward he was chiefly occupied with keeping his family together, getting them out of harm's way, and also with finding a source of support for himself and his family amid the disruptions of wartime. Even though state and sovereign were never absent from his thoughts and government service remained his most constant wish, in his lifetime Tu Fu found no scope for action in an area larger than his own life and his family. It is perhaps no use asking why. Tu Fu's life was probably typical of that of many men in the lower levels of the T'ang elite, who obtained a livelihood by a combination of family landholdings, patronage, and friendships (and perhaps literary commissions) and whose lives were punctuated by largely unsuccessful attempts to secure or retain an official post. Already under the T'ang dynasty, the supply of educated men far outran the demand for them; the *T'ang tien* notes that in Emperor Hsuan-tsung's *k'ai-yuan* era, "one out of one hundred" passed the advanced, *chin-shih* examination. In this respect, Tu Fu's life, as pieced together from the poems, provides an unusual glimpse of the life of a member of the official class. Without the compensations and prestige of office, such a life was far from secure, and, moreover, the next generations tended to disappear from the historical record. At the same time, however, given an exemption from taxes and corvée, patronage and kindnesses often proved sufficient. The vast number of others at this level, being undistinguished by literary achievement, left no trace of themselves. These others were likely not less deserving than Tu Fu. Although much sympathy has been focused on him, he quite possibly did not endure more hardships than did others of the elite during those dark years.

Viewed in this perspective, Tu Fu is an unlikely candidate for the adulation of posterity. But the ability of later ages to recover, by means

19. For the An Lu-shan rebellion and its widespread consequences, I use David Hawkes's fine adoption of the term "the Troubles." See Hawkes, *A Little Primer of Tu Fu*, p. 81.

of the poems, Tu Fu's life and personality from among the many unknown others has vested unusual significance in his experience. In fact,
so much has been learned about Tu Fu that the typicality of his life in its
outward aspect is easily lost sight of. The singular informativeness of his
poetry, added to his moral stature, have made of him an individual of
consuming interest to readers and scholars. Everything about him,
whether a lofty thought or a mundane detail, is received with equally
serious interest. Nonetheless it is important to remember that in this life,
the commonplaces of the life of a member of the T'ang official class are
preserved, and the questions that puzzle us about Tu Fu's life are not
unique to him. Why he failed to secure a post, why he failed the examinations, how he made ends meet at particular periods, what was his
place in the social and official world of his day – the answers are aspects
of the social history of the T'ang dynasty and not, as is often assumed,
matters peculiar to Tu Fu. His poetry kept him from disappearing from
the historical records and also provided the means for recovering the
details and feelings of that life. The picture of the times that is given in
the poems is not one that can emerge from official narrative history, nor
is the self-portrait of the poet one that can emerge from official biography. The record is unique, but the information to be gleaned from it
concerns issues that are part of T'ang history. The complex interdependence between the poetry's uniqueness and its value as a record of
the author and the times is explored from several perspectives in this
volume.

The cultural legacy

Since the twelfth century, it has been widely accepted that Tu Fu's work
represents the highest achievement of Chinese lyric poetry, setting a
standard of excellence in both moral and aesthetic terms. The supreme
position accorded Tu Fu, however, concerns more than his poetry. To
both traditional and modern critics, he has a unique significance. For
them, Tu Fu is not simply one of the greatest poets but exemplifies the
culture's highest ideals of moral responsibility and compassion. His
name represents a high cultural ideal of loyalty and social concern by
which later readers have judged their own conduct and that of others,
and by which they have also judged Tu Fu's poetry and that of others.
Such a Tu Fu has, in effect, been placed out of reach of the usual bounds
of literary criticism. Thus the objective tone that modern criticism tends
to assume is often perceived as too objective for him.

Until we understand the nature of Tu Fu's formidable reputation, the
study of his poetry, however subtle the methodology, can advance only

within the limits set by tradition. It is only when his more than literary standing is understood that we can begin to free ourselves to work with his intimidating stature. It is useful to begin by distinguishing between poetic and cultural factors in the legacy of Tu Fu. Of the two, his cultural legacy is the more daunting one. The traditional view of his character, derived, as it had to be, from his poems, once it had acquired a cultural and moral stature, became too firmly fixed to be shaken by merely literary criticism. Under such circumstances, the poetry becomes only a source. In a poetic argument that makes Tu Fu the greatest of poets, the criteria one has used are more or less deducible and hence can be, and have been, countered or modified. By contrast, the cultural argument that makes Tu Fu the greatest of poets has never been debated, for it has not even been perceived as an argument but received as a given, a fact of nature. Indeed the Confucian values embodied by this Tu Fu, being themselves axiomatic in traditional culture for at least the past millennium, have reinforced the seeming inevitability of Tu Fu's supremacy. His great and undoubted poetic powers, rather than siphoning off critical attention toward poetic issues, have simply confirmed the rightness of his primacy. It is the forces which created this monumental figure of Tu Fu that this section seeks to clarify.

It is important to emphasize that the moral interpretation of Tu Fu is not dryly moral but is phrased in highly personal terms. His sufferings and his concern for the hardships of others began as personal qualities in the poems before they were translated into moral values. Readers have found in Tu Fu qualities of unswerving loyalty, instinctive generosity, and unpretentiousness which have a moral dimension but which originate in human feeling. Intense participation in Tu Fu's difficult experiences after the rebellion and an empathy with him as a person are joined to an appreciation of his social conscience. Another important trait of Tu Fu's – his affection for his family and his neighbors – also came to notice once the personal appreciation of Tu Fu was established. Traditional critics regarded Tu Fu as a person whom they knew, and who was worth knowing because of his moral stature. The detailed portrait of Tu Fu reconstructed from the poems is infused with an intensely personal tone. This tone, too, is a part of the legacy of Tu Fu as cultural icon and is inseparable from the elevation of Tu Fu to moral and poetic supremacy. With the exception of T'ao Ch'ien, readers have not identified so closely with any other poet as a person.

In the discussion which follows, I examine the limits unconsciously placed upon approaches to the study of Tu Fu by analyzing the nature of his supremacy in two areas: his social and political views, and his personal reputation. As the foundation of his claim to iconic status, his political views have been considered irreproachable. I investigate the nature of this admiration and explore the role of Tu Fu's political views in the literary study of the poems. Next I analyze Tu Fu's personal reputation, examining its formation, content, and influence. Neither discussion rejects the traditional image of Tu Fu; instead, in each I attempt to reach an understanding of the poet's cultural legacy and its formation that will allow us to work with that tradition, rather than merely to follow it.

Tu Fu's political views

Tu Fu does not fit what is usually meant by a political thinker, nor do his views shed much light on political thought. Nonetheless, obtaining some kind of perspective on Tu Fu's political and social views is an indispensable key to understanding him and his enduring name, involving as it does a moral judgment. The issues associated with his views – their expression, their reception by readers, their role in his reputation – are intrinsic to the Tu Fu legacy as shaped by Confucian values. Acceptance of these views as ethically admirable is the foundation of the high regard in which he is held. One might ask, then, what in these views produced this remarkable consequence.

Let us first survey the relevant material. A wide and eclectic range of material falls under the heading of Tu Fu's political and social views. Most obviously political are his explicitly stated opinions on political subjects. These are plentiful: as has often been remarked, Tu Fu was deeply concerned with the political events of the time, and he expressed views on everything from officials and court politics, military policies and politics, battles (including advice on strategy and postbattle evaluation), to taxes, prices, punishments, local officials and regional militia, and the sufferings of the common people. His own constantly voiced desire to be an official is always presented as an aspect of his desire to serve and to alleviate the sufferings of the people. In his poems, Tu Fu may make criticisms, suggestions, or recommendations, or he may offer concern or express hopes or desires. Some comments are made in passing, whereas others form the main point of a poem or a section of a poem. Aside from such explicit statements, many more of his opinions can be surmised from particular poems. There are many less classifiable examples, for in the broadest sense, any mention of the contemporary situation potentially conceals a political or social opinion. Moreover, aside from content, there is the latent political comment that is built into the very act of writing poetry, especially when he uses the ballad and frequently when he employs the old-style form as well. In other words, the amount of material that can be encompassed under this heading is both large and varied.

Faced with such a range of topics and treatment, the most common critical approach has been, instinctively, a mixture of thematic organization and evaluation. An early reader who used this approach was Po Chü-i, who, writing in the year 815, singled out the political and social themes of "Three Officials" and two other poems for commendation. Po Chü-i praised Tu Fu's description of the common people's sufferings and lauded him for the concern represented by his choice of subject.[20] Subsequent readers have identified in Tu Fu's poetry many other themes that can be called political and social, and after twelve centuries of appreciative readers, many of these themes now bring instant recognition. Some themes have sat less well with modern readers (for example, his repeated professions of loyalty to his sovereign), and others have been updated (from a Confucian concern for the common people to a Marxist one). Left and right, conservative and iconoclast, each can find, and has found, something sympathetic in Tu Fu's earnestness. Less overtly personal studies also exist. For example, a recent work discusses three political themes from the K'uei-chou period: the poet's condemnation of rapacious officials who continue to exact taxes from exhausted peasants and of generals who put martial glory before all else (the latter a theme not often discussed); his longing for peace, to ameliorate the lot of the peasants; and his heartbreaking descriptions of untended fields, deserted villages, and displaced peasants.[21] Over the centuries, Tu Fu's sympathy for the common people, especially, has drawn comparisons with Mencius.[22] Comparison to the historian Ssu-ma Ch'ien is also often made, or the tag of "poet-historian" is applied, both with the purpose of invoking the moral responsibilities of the accurate recorder.[23]

Despite a now-ready critical recognition of the major social and political themes, the main body of material remains scarcely organized, probably because it is almost without boundaries. In theory the material can be covered methodically by analyzing all of its themes, and this analysis can also be extended over time to examine how Tu Fu's views changed as the An Lu-shan rebellion worsened and enveloped every facet of mid-T'ang-dynasty life. However, this would be a long undertaking, and its rewards are not clear, in part because the subject is so large. More useful than pursuing a detailed line of inquiry would be to examine in general

20. Po Chü-i, "Letter to Yuan Ninth" 與元九書, in *Tu Fu chüan*, 1:18.
21. Fang Yü, *Tu Fu K'uei-chou shih hsi-lun* (hereafter *K'uei-chou shih*), pp. 71–103.
22. For comparisons with Mencius, see Wei Ch'ing-chih, *Shih-jen yü-hsieh* (Preface 1244), 14.303; and Hsiao Ti-fei, "Jen-min shih-jen Tu Fu," in *Tu Fu yen-chiu*, pp. 248–52.
23. See the surveys of the term "poet-historian" in Yang Sung-nien, *Chung-kuo ku-tien wen-hsüeh p'i-p'ing-lun chi*, pp. 127–62 and 163–84.

terms the effect exerted on Tu Fu's poetry and on the reception of his poetry by its recurrent political and social themes.

In general terms, Tu Fu's views fall, not surprisingly, squarely within the traditions of Confucian thought. That is to say, the issues that Tu Fu holds important, his identification of the causes of social disorder, and the solutions he recommends are all in keeping with the Confucian analysis of society. It is the conventional nature of what Tu Fu says that provides a key both to an important level of meaning in his poetry and to the unparalleled reception of his work.

The earnest, unswerving concern for the state and for his fellow men that pervades his poems underpins the traditionally high esteem in which he is held and imparts to this esteem an unalterability that appreciation of his literary achievements alone could not have secured for him. His unassailable reputation needs no elaboration. The repercussions of this fact upon scholarship, however, are less obvious. It has in effect placed Tu Fu's work beyond the reach of usual methods of literary criticism. The irreproachability of his political and social attitudes has inhibited their objective discussion, and consequently the question of what criteria ought to be applied in such an evaluation has received little consideration. Studies that discuss his political views tend to commend, rather than evaluate, the themes isolated by the study: Tu Fu's descriptions and opinions tend to be paraphrased, elaborated, and then lauded. A general framework for analysis has yet to be formulated. For example, if we desired to evaluate the sagacity of Tu Fu's criticisms and recommendations in terms of the circumstances of his day, we would have to ask how they compared to the recommendations of men who saw active government service and military action, figures such as Yen Chen-ch'ing and Yuan Chieh.

In such a comparison, from today's viewpoint, Tu Fu might not come off so well. Yuan Chieh, for example, was twice able to obtain a remission of taxes for his province when he served as prefect of Tao-chou.[24] By contrast, although Tu Fu pleaded many times for more compassionate conscription policies and lighter taxes, when he was faced with a direct appeal by peasants he could only give rather lame advice. Conditioned by Confucian conceptions of social roles, he depicts himself as offering only a helpless recommendation for the peasant to comply with the demands of officialdom. In one instance, he describes himself as consoling conscripts and their families by noting that the conscription was only for local duties and saying that the commanding general was "like a father or older brother." In another instance, even through his sorrowful

24. In 764 and 766. See also his biography in *Hsin T'ang shu* 143.4681–6.

sympathy, Tu Fu said to a straitened farmer that he should not desert the land (and the tax rolls).[25] These are indeed lame responses, yet the objection might reasonably be made that Tu Fu's views should not be evaluated for consistency or practicability. The overall point to be made, however, is that if Tu Fu should not be held to such standards, what, then, would be fair criteria of evaluation? It may be that we will never have the information needed to make evaluations at the level of detail we may desire, but conscious choice must guide the application or rejection of criteria. This has generally not been the case. It is my hope that by understanding that the traditional Tu Fu transcends mere literary judgment, it will become possible to analyze his work in an objective, indeed, literary, fashion.

It is in this context that two points are argued here: first, that if we are to evaluate Tu Fu's social and political views sensibly, we have to admit, as a first step, that they are naïve; second, I would like to restate in a new way the obvious point that his social and political views are central to his poetry and should not be judged out of the poetry's context simply as political views.

To hear the word "naïve" applied to Tu Fu's views may disturb dedicated readers, but that naïveté is not hard to demonstrate. The point is difficult to follow up, however, for the task is to find a proper context in which to understand this naïveté. It is clear that, given the complex, crisis-filled situation from 755 onward, many of his views – or for that matter, anyone's – were bound to be inadequate. The naïveté in his poetry comes about because his recommendations often boil down to saying, "Let us all be less selfish, let us all do what we are supposed to do." Basically he asks for more integrity, more loyalty, more dedication. Moreover, he is always ready to do his part. Very early on, in 748, well before the rebellion, with no job and no prospects, he declares himself willing to serve his sovereign as did Yao and Shun, and he repeats this on the eve of the rebellion, this time comparing himself to Chi and Hsieh of antiquity. In old age, he writes of his willingness to die, if only his death could be of any use.[26]

Once the rebellion breaks out, Tu Fu begins an unusually large

25. In "The Official at Hsin-an," lines 25–8 (on this, see also Shih Chih-ts'un, *T'ang-shih pai-hua*, p. 258), and "Orange Grove," lines 31–2.
26. For an expression of the desire to serve dated 748 or 749, see "Twenty-two Rhymes Presented to Assistant Secretary of the Left, Wei Chi," 1/1/1, lines 15–16. For its expression six years later on the eve of the rebellion, see "Five Hundred Words Expressing My Feelings on the Way from the Capital to Feng-hsien County," 37/22/16, lines 3–4. The vow made near the end of the poet's life comes from "Year's End," 352/21/35, line 7. For other lines in this vein, see Chien Ming-yung, *Tu Fu shih yen-chiu*, pp. 2.50–3.

number of lines with a rhetorical question, as he pleads for or looks forward to a time of less self-interest, no corruption, lighter taxes. "When will" 何時, these lines begin, or, "Who can" 誰能, "How may" 焉能, 如何, or, again, "When?" 何日. The lines that follow these interrogatives are achingly wistful. Even toward the end of his life Tu Fu asks these questions:

> Who will knock upon the monarch's gate
> So he will order lightened conscription and taxes?[27]

Such sentiments are irreproachable, but despite their sincerity the examples, multiplied, cause Tu Fu's views to seem by turns ineffectual, limited, or naïve, both in the analysis offered and the solutions urged. This observation was made as early as Tu Fu's biography in *New T'ang History,* where it is said that he "loved to discuss affairs of state; he was idealistic and impractical."[28] No one could in good conscience dissent from his urgings; on the other hand, undesirable situations have complex histories and can scarcely be altered by goodwill or imperial fiat, as Tu Fu desired. It seems that his high political idealism, unchecked by harsher realities, could respond to them only by sorrow or reproach.

In a larger context, however, it should not be Tu Fu but the Confucian frame of analysis in a time of crisis that is at issue here. As heir to a Confucian mode of discourse, Tu Fu operated in a realm of idealism that ranged above the reality of politics, emphasizing intentions rather than the ability to reach goals successfully. His sentiments cannot be disputed, because they are precisely that – sentiments, which exist above the level of coherent political analysis. Tu Fu's inability to move from theory to events continues the ancient rejection, both Confucian and Mencian, of the expediencies and exigencies of politics. Men of ambition who are forced to live in obscurity remain his ideal figures.[29] When truly unable to accommodate theory to an imperfect world, Tu Fu fell back on the more thoroughgoing rejection of the world exhibited by Buddhists and Taoists; his few allusions to a desire to retreat from the world paralleled his political despair.[30] *Realpolitik* was outside his frame of reference.

Furthermore, in a time of continual military emergencies, Tu Fu's thinking remained firmly civilian. He accepted the way in which Con-

27. "Overnight at Hua-shih Garrison," 246/16/9, lines 19–20.
28. *Hsin T'ang shu* 201.5738.
29. Thus in the final lines of "Ballad of an Old Cypress" (108/7/10), Tu Fu emphasizes, not Chu-ko Liang's employment by Liu Pei, but his earlier obscurity. It is "men of ambition and you who dwell unseen" 志士幽人 that Tu Fu praises and encourages – "Do not cry out in despair! From old the really great has never been found a use for" (trans. David Hawkes, *Tu Fu,* p. 164).
30. See, for example, the parallels noted in Fang Yü, *K'uei-chou shih,* pp. 71–128.

fucian and Mencian thought focused on the problems of administering a state rather than on how to establish control over it or extend its boundaries. The use of force was clothed in the language of administration and its justifying morality: rebellious subjects and barbaric tribes alike were to be brought under the civilizing influence of Confucian models, whereupon they would voluntarily submit. Even under the extreme conditions of the years after 755, personal fame was more rightly to be assigned to the Confucian official than to the general. Tu Fu recognized the empire's critical dependence upon its generals – he wrote many sincere tributes to particular military figures – but, jealous for the dignity and honors of civilian officials, he always emphasized the generals' properly subordinate role in the state. He rejoiced at the peace settlement with rebel forces in 763, in part because it meant the appointment once more of civilians to frontier offices:

> The dynasty has seen much distress
> High officials are all military men
> Yu and Yen are open again to imperial envoys
> Where frontier officials are military men.[31]

Its orthodox Confucian content has meant that this naïveté has been relatively unproblematic for readers. Thus, for a string of well-intentioned advice and political analyses offered to an official in another poem from 763, a Ch'ing-era editor of the poems, Chang Chin, has only praise. He comments, "This poem could be held up as [stating] the rules of a well-governed state." Another poem elicited this admiring comment from Lu Shih-chun in the late Ming dynasty: "Who [else] would have dared to write thus? Who else would have been willing to write thus?"[32] Tu Fu, of course, does have his critics on this point. For example, the thirteenth-century critic Yen Yü, otherwise admiring, remarks mildly that Tu Fu's poems on seeing people off tend to end with exhortations.[33] Other criticisms are more pointed. I have mentioned the observation by *New T'ang History* that Tu Fu was idealistic but impractical. The poet's comparison of himself to Chi and Hsieh of antiquity also draws a stricture from Ke Li-fang as arrogant.[34] In the end, however, these remarks, eminently sensible though they are, seem churlish in the context of Tu

31. "Seeing off Prefect Lu of Ling-chou, Departing to Take up His Duties," 390/24/55.
32. Chang Chin's comment is made about the poem "Seeing off Wei Feng, Departing for Lang-chou as Military Administrator," 118/8/7, and quoted in Ch'iu Chao-ao, *Tu shih hsiang-chu*, 13.1156. Lu Shih-ch'ueh's comment concerns the advice in "Ten Rhymes for Lord Yen on His Return to Court," in the course of which Tu Fu reminds Yen Wu that even death is a part of service (374/23/17; see also Ch'iu Chao-ao, 11.913).
33. Yen Yü, *Ts'ang-lang shih-hua* 4.205.
34. Tu Fu compares himself to Chi and Hsieh in "Five Hundred Words," lines 3–4. For Ke Li-fang's comment, see his *Yun-yü yang-ch'iu, chüan* 8, in *Li-tai shih-hua*, p. 546.

Fu's earnestness. In the long run, critical, rational comments are unable to exert much influence on the interpretation of Tu Fu. He himself, after all, was only too conscious of the discrepancy between his power-lessness and what he wanted to accomplish: "I worry – but does it help?" 主憂豈濟時, he wrote.[35]

A second and important reason for the acceptance of his views despite their naïveté is that the political content has been interpreted in terms of personality. "It is not that the poets personalized their verse but that they versified their persons" 非詩其人而人其詩, a comment by Ch'ien Ch'ien-i, would be a view widely shared.[36] In Tu Fu's case, traditional readers on the whole preferred to attribute the poet's views to integrity rather than to naïveté. Instead of increasing the impression of naïveté, the iteration of such views caused tradition to value Tu Fu the more for his integrity. Tradition saw the persistence of his ideals and the way in which, with no sustaining enouragement, he still held onto them through thick and thin. "Sleepless – my thoughts on the fighting," he wrote, and, in the year before his death, he spoke of his "north-gazing heart"[37] [toward the capital]. Tu Fu was remarkably without the eccen-tricities of behavior that typically symptomized extraordinary integrity. Conscientiousness was his form of integrity.

With these observations we can come full circle and concur with the traditional view of Tu Fu – that broadly speaking it is his social and political views which constitute his permanent value. To say only that these concerns are simple would be to express a hard-hearted and blind attitude toward the suffering and destruction to which Tu Fu bore witness – the sole consistent witness in poetry, and certainly the most persevering and unselfish of witnesses. The ready sympathy with suffer-ing that Mencius detected as the psychological foundation of morality is here shown in lifelong consistency. It must be remembered that Tu Fu reacted to events as they unfolded, and that they unfolded in a far from tidy way. Repeated and dramatic changes in fortune in the main events of the rebellion, on the Ho-nan and Ho-pei plains and around the two capitals, raised repeated hopes only to have them dashed. As the main rebellion was prolonged, opportunistic local rebellions and foreign in-cursions complicated the general picture. It is true that the solutions and recommendations that Tu Fu urged in poem after poem were sadly inadequate to a political and military situation that daily grew more complex. What, however, could be sensible views, either then or in the

35. "Sojourn in the Thatched Hut," 152/11/10, line 35.
36. Ch'ien Chi'ien-i, in *Ch'u-hsueh chi*, p. 32.
37. The first quotation is from "Overnight in Rooms by the River," 487/31/4, line 7. The second quotation is from "Journey South," 395/25/12, line 6.

perfect vision of hindsight? One wanted, certainly, primarily views that would lead to effective action. This Tu Fu, who reacted basically in an ad hoc way, piling on more advice, more pleas, and (for us, fortunately) more poems, could not supply. Confucianism imposed a burden of activism on a person who could neither play an active role nor lay aside the burden imposed by conscience. In practical terms, to have social and political views was of little use or consolation to an individual. So we come back to the thought that it is as a person that readers identify with Tu Fu, with his hopes and despairs and his sense of powerlessness, and not through the conviction that his analyses are correct. Liang Ch'i-ch'ao, in calling Tu Fu a "sage of the feelings" (*ch'ing-sheng* 情聖) to complement the traditional sobriquet "sage of poetry" (*shih-sheng* 詩聖), seems to have had this in mind.[38] That Tu Fu's views are, in Confucian terms, unexceptional simply means that no obstacle is placed in the way of the traditional reader's identification with him.

In the end, Tu Fu's poetry provides the same answer: if we read it poem by poem, and follow in these poems the shifts and uncertainties of his life and the lives of others, the present desolation and the unknown future, then we see that the fundamental continuity in these poems is not the strictly social and political views but the ebb and flow of one person's experiences, those of a powerless man who could not help observing but who could only observe. He asked, of the suffering he saw, "When will the grief and sorrow of this song come to an end?"[39] It is impossible to read much of the poetry without having made vivid to one the widespread suffering caused by the rebellion, an enlargement of sympathy possible in part because the kind of suffering Tu Fu witnessed still exists. When the distress is made vivid, the emphasis placed by Confucian thought on alleviating or preventing the suffering of the populace may once again be appreciated as more profound than the commonplace it has become. The poems record the repeated hopes, the false hopes and temporary joys, the brief havens and swift tragedies felt and seen by someone caught involuntarily in the machinery of history.

Tu Fu and the tradition of Tu Fu

Tradition holds Tu Fu to be the supreme poet, the figure in whom Chinese literature culminated and from whom subsequent literature took its standards. Discussions of his place in literary history commonly assume that it is the impartial verdict of time which has established his

38. In his 1922 lecture, "Ch'ing-sheng Tu Fu," *Yin-ping shih he-chi*, 7:38–50.
39. 此曲哀怨何時終, "Song at Year's End," 229/15/12, line 18.

position at the apex of the poetic tradition. Usually only the simplest of histories is attached to the process that brought him from obscurity in his own lifetime to his rightful preeminence. In this account, Tu Fu, unknown and unappreciated in his own time, first began to be noticed in the next century by Han Yü and other eminent literary figures. Then, in the Northern Sung dynasty, this esteem became universal, and so it has continued for nine centuries down to the present time. The progression recounted in this manner is in one sense tantamount to no history at all, for it accepts the inevitability of his eventual ascendancy and lacks connection to specific historical causes. The ahistoricity which is a characteristic of myth is here fully displayed. A mutually reinforcing relationship has developed, for the veneration in which Tu Fu is held and the ahistoricity which is intrinsic to his legacy, one which persists today.[40]

This is not to say that knowledge of the historical development of his reputation is wanting. The development has more than once been carefully traced, insofar as the spotty preservation of T'ang and Five Dynasties records allows.[41] But in general this development is not conceived of as contingent upon historical particularities but rather as reflecting a particular cultural and moral pattern. In this case, it is the pattern of the neglected genius – moreover, a neglected genius of great moral stature. Made possible by hindsight, since his eventual triumph is known, the pattern here accommodates Tu Fu's death in obscurity and want and (three centuries later) the belated rendering of his due recognition. This pattern appears to gain further confirmation from the fact that it is the most famous of names that are associated with the recognition of his merits: Han Yü, Po Chü-i, and Yuan Chen in the ninth century, and in the eleventh century Su Shih, Huang T'ing-chien, and Wang An-shih. For here is proof that Tu Fu needed only to await vindication by time and – most notable vindication of all – by other geniuses. A secondary theme of the recognition of genius by genius here reinforces the original pattern of neglected genius. In this view, the insight that was originally possessed by an isolated few soon deservedly became widely accepted.

This pattern is of course correct in the facts upon which it is based (although even this attractive pattern cannot explain why it is that Tu Fu's merits, having been recognized in the ninth century, then had to be

40. This ahistoricity persists in the many modern critical works that employ the epithets "poet-sage" and "poet-historian" in their titles. Such usage in effect forestalls reevaluation.
41. Kurokawa Yōichi, "Chū-Tō yori Hoku Sōmatsu ni itaru To Ho no hakken ni tsuite," pp. 81–112; Tseng Tsao-chuang, "Lun T'ang-jen tui Tu shih te t'ai-tu," in *Ts'ao-t'ang* 1,1 (1981), 54–62.

rediscovered in the eleventh century before becoming widely acknowledged). But the pattern maintains its hold, not owing to the correctness of the underlying facts, but to the pattern's firm basis in the political culture of traditional China. The common acceptance of this attractive pattern has prevented a search for a historical process involving historical contingencies. Accepting the inevitability of Tu Fu's ascendancy has in effect placed restrictions upon other interpretations of the poet and other versions of how he came to achieve such supremacy. If, however, it can be shown that his reputation evolved out of particular contingencies rather than by destiny, then we are freed to add to or modify our sense of his legacy according to our own historical circumstances.

To understand Tu Fu, therefore, one must first understand the nature of our received legacy and how it came to be formed. The creation of Tu Fu's reputation should be regarded as a historical event, with identifiable actors and causes, rather than as an inevitable triumph. In this process, the Northern Sung era is the critical period, for its high valuation of Tu Fu permanently altered the terms of discussion for the poet. After the eleventh century, one could still ignore Tu Fu and deliberately leave him out of the listing of the great tradition; one might prefer Li Po to Tu Fu, or prefer Sung poetry to T'ang poetry – all of these views have indeed been expressed at some point – but the implicit or explicit standard of reference was always the position established for Tu Fu at the apex of literature by Northern Sung literati. After the Sung period, even negative criticism of Tu Fu is not genuinely negative but a way of criticizing a contemporary position. In traditional argumentation, debate over a contemporary matter tended to take place through discussion of a historical issue. After the Northern Sung era, Tu Fu was more and more put to use by one side or another in such debates. Negative criticism of him, therefore, tended not to be genuinely negative.[42] Opinions on him did vary in the succeeding centuries, and were occasionally updated, but they all referred to the common consensus first established by the Northern Sung critics, and therefore for our purposes here they hold a different, and lesser, interest. In essence, opinions after this time fill out, elaborate, or contradict the picture set out here, but their implicit reference is to the model first given form in Northern Sung times. Furthermore, Tu Fu's poetry became, fairly or unfairly, the standard by which the achievements of others were judged. After this time, a true

42. For instance, Chien En-ting's section on "Negative Views of Tu Fu" contains few items of geniune criticism. Essentially, the critics quoted are using Tu Fu's work to drive home a point about their view of the nature of *shih* poetry. (See Chien En-ting, *Ch'ing-ch'u Tu-shih-hsueh yen-chiu*, pp. 57–72.)

revision of his standing would have meant undoing the entire fabric of elite culture first woven during the eleventh century.

During the Northern Sung era, consensus was reached not only on the supremacy of Tu Fu's standing but also on the reasons for his high valuation. In addition, a new tone came into discussions of him – a tone of intense personal identification with the poet by the reader. Of these three points, the invulnerability of Tu Fu's reputation to detraction is sufficiently self-evident not to require discussion. I shall focus here on the content of that reputation as established in Northern Sung hands, and on the personal identification of the reader with Tu Fu.

Su Shih's opinion is typical of the comments which begin to appear in the eleventh century:

Since ancient times there have been a great many poets, but Tu Fu alone is preeminent among them. Is this not because all through his wanderings, through poverty and hunger, despite his unsatisfied desire to serve the state, through all his vicissitudes, he never for the space of a meal forgot his sovereign?[43]

Wang An-shih, writing about an (imaginary) portrait of Tu Fu expresses the same view:

> Chanting verses, faced with this extremity
> Still he did not discard that concern for the court.[44]

Out of the many possible summations of Tu Fu, Northern Sung literati emphasized one image: Tu Fu as the epitome of loyalty, at every moment of the day, but frustrated in his desire to serve his sovereign. Around this central theme of loyalty clusters a group of related themes – concern for the common people, warnings about policies and generals, and dedication to the state – in short, all the themes which are so familiar and which have been accepted as the essence of Tu Fu's achievement. The portrait which has been drawn is, in a word, a moral one. Moreover, it is morality as summarized by Confucian values. The Tu Fu that we have inherited has not moved beyond happy iteration of this view. His recent reputation as a lover of the people and of his country are modern Marxist and nationalist variations upon the same premise, integrated into the current structure of values.

To us there is nothing surprising in this portrait. It indeed contains the essence and the unavoidable cliché about Tu Fu. At most it holds

---

43. Su Shih (1037–1101), "Preface for the Collected Poems of Wang Kung" 王定國詩集
敍, in *Tu Fu chüan*, 1:99.
44. Wang An-shih, "Portrait of Tu Fu" 杜甫畫像, in *Tu Fu chüan*, 1:80.

special interest as being promoted by Wang An-shih and Su Shih, or as being an early expression of what is now the universal view. But the question which needs to be asked concerns exactly this: Why has this become the standard view of Tu Fu? If the poems are consulted, this view is not more accurate than another portrait which can be drawn from the poems, but it is the one which has prevailed, and indeed there is no real rival. The Tu Fu which Su Shih describes is decidedly to be found in the poetry, but this Tu Fu is given a focus which does not account for the many poetic achievements which Su Shih and others do recognize, but which are summarized in less ringing terms.

Tu Fu's legacy is plainly much wider than the image of the ever-loyal official that is described here. Nor is there any question that Northern Sung literati appreciated his other, poetic achievements. The modern critic Jao Tsung-i has noted that the aesthetic points on which Tu Fu anticipates Sung poetic emphases had contributed to Sung interest in his work:

"Meaningfulness and novelty" [*tso-yi hao-ch'i* 作意好奇] was precisely the path chosen by Sung poetry, and one of the main reasons Tu Fu is especially venerated by Sung figures is that he and they have chosen similar paths in poetry.[45]

Comments by Sung literati show the many different levels on which they were engaged – and often engaged intensely – with Tu Fu's poetry. Editions of Tu Fu's poetry, annotations, imitations, and explications began at this time. The aesthetic opportunities for expressing one's admiration – painting, colophons, poetry exchanges, and poetry re-marks – proliferated as well. However, it was in the Northern Sung period that for the first time appreciation of Tu Fu's poetic achieve-ments became inseparable from appreciation of his integrity. Moreover, appreciation took the form of an intense personal identification with his hardships. The generosity of spirit which he displayed and his character in general were taken as models for emulation. Wang An-shih, remem-bering Tu Fu's willingness to sacrifice his own roof if it could secure warmth and shelter for others (in "Song of My Thatched Roof Torn by Autumn Winds"), concludes his poem on the highest pitch:

> That is why when I see your portrait
> I bow twice and tears flow freely.[46]

The addition of a moral dimension to the portrait of Tu Fu that was at the same time deeply felt – this was the particular contribution of

45. Jao Tsung-i, "Tu Fu yü T'ang-shih," p. 187.
46. From "Portrait of Tu Fu," in *Tu Fu chüan*, 1:80.

Northern Sung literati, and this moral portrait was the summary that made possible the widespread appreciation to come of Tu Fu.

The modern critic Ch'en Wen-hua has pointed out more clearly than anyone the moral nature of the Northern Sung interpretation, the newness of it in that era, and the degree to which it is currently accepted without an awareness of this history. He writes, "Today in discussing Tu Fu's thinking, modern critics unhesitatingly place him among the Confucianists, but if we were to trace this concept historically, it would be apparent that this interpretation came about through an evolutionary process and was deeply influenced by the intellectual climate of the interpreters' own period."[47] The biography of Tu Fu in *New T'ang History*, a Northern Sung product, is among the earliest to show this moral emphasis clearly. It says that although he repeatedly experienced the devastations of the rebellion, his behavior remained above reproach. He composed poems that reflected his anguish about the times, he never forgot his sovereign, and for this "people were moved by his loyalty." In this passage, Tu Fu's conduct and the proof of his loyalty are mentioned first. The interest of *New T'ang History* in his words is filtered through the historians' interest in the author's personal conduct. Su Shih's comment is similarly premised. His is a personal version of the history's description and adds an evaluation ("there have been a great many poets, but Tu Fu alone is preeminent among them").[48] In the Southern Sung period, Lu Yu carried this view a step farther and lamented that Tu Fu was then seen only as a poet. If he had been born a century earlier, in the reign of the energetic T'ai-tsung, Lu Yu averred, he would certainly have been like Ma Chou (who both excelled at poetry and found favor with T'ai-tsung).[49] By the end of the Southern Sung, this image of Tu Fu is fluently delivered. A 1225 preface to an edition of his poems mentions all the reasons why his poetry is esteemed, "almost on a par with the *Classic of Filial Piety, Analects*, and *Mencius*": the disordered times in which he lived, the wife and children who suffered with him, the poverty and wanderings he endured, and how "not for the space of a meal did he forget his sovereign."[50]

One might ask why, out of the many possibilities, the image of Tu Fu as ever-loyal official has become dominant and inseparable from the appreciation of his poetry. As one might expect, the reason does not lie in Tu Fu but in the nature of the Northern Sung period. Ch'en Wen-hua

47. Ch'en Wen-hua, *T'ang Sung tzu-liao k'ao*, pp. 203–4. See also pp. 263–6.
48. For examples of the many comments which follow the leads of *Hsin T'ang shu* and Su Shih, see Ch'en Wen-hua, *T'ang Sung tzu-liao k'ao*, pp. 208–10.
49. Lu Yu, "On Reading Tu Fu's Poetry" 讀杜詩, in *Tu Fu chüan*, 2:614.
50. Tseng E, Preface to *Chiu-chia chi-chu Tu shih*, written upon the recutting of the 1181 edition.

explains his new renown as a result of the new interest in Confucian thought which arose during this period.[51] This seems reasonable. It makes sense that the prevailing interest in Confucian thought should have provided the direction of Tu Fu interpretation, and that its continued strength in the following dynasties should have ensured that morality continued to constitute his central identity. Any explanation, however, needs also to take into account the fact that other poets besides Tu Fu saw their legacy shaped during this period, and not always in a Confucian mode. The evolution of an interpretation of Tu Fu should be seen as a by-product of a larger contemporary preoccupation with self-definition, in which Northern Sung literati sought precedents in the figures of the past. In this evaluation and interpretation of the past, Tu Fu was only one of the T'ang and pre-T'ang poets who received interpretation or reinterpretation. Each of the major pre-Sung poets was evaluated by Northern Sung literati, and some, like T'ao Ch'ien, were elevated to the status of major poets. The separate histories of these evaluations add up to an intellectual enterprise that may be thought of as the formation of literary reputations. The undertaking to organize and understand the past proves to be part of the history of Northern Sung culture, a by-product of the literati's concern with aesthetic, political, and intellectual issues.[52]

In the context of Northern Sung interests, Tu Fu's case is not unique: rather it is one instance of the formation of literary reputation. When Tu Fu is viewed in the context of the poets read by Northern Sung literati, it becomes apparent that each poet was chiefly identified by a trait which carried philosophical and moral meaning within the literati culture. Tu Fu became identified with the central Confucian value of the moral, concerned official. Li Po was identified with the Taoistic themes in his poetry, and Wang Wei with the Buddhistic themes in his. The three thus divided among them the major alternatives of action and thought. From the pre-T'ang era, T'ao Ch'ien was elevated above all other poets and his retirement from office singled out as the key to his personality and poetry. Focused and solidified in this manner as cultural icons, the reputations formed during the Northern Sung era were firmly embedded in a cultural framework which no reinterpretation based merely on poetic evidence could meaningfully readjust.

The figure created for Tu Fu is composed of various traits of the persona presented in the poems, and this archetype is in turn validated by the poetry. As such, it is a cultural portrait rather than a literary one

---

51. Ch'en Wen-hua, *T'ang Sung tzu-liao k'ao*, p. 265.
52. This phenomenon is discussed in Chou Shan, "Wen-hsüeh sheng-yü te han-yi," *Chiu-chou hsüeh-k'an*, 3,2 (1989), 53–66.

that has been formed from the totality of traits in Tu Fu's poetry. Yet it is more powerful than a more thorough, literary portrait could be. Tu Fu as loyal subject functions as a focus for many other themes that traditionally belong to the concept of loyalty: sympathy for the common people, advice and admonition on political subjects. Because the role of loyal, concerned subject already existed in Confucian culture, a portrait based on it had great power. A cluster of values already long defined gave this cultural reputation a potency which overpowers other themes in the poetry. Similarly, the supreme accolades invented for Tu Fu, "poet-historian" (*shih-shih* 詩史) and "poet-sage" (*shih-sheng* 詩聖), evoke the two roles, historian and sage, which were most esteemed by Confucius.[53] Over time, the course of moral and political thought in the Chinese tradition tended to reinforce rather than to weaken the mutual dependence of culture and icon.

Some remarks by Edwin Muir on the Scottish poet Robert Burns are of interest in this connection. The process of cultural deification that Muir identifies for Burns is remarkably similar to what we find in Tu Fu's case. The hard-living, hard-drinking Burns who is the object of national admiration has little in common with Tu Fu, yet many of Muir's comments about the fit between icon and cultural needs apply to Tu Fu with surprisingly little adjustment. For example, Muir describes Burns as "a man whose life and poetry are very difficult to separate; for the best of his poetry sprang directly out of his life." An identifying trait in the poet – Confucianism in the case of Tu Fu, what Muir calls "sentimentalism" in the case of Burns – forms both the foundation and the vigorously guarded necessity of the heroic figure. The result, in Muir's words, "is not a literary cult but a social one," an observation that is true of Tu Fu as well. The culture which creates the hero creates other legends as well. Scotland, in the face of its declining power, elevated in Burns, and in its other heroes, the attributes of "heroism, beauty and grace heightened by weakness or misfortune,"[54] just as the Chinese gave to their most admired poets the traits especially celebrated by their culture.

Why the reexamination of the literary past should have occurred among Northern Sung literati is a question which cannot be explored here. It seems that their interests drove them to ascertain what should be counted as best in every area of humanistic endeavor. Poetry was only one of several skills evaluated. "Tu Fu's poetry, Han Yü's prose, Yen

53. The earliest uses of the term "poet-historian" are in Yuan Chen's grave inscription for Tu Fu (in *Tu Fu chüan*, 1:14–15) and in Meng Ch'i's *Pen-shih shih* (Preface 886), *chüan* 3. Tu Fu's *Hsin T'ang shu* biography quotes Yuan Chen. The term "poet-sage" is of later date, generally said to be first used by Yang Wan-li (1127–1206). See his "Preface to *Poems of the Chiang-hsi School,*" in *Tu Fu chüan*, 3:645.
54. See the penetrating discussion in Edwin Muir, *Scottish Journey*, pp. 87–94.

Chen-ch'ing's calligraphy is each the summation of its genre." Such a statement encompassing several arts is frequently made.[55] A history of this phenomenon would likely show that the structure of hierarchy and values assigned in this period is a perfect one for its purposes – but that purpose is not ours. It is not our task, therefore, to readjust the traditional interpretation of one or another poet, for a single item can be altered only by removing it from the framework that gives it meaning. Criticism in our time seeks to evaluate the poet in his or her multiple contexts. To translate a Northern Sung framework into ours would be an injustice to and a distortion of both purposes. We are better off seeing that any new interpretation relies greatly on the judgments of tradition but that it does not have the same purposes and hence does not have the same focus or framework. Understanding the forces which strengthen such reputations makes it easier to lay them aside.

Once we understand the Northern Sung evaluation of Tu Fu as an innovation and departure, we may turn with a clearer purpose to examining the praise that he received from T'ang-dynasty voices. The three centuries between Tu Fu's lifetime and the Northern Sung period had certainly not been blank. Notable ninth-century literary figures stated their admiration for him more than once and in unmistakable terms. Han Yü wrote:

> Shao-ling is no more, the Banished Immortal dead,
> My talents are thin, of what use to sing of the Stone Drum![56]

("Shao-ling" refers to Tu Fu, "Banished Immortal" to Li Po.)

In his grave inscription for Tu Fu, Han Yü's contemporary, Yuan Chen, went beyond the obligatory compliments and reviewed the history of poetry in order to cap his survey with a ringing conclusion: "Since the dawn of poetry, there was no one to compare with Tzu-mei."[57] Yuan Chen may have been implying that subsequent to Tu Fu, poets of comparable standing did appear, for example in his (Yuan Chen's) own day. But even so, this praise is high, and furthermore, Yuan Chen's views must have been known in order for Tu Fu's grandson to have made the request for an inscription from him. Other ninth-century men prominent on the literary scene, such as Po Chü-i, Li Shang-yin, Chang Chi, and Tu Mu, added their voices.

How do such comments fit into the evolution of Tu Fu's reputation? The admiration they express would seem to simplify their relation to the

---

55. This comment is recorded twice in Ch'en Shih-tao, *Hou-shan shih-hua*, in *Li-tai shih-hua*, pp. 304 and 309.
56. Han Yü, "Song of the Stone Drum" 石鼓歌, in *Tu Fu chüan*, 1:9.
57. *Tu Fu chüan*, 1:15.

later Northern Sung view of Tu Fu, and indeed they are usually regarded as auguries of Northern Sung acclaim. Analyses therefore tend to focus on particular arguments they made, for example, their relative ranking of Li Po and Tu Fu, a comparison which Yuan Chen initiated,[58] or the social conscience for which both Po Chü-i and Yuan Chen lauded Tu Fu. For present purposes, however, it is probably most useful to take another approach and examine T'ang comments about Tu Fu in the perspective of their end point in Northern Sung criticism. In this way, the newness of the Northern Sung project may be thrown into relief; equally import-ant, we may more properly give a renewed consideration to the views which antedate that period.

T'ang comments on Tu Fu may be divided into two groups: those made during Tu Fu's lifetime (712–70) and those made in the century that followed. Neither group is large, for comments contemporary to Tu Fu are a bare dozen or so, and ninth-century comments occupy fewer than forty printed pages.[59] The first group consists of the surviving poems addressed to or connected with Tu Fu. These number eleven poems from six hands.[60] In addition, six poems were composed on occasions for which Tu Fu also contributed a poem, although the grouped poems make no reference to Tu Fu or to each other.[61] The second group of early comments about him consists of various remarks, of which those by Po Chü-i, Yuan Chen, and Han Yü are best known and of the most interest.

In his own lifetime, the comments made by friends and colleagues in surviving poems are not particularly effusive, especially in light of later adulation and also in light of the warmth of Tu Fu's own feelings for these friends.[62] In nearly all of the surviving eleven poems addressed to Tu Fu, poets such as Kao Shih, Ts'en Shen, and Li Po and friends such

58. Also in the grave inscription for Tu Fu, *Tu Fu chüan*, 1:15.
59. Collected in *Tu Fu chüan*, 1:1–6 and 1:6–44.
60. Collected in the first six pages of *Tu Fu chüan*, vol. 1. The poem "For Tu Fu, in Jest" 戲贈杜甫 (*Tu Fu chüan*, 1:2), attributed to Li Po by some mischievous hand, is not counted here, nor is a poem sometimes attributed to Ch'ien Ch'i (*chin-shih* degree, 751) but also attributed to one Ch'ien Hsu (*Tu Fu chüan*, 1:3). For a different count, see Liu Hsin-sheng, "T'an T'ang-jen ch'ou-tseng Tu Fu shih," *Tu Fu yen-chiu hsueh-k'an* 2 (1988), 46–51.
61. The occasions are a climb up Tz'u-en Temple and a morning court audience. On the first occasion, Tu Fu, Ts'en Shen, Hsueh Chü, and Ch'u Kuang-hsi match a poem by Kao Shih (Hsueh Chü's poem does not survive). On the second, Tu Fu, Wang Wei, and Ts'en Shen match a poem by Chia Chih. Tu Fu's poems are "Climbing Tz'u-en Temple with Other Gentlemen," 18/1/22, and "Written to Match Chia Chih's 'Morning Court at Ta-ming Palace,'" 309/19/34.
62. See Li Ju-lun, "Tu Fu t'ung-tai jen p'i Tu" 杜甫同代人批杜, in *Tu shih lun kao*, pp. 159–63, and Tseng Tsao-chuang, "Lun T'ang-jen tui Tu shih te t'ai-tu," *Ts'ao-t'ang* 1,1 (1981), 54–62.

as Yen Wu speak of him in friendly terms, as a pleasant companion, a dear friend even, but not as an esteemed poet and never as a man of extraordinary Confucian character. By contrast, Tu Fu's tender concern for each of these men through each turn of fate in their lives is famously expressed in his lopsidedly numerous poems.

Praise of Tu Fu for his writing comes solely at the beginning and at the end of his life. For a number of reasons, in neither period does the praise seem particularly reliable. For the early years, we have only Tu Fu's own retrospective accounts. He tells of his warm reception as a writer of poetry and rhapsodies. He says that he has been compared to Yang Hsiung, Ts'ao Chih, and Pan Ku, and that in his early years in Ch'ang-an men of literary eminence such as Li Yung and Wang Han sought him out.[63] More than once Tu Fu recalls that brief moment of glory when the emperor himself expressed admiration for a rhapsody he had offered the throne.[64] Gratifying though these bits of evidence are to Tu Fu's later admirers, one must note that any appreciation of Tu Fu at this time would have had to be on the basis of his more conventional literary abilities, not on his distinctive themes, which were still to come. It is not until the last year of his life that Tu Fu again receives praise for his poetry. This time the evidence is not dependent upon Tu Fu's statements alone. Praise comes in poems by two men who were officials in towns on the Hsiang River. Each of the men lauds him in extravagant terms, one writing "Your new poems have traveled throughout the empire" and the other, "Your great name [is owing] to your unparalleled poetry."[65] These sentiments, too, have gratified later readers, aggrieved on Tu Fu's behalf, but they are hard to give credence to, for the fame claimed for Tu Fu is not corroborated by the available and extensive information in Tu Fu's own poems. Even if we suppose the lines are

---

63. In "Wanderings of My Prime," Tu Fu recalls the comparison with Pan Ku and Yang Hsiung when he was fifteen (line 2). In "Twenty–two Rhymes to Wei Chi," he recalls the comparison with Yang Hsiung and Ts'ao Chih (lines 9–10) and also says that while in Ch'ang-an, Li Yung and Wang Han sought him out (lines 11–12). Susan Cherniack provides references to the critics who point out the chronological impossibility of the claim about Wang Han. See her "Three Great Poems by Tu Fu," pp. 24–9.

64. "My lines moved the emperor" 詞感帝王尊 ("Left as Farewell for Two Gentlemen of Chi-hsien yuan, Ts'ui Kuo-fu and Yü Hsiu-lieh," 293/19/1). "In those days, my brilliant words moved the emperor" 往時文彩動人主 ("Don't Doubt Me," 134/9/23, line 7). "The emperor left his food to issue a summons" 天子廢食召 ("Wanderings of My Prime," 171/12/7, line 57).

65. The first comment is made by a Kuo Shou, in his poem "Auxiliary Secretary Tu was kind enough to show me his poem, whereupon I wrote this respectfully to send to him" 杜員外兄垂示詩因作此寄上, in *Tu Fu chüan*, 1:5. The second is by a Wei T'iao, in his poem "At T'an-chou, Taking Leave of Auxiliary Secretary Tu" 潭州留別杜員外院長, in *Tu Fu chüan*, 1:4. A third poem, attached to Jen Hua's name, is convincingly refuted by Ch'iu Chao-ao as false, *Tu shih hsiang-chu*, pp. 2258–9.

meant only as figurative praise (meaning, in effect, "Your poems are so great as to deserve to travel throughout the empire"), we must still note that the praise comes from two men who were not themselves known as poets. Indeed, according to the poet himself, recognition of any kind was rare. In that last year of his life, Tu Fu writes, "I have not yet met one who appreciates me."[66]

How shall we explain this neglect? That Tu Fu should be so unappreciated by his contemporaries, often by men who are themselves considerable poets, is for many readers a reproach to his times. His obscurity is often referred to in tones of alternating indignation and sorrow. Huang T'ing-chien, writing of both Yuan Chieh and Tu Fu, invokes a familiar archetype of neglected virtue:

> Who knew that faithful officials would suffer such bitterness?
> The world loved only words of lustrous jade.[67]

A literary historian, by contrast, would suggest that Tu Fu's obscurity is, if anything, further proof that the High T'ang era in literature constitutes a grouping and hierarchy arranged by later critics according to standards which, as we have seen, had a large moral component.[68] Tu Fu's modest position among his friends and acquaintances is a hint that a reconstruction of T'ang views will show much divergence from that transmitted by the Northern Sung writers, that T'ang views will bear a closer resemblance to those expressed in the surviving T'ang anthologies of T'ang poetry than to our current conceptions. The modern critic Jao Tsung-i makes this argument specifically in relation to Tu Fu. He argues that Tu Fu was overlooked because he did not write to contemporary taste, and thus he did not meet with appreciation until poetic values changed.[69] To show the aesthetic dimension of Tu Fu's obscurity, Jao Tsung-i examines T'ang taste as represented by the nine surviving T'ang anthologies. For each anthology, he quotes prefatory comments that reveal the compiler's aesthetic criteria and notes that Tu Fu's poetry does not conform to them. Jao Tsung-i points to a particularly telling omission made in *Ho yueh ying-ling chi*, one which could not have occurred from ignorance of Tu Fu's work, as might be argued

---

66. From "Journey South." 395/25/12, line 8.
67. Huang T'ing-chien, "Written at the End of [the Text of] Mo-yai Tablet" 書磨崖碑後, in *Tu Fu chüan*, 1:119. The Mo-yai Tablet is an inscription on stone that employs the text of Yuan Chieh's "Hymn on the Renaissance of the Great T'ang" 大唐中興頌 (*Ch'üan T'ang wen, chüan* 380) and the calligraphy of Yen Chen-ch'ing. Yuan Chieh, therefore, is a natural subject for Huang T'ing-chien's poem; the inclusion of Tu Fu is interesting.
68. Ou-yang Hsiu and Sung Chi, in their preface to "Biographies of Literary Men," in *Hsin T'ang shu* 201.5727.
69. In Jao Tsung-i, "Tu Fu yü T'ang-shih," pp. 173–88.

about other anthologies. This anthology was compiled in the very year (753) in which a group of five men, including Tu Fu, composed a set of poems upon the occasion of a visit to Tz'u-en Temple. Yet whereas work by each of the other four poets was included in *Ho yueh ying-ling chi,* Tu Fu was excluded.[70] T'ang taste, Jao Tsung-i concludes, shows a preference for surface ornament of the kind best suited for success in the examination system, and he notes that in fact some of the T'ang anthologies were intended as study guides for the examinations.[71]

Jao's explanation persuasively accounts for Tu Fu's omission from most T'ang anthologies. The remaining puzzle, perhaps, is Yuan Chieh's *Ch'ieh-chung chi.* The other anthologies appear to have been formed on aesthetic grounds, but Yuan Chieh's most definitely was not, for he states clearly in the preface its Confucian inspiration and principles. His life and Tu Fu's intersected at a number of points, and it is tempting to compare two men seemingly so well matched in poetic inclinations. Tu Fu was familiar with and admired Yuan Chieh's poetry, but it is not clear whether Yuan Chieh in turn knew of Tu Fu's.[72] Yuan Chieh formed his anthology in 762, during the An Lu-shan rebellion, while he was serving on the Ho-nan front. Making a virtue of restricted circumstances, Yuan Chieh claimed to have put together the collection from "what he carried in his bag." That bag was most admirably principled, for only seven men and twenty-two poems made their way into his anthology. Tu Fu was not among them. Perhaps the simplest answer is that his work was not known to Yuan Chieh. Certainly Yuan Chieh's views of Tu Fu would have been most interesting to have.

In any case, Tu Fu's lack of influence in his own time has ensured the uniqueness of his achievement. When imitations did come, enough time had elapsed so that there could be only one first occurrence.

In the next century, the ninth, comments about Tu Fu tend to be on a level of the superlatives with which we are familiar. They tend today, therefore, to be subsumed into later views as enlightened precursors. I would argue, however, that ninth-century opinions should be viewed as favorable assessments of Tu Fu which nonetheless did not prevail nor exerted much influence. Although the ninth-century superlatives

70. Ibid., pp. 174–5. The other four poets were Kao Shih, Ts'en Shen, Ch'u Kuang-hsi, and Hsueh Chü. (See note 62 to the present chapter.) William Hung (*Tu Fu,* p. 72) dates the excursion to 752 rather than 753, but, whichever the date, Jao's point is still valid.
71. Jao Tsung-i, "Tu Fu yü T'ang-shih," pp. 176 and 186. Each of the T'ang anthologies just discussed, as well as Yuan Chieh's anthology discussed next, is reprinted in *T'ang-jen hsuan T'ang-shih.*
72. Tu Fu wrote a poem in response to one of Yuan Chieh's that he had seen, without, however, sending the poem to Yuan. In its preface, Tu Fu writes, somewhat obscurely, "I will send this to those who know my feelings; it is not necessary to send it to Yuan" ("Matching Prefect Yuan's 'Ch'ung-ling hsing,'" 154/11/15).

are carried on, Northern Sung writers do not follow them in either emphases or perspective. All three characteristics of the later consensus on Tu Fu are missing: the agreement that he is paramount among poets; the attribution of his uniqueness to his Confucian sense of responsibility; and the intense sense of identification with the man on the reader's part.

Han Yü's well-known praise for Tu Fu is one example. It is primarily aesthetic, focused upon the poetry, not his character. In his longest discussion of the matter, a forty-line poem about Li Po and Tu Fu ("For Chang Chi, a Light Poem"), Han Yü begins with a brief defense of the two against their detractors and continues by praising their poetry in extravagant terms.[73] The language he employs is almost entirely metaphoric, a figure rarely used because usually reserved for suggesting, as here, the ungraspable essence of works of art or personality. Who the poets' detractors were we do not know, but since Han Yü's emphasis is aesthetic we may guess that the objections were aesthetic ones too. It appears, then, that Tu Fu was prominent enough to attract debate, but that the terms of discussion were not those of subsequent centuries. Although Han Yü's praise for his achievement is unstinted, it is focused on his artistry and does not mention the excellence of his character or the worthiness of the poems' content, as Sung and later commentators inevitably did.[74] Nor does he separate Li Po's traits from what we now see as Tu Fu's very different qualities. Rather he refers to them jointly – in the pronouns *ch'i* 其 (line 7) and *chih* 之 (line 9) and also as "the two gentlemen" *er fu-tzu* 二夫子 (line 17). Finally, unlike Northern Sung comments, praise like Han Yü's had no influence on his contemporaries. Yuan Chen and Po Chü-i, two other major literary figures who were admirers of Tu Fu, corresponded about many matters, including the mission and future of poetry and Tu Fu's part in them. But they made no reference to the reading of Tu Fu by their contemporary, Han Yü. It was presumably only his followers such as Chang Chi, to whom Han Yü addresses this long poem, that Han Yü sought to influence.

When other ninth-century comments are examined more closely, they also turn out to be only superficially similar to Sung views. The superlatives are to be found, but not the context which made Tu Fu unique to later readers. Yuan Chen perhaps best anticipates various themes in Sung interpretations. For example, the following couplet, in which he writes of the sense of kinship he feels with Tu Fu when reading his poetry, shows that among ninth-century writers his attitudes are the closest to Northern Sung views:

73. Han Yü, "For Chang Chi, a Light Poem," in *Tu Fu chüan*, 1:9.
74. This point is also made in Ch'en Wen-hua, *T'ang Sung tzu-liao k'ao*, p. 219.

> Tu Fu's heavenly gifts are quite without peer,
> Every reading of his poetry is like meeting an intimate.[75]

In the main, however, Yuan Chen's comments only coincide with later views; they do not presume the same context. He puts Tu Fu at the top of a long list of past poets, assigns a characteristic to each poet, and concludes with the rhetorical flourish that Tu Fu both encompasses and surpasses them all.[76] This presages the supreme position in the poetic tradition later accorded Tu Fu. It also sounds the theme, later so common, of Tu Fu as a universal talent and does so in the same manner, by listing single skills for other poets and combining them all for Tu Fu. One notes, however, that the qualities named by Yuan Chen are aesthetic rather than both aesthetic and moral. As Ch'en Wen-hua points out, Yuan Chen limits himself to characteristics of the poetry and excludes the person.[77]

In his "Preface to *Ancient Ballads*," Yuan Chen does discuss the content of Tu Fu's poems in terms of their social commentary, and he views their depiction of contemporary events as a revival of the ancient tradition of the ballad. But it is notable that when social commentary is at issue, Yuan Chen is interested exclusively in the ballad form. It is the ballad which he advocates as the best form for exposing and reforming, and of the whole body of Tu Fu's work, it is only the ballads which he commends.[78] He does not mention the pervasive social concern expressed in nearly all of Tu Fu's poems, which are composed in all the available prosodic forms. And although the subject is clearly close to Yuan Chen's heart, he does not display that Northern Sung manner of slipping instantly onto the highest moral level when discussing any remonstrance made by Tu Fu. He does not anticipate the exalted tone easily assumed in the Sung era, as in this remark by Su Shih: "This is more than just remonstrance without overstepping, which would only be correctness. Rather this is a thoroughgoing, complete dedication to moral responsibilities on the part of Tu Fu."[79]

Another topic in Tu Fu criticism first proposed by Yuan Chen but continued in a different way by the Sung, is the comparative ranking of Li Po and Tu Fu. Yuan Chen began this competition, perhaps inadvertently, when he compared the two poets in his grave inscription for Tu Fu and pronounced Tu Fu the superior. It is a not unnatural

---

75. In "Ten Poems in Reply to Poems Received from Hsiao Fu" 酬孝甫見贈十首, poem 2. In *Tu Fu chüan*, 1:13.
76. Yuan Chen, "Grave Inscription," *Tu Fu chüan*, 1:14–15.
77. Chen Wen-hua, *T'ang Sung tzu-liao k'ao*, p. 219.
78. Yuan Chen, "Preface to *Ancient Ballads*" 古樂府題序, in *Tu Fu chüan*, 1:14.
79. Su Shih, in *Tu Fu chüan*, 1:99.

conclusion, considering Yuan's commission, but *Old T'ang History* makes it more than a passing comparison by labeling it as a competition between Tu Fu and Li Po. Inevitably, adjudicating the relative standing of the two stars of High T'ang poetry came to be a favorite sport.[80] To this occupation, however, Northern Sung writers brought an intensely personal dimension in their feeling for Tu Fu which Li Po could not arouse and which prejudiced the outcome of the comparison from the beginning.

My argument here is corroborated in an interesting way by the Ch'ing-dynasty commentator Ch'iu Chao-ao in the preface to his 1703 *Tushih hsiang-chu*. Ch'iu's entire preface is rhetorically structured as a repudiation of Han Yü and Yuan Chen's words on Tu Fu, positive though they are. Ch'iu Chao-ao quotes their high praise of Tu Fu, but he does so in order to take issue with these evaluations. These are, he points out, only words about style, about the style of the pen and of the spirit. Their criteria are, in other words, merely literary. "In discussing other poets, one may compare the skill of various lines, but in the unique case of Tu Fu, one cannot seek him only in the lines."[81] Ch'iu Chao-ao rejects Han Yü's and Yuan Chen's views for a reason that we are now in a position to understand as anachronistic. He objects to them because they failed to anticipate the later veneration of Tu Fu; they failed to reserve a special, unique position for the poet whom Sung writers later enfeoffed as poet-historian and whom the Ming canonized as poet-sage. "What Yuan Chen and Han Yü wrote," Ch'iu Chao-ao concludes, "would make Tu Fu no different from other poets".[82] and that was indeed the case.

To be sure, enthusiasm for Tu Fu was evident in many ninth-century comments, but each writer focused on his own interests. Po Chü-i and Yuan Chen were close friends and exchanged views on the function of poetry. Han Yü, although an exact contemporary, wrote independently of them. Without debate and interaction there can be no general agreement about the meaning of a poet's achievement. The lack of consensus in the ninth century, even among Tu Fu's supporters, is itself an indication that his standing, though high, was not paramount. As late as Wei Chuang (838?–910) and Wei Hu (fl. 950), the record is quite inconsistent. Both men were great admirers of Tu Fu. Wei Chuang went so far as build a new Thatched Hut on the (putative) site of Tu Fu's hut, and his own collected works, *Wan-hua chi* (Flower-washing collection), was

---

80. An early compilaton is found in Wei Ch'ing-chih, *Shih-jen yü-hsieh* 14.296–8. Lu Chih-hsuan, *Tu kung-pu shih-hua chi-chin*, pp. 1–16, collects many of these comparisons but omits Yuan Chen's.
81. Preface, *Tu shih hsiang-chu*.
82. Ibid.

named after the site as a homage to Tu Fu.[83] Yet Wei Chuang's other work, *Yu hsuan chi*, an anthology of T'ang poetry, included only seven poems by Tu Fu, an absurdly small number by later standards. (Li Po had forty-four.)[84] It is true that the anthology is an earlier work, dating from 900, the year before Wei Chuang's removal to the Tu Fu territory of Shu and presumably before the onset of his admiration for Tu Fu. Still, in that case one must wonder whether it is geography rather than, say, morality or aesthetics that exerted the primary influence upon Wei Chuang. As for Wei Hu, he singles out only four men for praise in the preface to his anthology, *Ts'ai-tiao chi*. Tu Fu is one of the four, together with Li Po, Yuan Chen, and Po Chü-i, but no poem of his is included in the anthology.[85] Such inconsistencies show that despite our ability to gather proof that Tu Fu was known and much admired, his standing at this time was not the fixture of nature it was to become. Only in hindsight do T'ang comments fall into a line that is continuous with subsequent views of Tu Fu.

The evidence from the two T'ang histories corroborates this timetable. *Old T'ang History*, completed in 945, makes no independent evaluation of Tu Fu in its biographical notice of the poet. It shows awareness of his importance, but to illustrate and support its estimation of him, it depends entirely on quoting an extensive passage from Yuan Chen's grave inscription for Tu Fu.[86] By choosing to quote Yuan Chen's highly laudatory words, it does give a prominent place to Tu Fu, but in the matter of theoretical support, it adds nothing of its own. By contrast, *New T'ang History*, completed in 1060, establishes Tu Fu's character as the centerpiece of an evaluation now confidently and explicitly carried out. *New T'ang History* states easily the thesis that Tu Fu was unceasingly steadfast in a perilous time, and that for this reason people loved his poetry.[87] This was, presumably, by that time (1060), the common view of Tu Fu.

Much of the evidence frequently cited to argue for Tu Fu's high standing in the ninth century looks different if its inconsistencies are not glossed over. One more may be briefly mentioned here. This is the

---

83. So says Wei Hsu, younger brother of Wei Chuang, in his Preface to *Wan-hua chi*. In *Tu Fu chüan*, 1:50.
84. This is reprinted in *T'ang-jen hsuan T'ang-shih*. In 1928, a very different edition of *Yu hsuan chi* was discovered in Japan, but that too contained only seven poems by Tu Fu. See Ling Tzu-liu, *T'ang-shih hsuan-pen Tu Fu shih ts'ai-hsuan t'ung-chi*, p. 38.
85. *Ts'ai tiao chi*, reprinted in *T'ang-jen hsuan T'ang-shih*.
86. Quotation from Yuan Chen's grave inscription takes up nearly half of Tu Fu's biographical notice in *Chiu T'ang shu* 190C.5054–7.
87. *Hsin T'ang shu* 201.5736–8.

pairing of Li Po and Tu Fu, made most notably by Han Yü.[88] Since Li Po was indisputably famous in his own time, the pairing would seem to imply that Tu Fu's standing had come to equal Li's. One could just as well argue, however, that Han Yü used Li Po to bring Tu Fu's standing up to a higher level.[89] Indeed, although Han Yü wrote in this vein, he was not influential enough to produce a consistent pairing of the two poets. Later, of course, Li–Tu did become a byword for T'ang poetry. In T'ang times, however, although Li–Tu was a common pair, others also existed. Lu–Tu, for example, where Lu is Lu Hsiang. The conjunction is based on the same type of trivial commonalities that produces other groupings of minor poets. Lu Hsiang happened to have held a post, as *kung-pu*, that Tu Fu also briefly held. He also had at least Tu Fu's standing as a poet: he was an associate of Wang Wei's and his work was included in two T'ang anthologies.[90] By Sung times, however, it would be inconceivable casually to pair Tu Fu with someone other than Li Po.

The isolation of T'ang comments contrasts with the speed with which ideas about Tu Fu infected Northern Sung literati. In the Northern Sung, once a theme is started, it is taken up and repeated, echoed, embellished, elaborated, and particularized. The characterization of Tu Fu as "poet-historian" might have been broached by Yuan Chen and Po Chü-i, but it did not hold until the Sung era, whereupon it was repeated tirelessly and continually.[91] Su Shih's comment that Tu Fu did not for the space of a meal forget his sovereign was also unabashedly repeated by everyone.[92] A sense of personal identification with the poet made repetition a personal affirmation rather than the sign of an embarrassing lack of originality. In the Sung era, the regard for Tu Fu also easily spilled over into other facets of the literati's newly defined activities: in calligraphy, writing out his poems; in poetry, writing variations on his poems; in painting, illustrating episodes from his life; in examinations, using his poems for setting questions. Pavilions, buildings, and other structures, as well as scenic sites, are named with lines from Tu Fu.[93] T'ang interest, by contrast, had not been nearly so all-

88. "For Chang Chi, a Light Poem," in *Tu Fu chüan*, 1:9.
89. As Wang Ssu-shih observed in the Old Preface to his *Tu i*.
90. His poems are included in *Ho-yueh ying-ling chi* and *Kuo-hsiu chi*. See Jao Tsung-i, "Tu Fu yü T'ang-shih," p. 177.
91. For an extensive list of adumbrations on Tu Fu as poet-historian, see Yang Sung-nien, "Sung-jen ch'eng Tu Fu wei shih-shih shuo hsi-p'ing" 宋人稱杜甫為詩史説析評, in *Chung-kuo ku-tien wen-hsueh p'i-p'ing lun chi*, pp. 127–62, and Tseng Tsao-chuang, "Lun T'ang-jen tui Tu shih te t'ai-tu," *Ts'ao-t'ang* 1,1 (1981), 54–62.
92. Yang Sung-nien, ibid., p. 132.
93. For the examples of Tu Fu in other cultural activities, see Ch'en Wen-hua, *T'ang Sung tzu-liao k'ao*, p. 274.

pervasive, nor had T'ang writers had as many avenues of expression for their interest.

It is easy to underestimate the newness of the Tu Fu created by Northern Sung literati. For instance, it is easy to fall into line with the view that Po Chü-i, in singling out Tu Fu's concern for the common people, anticipates the later view of Tu Fu as moral exemplar. But in fact as strong a case can be made for the opposite view. One could say that Po Chü-i failed to make exactly those points that were to prove important to Sung literati. He did not make a generalization to suggest the overall emblematic significance of Tu Fu's moral concerns. Indeed, as is frequently and uneasily noted, his praise of Tu Fu was highly qualified. He seemed to value Tu Fu for the single trait of social protest. Even then he lacked a sense of intense identification with Tu Fu's concerns. The poems he did single out (the set "Three Officials," in ballad form, "The Pass at Lu-tzu," and "Detention at Fort Hua-men," in five-character old-style form) were neither the poems nor the prosodic forms favored by later critics. (Admittedly, Po Chü-i was accurate in singling out the since-famous couplet from "Five Hundred Words" in which surplus rotting meat within the palace gates is contrasted with starved corpses outside.) Most remarkable is that although almost every poem by Tu Fu illustrates his sense of social responsibility, Po Chü-i found only 5 poems to commend for this quality out of the "more than one thousand" that he had seen, and referred to a possible total of only some 13 or 14 such examples.[94] Did he include among these a poem like "Song at Year's End," so like one of his own "New Ballads" in its explicitness? His friend Yuan Chen added 4 more titles to this list, although he did applaud all of Tu Fu's ballads as a group.[95] It may be that at the time of writing, 815, Po Chü-i's interests were narrowly focused on a particular subgenre (exemplified by his earlier "New Ballads"), and so he found only a few examples to match his own interests. At the same time, the surprisingly small number of examples may indicate how new Po's view was, how novel it was to single out the moral themes in Tu Fu's poetry, and how invisible they were before a theory brought them to our notice. Operating without such a theory except as he devised one, Po Chü-i had to make the first such selection. If he had been able to recognize a wider range of examples, perhaps his own "New Ballads" would have been different.

It should be noted at this point that we do not know what the effect

94. Po Chü-i, "Letter to Yuan Ninth," in *Tu Fu chüan* 1:18.
95. Yuan Chen, "Preface to *Ancient Ballads*," in *Tu Fu chüan*, 1:14. The four poems Yuan Chen named are "Lament for Ch'en-t'ao," "Lament by Serpentine River," "Ballad of Army Carts," and "Ballad of Beauties."

was upon early critics of their incomplete knowledge of Tu Fu's work. Shortly after Tu Fu's death, Fan Huang made a small collection of 290 poems. Only the brief preface survives; 69 of the titles included are known from their citation in other sources. In the preface Fan Huang says that in the Chiang-nan area sixty scrolls (*chüan*) of Tu Fu's writings were circulating, but that most knew Tu Fu's work only through poems that were written in jest or casually. Po Chü-i, however, saw a great many more poems. He mentions that "more than one thousand" are worth preserving, a figure not surpassed until the complete editions of Tu Fu's poetry in the Sung. Yuan Chen says, "After a long time, I got hold another several hundred poems." It is not clear how many poems were accessible before the complete Sung editions. In these, the number seems to have been substantial but still with many fugitive pieces. Wang An-shih writes of the delight he felt when a guest gave him "more than two hundred" poems he had never seen before, poems so wonderful he knew they had to be by Tu Fu. Yet his contemporary, Wang Chu, seems to have seen everything available; his complete edition of Tu Fu, dated 1039, now lost, is known to have had a total of about 1,400 poems, about the same as today's number.[96]

It is not possible in this survey to analyze all the evidence for ninth-century reactions to Tu Fu. Concerning one large remaining category of evidence, however, a few remarks are necessary. This is the category consisting of poems influenced by Tu Fu's work. Tu Fu's influence in the late T'ang era, especially his influence on Li Shang-yin, has been noticed since Northern Sung times.[97] The nature and the context of this influence are relevant to the interpretation of Tu Fu's legacy proposed here. The evidence from the ninth century shows that on the whole his influence was not exerted through his dominant subject matter of the Troubles. In the poems by Li Shang-yin, Han Yü, and others that show his influence, Tu Fu's subject matter, to us inescapable, is quite absent. Instead, his influence tend to be exerted in matters of style.

The poetic influence that Tu Fu had in the ninth century on poets such as Li Shang-yin he continued to exert in after centuries as well upon

96. For F'an Huang's preface, see *Tu Fu chüan*, 1:7, and Chou Ts'ai-ch'üan, *Tu chi shu lu*, pp. 255–8. The 69 recoverable titles are discussed in Kurokawa Yōichi, "To Ho no hakken," pp. 81–3. Po Chü-i's comment about the number of poems he had seen is in his "Letter to Yuan Ninth," in *Tu Fu chüan*, 1:16; Yuan Chen's is in "Letter to Lo-t'ien on Poetry," in *Tu Fu chüan*, 1:14. Wang An-shih, "Preface to *Tu kung-pu hou-chi*" 杜工部後集序, in *Tu Fu chüan*, 1:80. For Wang Chu's edition, see Chou Ts'ai-ch'üan, *Tu chi shu lu*, pp. 3–6, 6–17, and 23–4.
97. Tu Fu's influence during the Late T'ang period is briefly surveyed in, among others, Tu Ch'uan-an, *Shih-sheng Tu Fu*, pp. 51–86. These pages quote generously the terse remarks in *shih-hua* concerning the influence of Tu Fu upon Han Yü, Chang Chi, Po Chü-i, Yuan Chen, and Li Shang-yin.

other poets. The important difference lies in the historical context. In the ninth century, his poetic example operated in a universe of poetic influences. Li Shang-yin and others could not identify, as Northern Sung literati could, the permanent value of Tu Fu's words as lying outside the aesthetic realm. Thus Ou-yang Hsiu could write of Tu Fu,

> Alive he lived in poverty,
> Dead he was the jewel of posterity.
> If his words can live on,
> A gentleman need not be ashamed of lowness and poverty.[98]

To his T'ang admirers, the poetic experiments and intricate technical experiments in which Tu Fu delighted were observed, imitated, and – what is most important – were not overshadowed by the potency of his cultural legacy. Once the moral theme did emerge and established its hegemony through cultural values, the experience of the purely literary legacy as practiced by Li Shang-yin and others remained possible, but always morally suspect.

An instructive comparison can be made between the ninth-century experience and the poets of the Chiang-hsi school in the eleventh century. Led by Huang T'ing-chien, the Chiang-hsi poets also devoted themselves to studying the poetic experiments and technical intricacies of Tu Fu's poems. But to many critics and historians, the distinction between the two groups of admirers is clear: Chiang-hsi poets willfully focused "only" upon the technical intricacies of the poetry, thus trivializing the monumentality of his achievement as a whole. Although the imitations of Li Shang-yin and others have also drawn ambivalent critical reactions, their poems have a second, redeeming function as evidence of Tu Fu's standing in the ninth century.

One wonders what would have happened if Tu Fu's moral stature had not been so much emphasized in the Sung period and had not come to carry such weight in our responses to his poetry. In a way, the ninth century illustrates the path not taken, and, in particular, certain ninth-century poems show clearly the strength of Tu Fu's poetic influence when acting in isolation.

The newness of Northern Sung views has not been fully appreciated. The tradition of Tu Fu prior to the eleventh century cannot be fashioned into a consecutive, causal account. It is easy to think that since the first recognition of Tu Fu's work came from men who were themselves major literary figures, this segment of time fits easily into a continuum in which great literary figures confirmed their talents by their ability to recognize

98. "On the Portrait in the Hall, I Received the Subject Tu Tzu-mei" 堂中畫像探題得杜子美, in *Tu Fu chüan*, 1:69.

earlier geniuses. But the changes in Tu Fu's reputation in the three centuries from his lifetime to the beginning of the Northern Sung era show none of the internal connections necessary to a history; indeed, placed in the context of Sung opinion, they show lack of continuity with it. In these three centuries, the three main periods in the formation of Tu Fu's reputation – during his lifetime, from after his death to the eleventh century, and during the eleventh century – do not constitute a growth or an evolution that points toward the eleventh-century culmination. On the contrary, they simply constitute three separate periods, for no stage grew out of the previous one, no stage either accepted significant influence or showed a notable reaction against the previous stage. Whereas we might expect, for example, the men of the century after Tu Fu's death, such as Han Yü and Po Chü-i, to deplore Tu Fu's neglect by his contemporaries, this did not happen, at least not in surviving materials. Han Yü's defense of Tu Fu is a vigorous one, he thinks Tu Fu's critics benighted, but he lacks that tone of incredulity that later critics were to use. He still had to assert his case, whereas later literati simply stated their views as to how earlier poets should be ranked. And whereas we might expect the Northern Sung admirers of Tu Fu to look back to Han Yü and the others as their predecessors, as they did in their polemics and in writings concerned with the reform of the essay,[99] this too did not happen.[100] Northern Sung men made their appraisals without reference to late T'ang and Five Dynasties critics, and, as we have seen, they did not emphasize the same issues.

To sum up, one might say that the history of the growth of Tu Fu's reputation shows no clear evolution – no connection between one writer and another, either through influence, reaction, or claimed lineage. A lineage-conscious culture which emphasized transmission over invention would, one would think, devise a tradition if one was absent. The lack of such a lineage until the Southern Sung period indicates perhaps the newness of the enterprise of ranking Tu Fu and also the newness of the larger enterprise of ranking poets. This view of history, incidentally, is consistent with the "delay" in recognition of Tu Fu, the fact that his merits were first recognized in the ninth century and then had to be "rediscovered" in the eleventh century before becoming widely accepted. It remained for the more scholarly and systemizing Southern Sung literati to place all such remarks in chronological, and implicitly historical, order and to imply a history for them by comparing them to the unfavorable judgments which had prevailed in the early Five Dyn-

99. See Ronald C. Egan, *The Literary Works of Ou-yang Hsiu*, pp. 14, 20.
100. The trivial exception is the continual debate over the relative merits of Li Po and Tu Fu, discussed earlier.

asties era among the Hsi-k'un school. The strong iconic image of Tu Fu as loyal subject which emerged has forestalled the full formation of other interpretations. The chapters which follow acknowledge the central importance of this view of Tu Fu but propose interpretations that enlarge our sense of his achievement.

The poetic legacy

Tu Fu's work bequeaths a poetic legacy whose influence on subsequent literature has been inexhaustible. The many inventions, innovations, and improvements that he made in lyric poetry (*shih*) resulted in a body of work whose only consistent characteristic is its richness. In both content and technique, Tu Fu shows an enormous variety and range, as well as a willingness to experiment and to feel his way toward initially unclear goals. His poems range from the sonority and magnificence of court poems to unadorned and warm scenes of daily life, from the almost offhand journal entry to the carefully plotted lyricism of the last great poems in regulated verse. Indeed, the comprehensiveness of his talent is one of the points most frequently made about his poetry. The phrase commonly used, both in tradition and today, is a metaphor originating from music, of Classical provenance. This term, "a complete symphony" (*chi-ta-ch'eng* 集大成), is borrowed from Mencius's description of Confucius as someone who was able to bring the voices of individual instruments into a concerted whole.[101]

The comprehensiveness of Tu Fu's range is first noted in Yuan Chen's grave inscription, in which he compares his poetry to all of Chinese poetry, from *Classic of Poetry* down to the great names of the generation before Tu Fu's own, Shen Ch'üan-ch'i and Sung Chih-wen. Yuan Chen invokes by pairs the names and poetic achievements of Su Wu and Li Ling, Ts'ao Ts'ao and Liu Chen, Yen Yen-chih and Hsieh Ling-yun, and Hsu Ling and Yü Hsin. (Note, incidentally, that in the ninth century, T'ao Ch'ien is not yet automatically included.) Tu Fu, Yuan concludes, "united in his work traits which previous men had displayed only singly." Beginning with the Northern Sung era, this verdict is found frequently. Ch'in Kuan, using slightly different pairs of names and qualities from Yuan Chen's, similarly praises Tu Fu's universal talents. Wang An-shih writes that in Tu Fu one may find joys and sorrows, depth and sparkling surface, simplicity and ornateness, weightiness and fleetness, purity and

101. *Mencius* 5B.6. Legge translates the term as "a complete concert," *The Works of Mencius*, p. 372. The analogy between Tu Fu and Confucius is made explicit by Ch'in-Kuan, who prefaces the term's application to Tu Fu by first quoting the whole of Mencius's praise of Confucius ("On Han Yü" 韓愈論, in *Tu Fu chüan*, 1:139).

ornamentation. For this reason, Tu Fu supercedes all predecessors and has no successors. Hu Ying-lin concurs: "The one whose style comprehends an entire era – that one is Tu Fu."[102] Contemporary criticism echoes its agreement, although its method of proof is necessarily different.[103]

Commendation of the comprehensiveness of Tu Fu's poetry is also closely linked to a number of other frequently made judgments: that his work is the culmination of developments set in motion at the dawn of belles lettres in the Han dynasty; that he broke new ground in many areas; and that his poetry is unique (*tzu ch'eng yi-chia* 自成一家).

Critical agreement exists concerning these characterizations of Tu Fu's poetic achievement. Paradoxically, however, problems soon arise when the critic attempts to refine this consensus by further analysis. A wealth of topics appears to present itself for studying, yet often little is produced beyond promising initial results. It seems that in evaluating Tu Fu's poetic legacy, the problems lie not in the nature of the legacy, which is seldom under debate, but in the unexpected barriers encountered. Let us consider three situations of this type: the connection of the poetry with the life, the periodization of Tu Fu's work, and the functions of the prosodic forms. A variety of causes seems to be responsible for the unexpected limitations that attend the study of Tu Fu's poetic legacy.

In the first case, that of the connection between Tu Fu's life and his poetry, the methodological problem is that a thesis about the poetry that is manifestly true resists amplification. It is obvious that Tu Fu's poetry is intimately related to his life, and a large class of examples is available to support this thesis. Yet the thesis is usually extended only by repetition of the initial point rather than by development. Its amplification comes down to drawing a portrait of his life that is more sensitive and more comprehensive than earlier attempts. (The question of Tu Fu's political and social views, discussed earlier, also runs into this type of methodological limitation.)

In the second situation, that of periodization, we find that the distinctions made by a widely accepted, indeed an essential, model are unexpectedly difficult to render productive. To study any poet, it is helpful to determine whether his poetic development can be viewed in

---

102. For Yuan Chen's grave inscription, see *Tu Fu chüan*, 1:14–15. (Hu Tzu holds that Yuan Chen is the source of the subsequent adumbrations on this theme; see his *T'iao-hsi yü-yin ts'ung-hua, hou-chi*, 8.57–8.) Ch'in Kuan compares Tu Fu to Li Ling and Su Wu, Ts'ao Chih and Liu Chen, T'ao Ch'ien and Juan Chi, Hsieh Ling-yun and Pao Chao (*Tu Fu chüan*, 1:138). For Wang An-shih's remarks, see Hu Tzu, *T'iao-hsi yü-yin ts'ung-hua, ch'ien-chi*, 6.37. For Hu Ying-ling, see his *Shih sou*.
103. For example, Stephen Owen stresses "multiplicity" as the key to Tu Fu's achievement in his chapter on Tu Fu in *The Great Age of Chinese Poetry*, pp. 183–224.

terms of stages. In Tu Fu's case, the stages of development have been established for some time, so that differences of opinion are only variations of the basic model. Yet, as we shall see, the usefulness of the model is limited.

In the third situation, that of the function of the prosodic forms, we find that the assignment of functions is difficult to verify except in the most general way. That Tu Fu commonly uses certain prosodic forms for certain purposes can readily be proved by examples. Thus it is easily shown that he likes to use the five-character old-style form for journal-like records or recollections: "Journey North," "Wanderings of My Prime," and "Living as a Sojourner" are prominent examples. In fact, however, refinements of this first impression are difficult to devise, and consequently the same examples are used repeatedly to support the model.

The three types of methodological problems that I have just described are issues central to studying Tu Fu's poetic legacy. The reasons for our inability to advance beyond current knowledge are worthy of our attention, and in the remainder of this chapter I shall examine each of these issues more closely as preparation for the chapters to follow.

The relationship between poetry and biography

Tu Fu's poetry constitutes an autobiography, both by intention and by happenstance. Lacking any other major contemporary sources, it provides our only detailed firsthand knowledge about his life. Two related questions are of interest: (1) what do the poems tell us about Tu Fu? (2) what is the relationship between his poetry and his life? An obvious distinction between his poetry and that of his contemporaries Li Po and Wang Wei is that to understand Tu Fu's poetry, answering these questions is essential, whereas for Li Po and Wang Wei they are not of the first order of importance. The answer to each question begins in an obvious way but is quickly followed by uncertainties and complications, which in turn have implications for methodology.

To the first question of what the poems tell us about Tu Fu, the answer is, as is well known, "a lot." The many-sided portrait of him that emerges from his poems has often been noted and studied. First and most basic, a chronology of his life can be outlined. The reader sees quick snapshots of Tu Fu at a precocious seven years of age singing of phoenixes, at nine practicing large calligraphy, and, in a reversal, at fifteen scampering up trees for fruit.[104] The reader also learns about Tu Fu's family, his friends,

---

104. From "Wanderings of My Prime," 169/12/7, lines 6 and 7; "Ballad of One Hundred Accumulated Worries," 111/7/15, lines 1–4.

the servants; events he has witnessed, his thoughts, his opinions, his moods; his views on poetry, on the war, on taxation; farms and houses he has owned and trees he has planted; the climate where he lives, his illnesses, the medicines he takes, his convalescences; and much, much more.[105] Tu Fu relates an astonishing number of things about himself. We know more about Tu Fu than about anyone of his time or before him, such as Wang Wei or Li Po.[106] (With Han Yü and Po Chü-i, in the next generation, information increases severalfold, there being many nonpoetic sources as well.)

The biographical information is of two kinds. The first consists of the sort of facts which make up a chronological framework: dates, offices held, places lived, journeys made. For the early years, from which only a few poems survive, chronology is derived from later poems of reminiscence. Many facts Tu Fu states explicitly: "For five years I sojourned in Shu, / For one year lived in Tzu-chou," and "I lay pillowed in Yun-an County, / Then moved to live in White Emperor City."[107] Other information can be inferred with some accuracy, such as the number and ages of his children. Much of the material is enticingly buried in the poetry and has presented chronologists with challenges of great textual difficulty, brought to conclusion only through collaborations extending over centuries. This broad endeavor, though complex, is straightforward, in that the methodological problems are chiefly logical and the logical traps are well understood. Facts of this chronological kind are quite plentiful for Tu Fu (compared with, say, Shakespeare). Even the most conservative application of standards of evidence will give a fairly full chronology of Tu Fu's movements, and even the most conservative critic will agree that this chronology is solid.

In the establishment of a chronology, the interdependence between the life and the art is straightforward. Usually thought of as a relationship of some subtlety and elusiveness, here it is purely informational – a matter of what can be learned from the art about the life. In theory, we can wring all the information from the poems and leave the poems behind, and we would still have a good biography (not that anyone does this). In that sense the poetry is unnecessary (not that anyone thinks this).

Solid as its results are, the point of diminishing returns has been reached for this approach. Because there is such a wealth of infor-

---

105. *Tu Fu nien-p'u* keeps excellent track of this multitude of information.
106. Lü Cheng-hui also makes this point in "Tu Fu yü jih-ch'ang sheng-huo," in *T'ang-shih lun-wen hsuan-chi*, p. 286.
107. The first couplet is from "Quitting Shu," 413/27/1, lines 1–2, and the second from "Moving to Live in K'uei-chou," 420/27/27, lines 1–2.

45

mation, much scholarship has been devoted to establishing a comprehensive chronology and to putting together all the little pieces that together form the whole picture. Yet it must be admitted that not much more can be learned about Tu Fu's life by doing more of the same. It is true that many topics along those lines still await tidying up – a patron or acquaintance not yet studied, the poet's illnesses analyzed in the light of modern medical knowledge, boats and trees considered from an expert's viewpoint, and so on – but basically, little more can be extracted by sifting out the facts from the poetry.

It is on the second kind of biographical information contained in the poems – Tu Fu as a person – that much of nontextual criticism is focused. This information also centers on Tu Fu, but it is more problematic. It begins in a seemingly solid fashion by ascertaining facts, such as what the poet has been doing (visiting a friend or a site, making plans, attending a party), but it inevitably goes on to deduce the feelings and states of mind hinted at or stated in the poem: why he chose to do this rather than that, how such and such an event affected him. Tu Fu wrote constantly and copiously about his reactions, and these poems are all attached, as lyric poetry usually is, to specific occasions. The poems reveal Tu Fu more intimately than if all one's information about him came from public documents, funeral steles, and such. A close, sensitive reading of poems composed over a brief number of years will show that much can be elucidated by reading Tu Fu's poems for a sequence of moods.[108] Cumulatively the reader comes to feel that he knows Tu Fu in a personal way that is not true of or possible for any poet up to his time.

Yet although this is knowledge of Tu Fu, it is neither solid nor simple. The reliability of information of this kind fades rapidly when one begins to generalize, as one must. One may safely assume, to begin with, that a poem reflects the poet's mood at that moment, however transient the moment. In addition, one has the impression, in old-style poems (*kushih*) at least, that little contrivance attended the passage from experience to poetic expression. The difficulties arise from the uncertainties attendant upon converting momentary psychological information into biography, especially given the ephemeral context of most lyric poems. Nearly always, literary-critical convention guides the reader to extrapolate from the poems to the man. This practice, however, tends to produce a particular problem of interpretation, a problem in reconciling certain poems with one's impression of the poet already established from information in other poems. In such cases, the common solution is to soften the counterexamples in some way that allows the poet's portrait

108. See Fang Yü, *Chan i hua yü*, pp. 1–31, and also her *K'uei-chou shih*, pp. 9–21, for excellent examples of this approach today.

to remain consistent. Less often is the choice made to alter the prevailing portrait of the poet. That is to say, usually the poems are made to give way, rather than the readers' conception of Tu Fu being modified.

This critical phenomenon is worth a more detailed examination, since readings of some poems differ drastically, depending upon one's understanding of the biographical context. These interpretations are sometimes much controverted, and for this reason it is important to observe that they owe their ambiguity not to strictly literary issues, but to the competing claims of biography and the individual poem. An example will clarify the characteristic ways in which the reader's convictions about Tu Fu's life may both interfere with and contribute to a reading of his poetry. A well-known instance of this phenomenon is the interpretation of the second of the two "Serpentine" poems.[109] This set of two poems was composed in 758, when Tu Fu had returned with Emperor Su-tsung's court to a Ch'ang-an newly wrested from the rebels. The second poem reads:

> Every morning, released, I always pawn my spring clothes,
> And every day I return from the river completely drunk,
> Routine are my wine debts, found wherever I go,
> Rare has been the person who lives to be seventy.
> Butterflies thread through the flowers, visible in their recesses,
> Dragonflies touch down on water, then dart on.
> I say to the spring scenery: we make our rounds together,
> I have only a moment to enjoy you, please don't be aloof.

If there were no accompanying biographical information, this would be an unproblematic poem. The speaker seems to be a buoyant, irresponsible person, resembling Li Po. He takes his court duties lightly, finding that court clothes can be useful for other purposes than wearing to court. Carpe diem is his philosophy, and he has an easy mastery of light yet intricately constructed lines that sweep the reader along with him.

The problem is, the author is Tu Fu, and the court appointment airily mentioned in the poem is the one which he had long sought, finally received, and then frequently and gratefully mentioned in other poems. This poem seems to contradict everything we know and believe about Tu Fu. By contrast, other poems from this period in Ch'ang-an more expectedly show his total dedication to duty. In one he sits up the whole night to await a court audience at dawn, with a memorial at the ready for presentation. In another, after the dawn audience, rather than moving on to drinking bouts, as in this poem, he returns to his office and works

109. "Serpentine," Two poems, 308/19/30A–B.

through the day on drafts of a memorial.[110] Even the first "Serpentine" poem, although similar in setting and action to the second (here also the poet drinks amid spring scenery by the Serpentine River), that poem is at least openly melancholy and does not boast of pawning court clothes and running up wine debts everywhere. This particular poem, by contrast, gives us a damning portrait of a Tu Fu derelict in his duties even though the rebel emergency was far from over. Li Po might behave this way, or Tu Fu's talented, eccentric friend Cheng Ch'ien (with whom he drinks by the Serpentine River in another poem from this time),[111] but not Tu Fu, and so the Ch'ing commentator Wang Ssu-shih wrote, "At first I was unhappy with this poem. The state still faced many problems, Tu Fu held an office as remonstrator – is this the time for an official to be pursuing pleasures?"[112]

Wang Ssu-shih's criticism is a moral one, or, in the terms suggested here, his basic framework is biographical. He faulted not the poems but their writer for what appeared to him (though only initially) as a lapse in the person he felt Tu Fu to be. Accordingly, when upon reflection Wang decided that he had misjudged the poem, his self-correction was arrived at through a reconsideration of the biographical context. First, he says, it suddenly came to him what the set of two poems really meant in Tu Fu's life, and then that insight in turn enabled him to grasp the true tone of the poem. Tu Fu, he realized, is not seeking wine for its own sake but as a release for his pent-up anxiety. As for his seeming to have forgotten the problems of empire, he in fact felt keenly the frustration of holding office while being permitted no scope for action. Wang Ssu-shih reminded himself that in just six more months Tu Fu would be demoted to the small town of Hua-chou, so we can surmise that injurious talk must even now be circulating at court. "The composition of these two poems," he concluded, "is owing to his worrying about slander and derision."

The biographical context Wang Ssu-shih sketched is indeed confirmed by (and derived from) other poems of this period, which do express their author's unease and dissatisfaction. For Wang, a reminder of Tu Fu's circumstances was sufficient to allay his misgivings about the hedonism in the second "Serpentine" poem: presumably the hedonism now represented a legitimate outlet. Critics today, however, must continually test the linkage between biography and poetry that Wang Ssu-shih was free to take for granted. In this light, the poem may well be a

---

110. "Overnight in Spring at the Imperial Chancellery," 310/19/39, and "Leaving the Imperial Chancellery Late," 311/19/41.
111. "Drinking by Serpentine River," 308/19/31.
112. Wang Ssu-shih, *Tu i* 2.65.

perfect candidate for the exhibition of the possible freedom of the work of art from gross, direct biographical connections. To such a critic, less invested in protecting Tu Fu's reputation, the poem may be self-explanatory. After all, no question is raised in it which the poem itself cannot answer; questions arise only by comparing the poem's sentiments to an external factor, to the prevailing conception of Tu Fu's character. Thus the poem may constitute one small proof that he was occasionally, when writing for himself, capable of writing a poem in which poet and persona are two separate entities. Perhaps, even though the author is Tu Fu, it may be possible to divorce the poem from his seriousness and read it as a Li Po–style composition.

This poem has been discussed at such length here because one might especially expect modern critics to notice and exploit this discrepant moment. If it can be shown, even in one case, that the poet's life is not relevant to reading a poem, then a small wedge between life and poems has been inserted. Other examples might then be found to widen this wedge, and our conceptions altered of a poet who is, of all poets, quintessentially defined by his own words. Yet, despite this inviting opportunity, it seems that where Tu Fu is concerned, a divorce of poetry and biography is instinctively unconvincing. Certainly it continues to be eschewed by modern critics, who agree with tradition in rejecting a purely hedonistic reading of the poem. Instead, modern readings supply a needed refinement of traditional views by isolating more persuasively the necessary textual support. This approach leaves intact the traditional conjunction of poetry with biography, for the more precise reading is then fashioned into a more complex portrait of the poet, along the lines suggested by Wang Ssu-shih.

The second "Serpentine" poem proves amenable to this procedure. Since in other poems of the Ch'ang-an months, idealism and dissatisfaction do contradictorily coexist, to fit in the second "Serpentine" poem with them critics need to uncover in it darker strains amid the careless dissolution. The poem's theme helps here. Carpe diem, after all, tends to conceal a disillusioned view of life only just below the surface. Thus, once motivated to do so, one now notices the subdued sense of powerlessness in the last couplet ("I say to the spring scenery: we make our rounds together / I have only a moment to enjoy you, please don't be aloof.") The request now seems a plea and more significant than one had realized. More subtly, Yeh Chia-ying has convincingly pointed out that the first couplet, which in one reading is blithely carefree, is in fact ambiguous. Its forgetfulness is forced, she feels, and she notes how weariness permeates the phrases "every morning," "every day," "always," and "completely." In them, she notes, fatigue is expressed four times in two lines.[113] Similarly, Ronald Egan has pointed out that, far from being carefree, every line alludes to the poet's worries.[114] More attentive readings such as these reveal a darker range of moods and hence a more subtle view of Tu Fu than one's initial impression of cheerful dissipation. The second thoughts about officialdom that experience is known to have brought Tu Fu are shown to be latent in the poem, not merely imported.

Readings such as these seek to establish the poem as the source of information, rather than require that supplementary, justifying facts about Tu Fu be borrowed from his other contemporary poems. These readings are better in that they are better supported, and they have in fact led to a subtler, more shaded portrait of the poet. In the best of them, whether or not the initial motivation is biographical, the analyses scrupulously adduce only internal evidence for support. The personality of the poet remains, however, a permanent reference point. It seems that it is impossible to write about Tu Fu's poetry without being engaged on some level with filling out the picture of his life.

An instructive contrasting example to the second "Serpentine" poem is provided by a later poem, "Return in Spring" (356/21/43), dated to 764. The "return" of the title refers to Tu Fu's return in that year to his Thatched Hut outside the city of Ch'eng-tu, after nearly two years' absence in Tzu-chou, one hundred miles to the east. This poem too declares the poet's intention to stay as drunk as possible, and his reason again is the shortness of life. The last six lines of the twelve-line poem are especially pertinent:

> Far off, the gulls are still, afloat on the water,
> Swallows light and aslant, sheered in the wind:
> One's path through the world is filled with thorns,
> And my life too has its end.
> This person will sober up just to drink again,
> And, if my inclination holds, this will be home.

Seated by the riverbank, the poet pours for himself. In these lines he shows none of the cares that he expresses in other poems written upon the same return, such as:

> Rootless, in the world's wind and dust,
> Where may an old man be set down?[115]

---

113. Yeh Chia-ying, "Lun Tu Fu ch'i-lü chih yen-chin chi ch'i ch'eng-hsien ch'i-hou chih ch'eng-chiu" 論杜甫七律之演進及其承先啟後之成就, in *Chia-ling t'an shih*, pp. 92–3.
114. Ronald Egan, *Ou-yang Hsiu*, p. 90.
115. "Thatched Hut," 143/10/18, lines 55–6.

The somewhat irresponsible sentiments of "Return in Spring" reveal no such gloom, yet they have never really created problems. One speculates that they are felt, even given evidence to the contrary, to be consistent with the poet's life at this time. His second stay in the Thatched Hut lasted about a year, after which the poet left Szechuan altogether for the middle Yangtze region. This year is seen as largely a continuation of the first halcyon Thatched Hut years. The contentment and personal tranquillity of these two periods are considered to provide a countermotif to the poems concerned with the recurring military and political crises. Nonetheless, if the criterion used in the second "Serpentine" poem were used here, the attitude in this poem might be criticized as verging on the casual. No objections, however, have been raised by critics. The poet is known to be living in retirement, when a carpe diem attitude might be considered a right.

This discussion has illustrated some of the assumptions made in the Chinese critical tradition about the connection between the poet and his work. If these common working assumptions are correct, then some of the major premises of modern Western literary criticism are simply inapplicable to Tu Fu. Two of these premises are especially pertinent here. One is the distinctions made between person, poet, and persona. The second is the assertion that meaning is ultimately indeterminable.

The distinction between poet and "persona" was first made popular as a principle by the New Critics, who saw the methodological advantages, at least in an early stage of analysis, in being able systematically to divorce the poet's personal views from the artifice by which he made them known. Deconstruction has taken this up more rigidly, enforcing a distinction at all stages and adding a distinction between the "person" and the poet. According to this reasoning, it is no longer possible to accept a complete identification between the author and his or her words. Whatever might be the validity of this assertion in philosophical terms, in practical respects it goes completely against the context in which lyric poetry is written, as well as the way it is received. In the writing and reception of lyric poetry, poets and readers have acted as though the three roles are one. The sentiments and views in a poem are assumed to reflect the poet's, and the poet's views are assumed to be the man's. On this assumption, poems are written, received, and acted upon, sometimes with grave consequences. These assumptions are made about everyone's work but apply with particular force to Tu Fu because he writes more about genuinely personal subjects and less on conventionally personal ones. By contrast, with Wang Wei and Li Po we may make do with the poet and the persona, for the person is absent for lack of information in the poetry.

In Chinese lyric poetry the exceptions to this convergence of identities are instructive because they are conventional exceptions and hence are considered separately from the main body of lyric poetry. Subject matter, voice, point of view, plot development, and style may each be conventionalized, and choices made in each determine the subgenre of the work. The ballad provides the most prominent category of conventional exceptions, yet even in such categorical exceptions, concealed personal views are often suspected. Poems on objects (*yung-wu shih*) are often searched for hints of authorial attitudes toward events. Furthermore, conventional exceptions such as court poems are often roundly condemned as empty frivolity precisely because the poet's own self is not to be found in them.

A partial exception is the category of names that are adopted by oneself or given by others. By this means the poet can refer to himself in the third person and thus put a distance between himself and his portrayed self. Tu Fu uses at least five. His choices emphasize his status as a nonofficial, an ordinary person: "the rustic old man of Tu-ling," "the guest from Tu-ling." Bestowing attributive names on oneself is a custom that flourished in the Sung and later dynasties. Such names form only a partial exception, however, for these identities are transparently assumed and reveal more distinctly some aspect of the poet's personality, rather than distancing the poet from his words. Thus, although the identity of person, poet, and persona is an unexamined assumption in the Chinese poetic tradition, it is one that is corroborated by the history of poetic practice and reception.

Another major premise in modern Western criticism which does not apply to much of Chinese lyric poetry, especially that of Tu Fu, is the assertion that the poetry's meaning is indeterminable. Borrowed from analytic philosophy and set up as a premise of literary interpretation, this idea, applied by deconstructionist criticism, undermines the authority of the author in assigning meaning to his words but places that authority with no one. In addition, doubt is also cast on the epistimological ability of readers to agree on a work's meaning. However, the assumption of authorial sincerity that pervades every aspect of Chinese lyric poetry, its writing, its reception, and its criticism, is fundamentally at odds with this assertion. In the lyric tradition, sincerity can be assumed, because the poem's expression is the poet's and the poet speaks with the man's voice. (Again the exceptions are conventionally known.) Meaning is indeterminable only if the poet has been deliberately (and usually politicly) oblique. Both aesthetic and moral criticism are founded upon the conviction of sincerity in a lyric poem. In Chinese criticism, sincerity is not viewed as a tautological trap, as it is in the recent West, but rather as the quality that serves to transport the reader directly from the poem to its author's life.

One implication for investigating the intimate connection between Tu Fu's life and his poetry is that studies of Tu Fu ought to advance on two fronts simultaneously, his life and his poetry. This may seem an obvious point, but in fact, whatever the initial point of departure, works of criticism have tended toward biography and have, comparatively, neglected poetry. Tu Fu's poetry is so copiously about himself that it begs for biographical criticism, which it has received, in great amounts. Consequently, in practice the problem is to do justice to the poetry's poetic aspects. In the existing scholarship, biography has proved primary, elemental, in a way that poetry has not, even though nearly all the primary material we have is in the form of poetry.

For several reasons it has proved easy to slight the poetic aspects in favor of biography. First, we feel we know what biography is: it is a life, and therefore we should know as many details about it as possible. One's task is thus already delineated. The kind of life we think it is and the details deemed desirable may vary according to the culture of one's era – the Sung had theirs and we have ours – but either way readers feel they have a firm idea of what biography is. Then, too, because the life has to be painstakingly reconstructed by working with the poetry, it is natural to feel that the poetry has been dealt with. Third, it is natural to be guided by the direction of the existing scholarship. Interpretation, solidified since the eleventh century, has in general, if not in detail, been an interpretation of the life rather than the poetry. This is particularly the case when an intense and personal sense of identification with the poet constituted the primary mode of appreciation. Modern work updates that approach by passing lightly over the moral overtones wherever possible, but it is unable to escape the underpinning of biography. This leads to a fourth reason, which is that in the end we do have to refer back to the life, for the poetry is so evidently biographical and personal that any other course would be perverse. The moral critics of the Sung dynasty, with their interpretation of the poetry in terms of the person Tu Fu, have emphasized a vital connection. When these causes are added together, the unintended consequence is a tendency to jump to the end, to the poems' inevitable connection to their author, and wittingly or unwittingly to direct the work toward framing, filling in, and refining the poetry's biographical context. The poetic context has been far from well understood, and in most studies one tends in the end to have learned a great deal about Tu Fu and rather less about the poetry.

In planning a new study of Tu Fu, one major concern is to explore ways of extracting more, and different, information from the poems.

Nearly all that we must know about Tu Fu we can learn only from him. The scant biographical material that is contemporary or nearly contemporary and that does not originate with Tu Fu reveals little by comparison with the wealth contained in his poetry. At the same time, we find that that information is conveyed by an entity – poetry – whose nature is far from fully understood or acknowledged. A study, whether focused on the poet or on the poetry, must make a series of successive forays from the poetry to the life and back to the poetry. The critic cannot plan to solve a set of questions about the life once and for all and then to use that knowledge to work with a set of questions about the poetry.

In order to work at the same time with both the poetry and the poet, the methodology employed in this volume is to devise concepts that can operate in both realms – biography and poetry – and to use these concepts as the methodological pivot of each chapter. In Chapter 2, I focus on the concept of topicality, which both functions as a neutral equivalent to the usual emphasis on the poet's compassion and also allows us to address the poetic issue of how contemporary events are treated in poetic form. In Chapters 3 and 4, two such concepts are defined. One is the structure of "juxtaposition," which points to an author whose feelings at times overpower him and at the same time characterizes a certain mode of composition. The second concept, that of themes, complements the lessons of juxtaposition. In Tu Fu's poetry, there is a natural continuity between the themes of the poetry and the preoccupations of the poet. Thus his themes provide a means by which we may both study motifs in the poetry and understand the poet who uses certain themes so plentifully. The conclusion examines the concept of sincerity, which also has been applied equally to the poet and to his works. As such it allows us to consider again, from another angle, the mutual dependency of our admiration of the poet and of his poetry.

Periodization

Schemes that divide Tu Fu's work into periods vary, but all use the onset of the An Lu-shan rebellion as the major division and make further subdivisions according to his geographic movements after 755. A common scheme uses four stages: (1) the pre-An Lu-shan years; (2) the years from 755 to 759, when the poet left the Central Plains; (3) the years in Ch'eng-tu (759–66); (4) the years in K'uei-chou (766–8) and Hunan Province (768–77), the last chiefly along the Hsiang River. Some schemes conflate the last two periods, for a total of three; some separate the K'uei-chou and Hunan years into two periods, for a total of five. The brief time spent in Ch'in-chou between leaving the Central Plains and

54

arriving in Szechuan Province, is sometimes counted separately, because of the poet's great productivity in those months.

It is not possible at present to write a history of Tu Fu's development as a poet. When one is written, its broad outlines likely will reflect the now commonly accepted divisions. Overall, no serious objections can be made to this scheme: we must have some scheme, and this one serves well in several important respects. Its first advantage is that although the stages coincide suspiciously closely to the major stages of Tu Fu's life, external changes did profoundly affect the poetry, and shifts of residence must be taken into account in any discussion of the poetry. Furthermore, in some analyses of the poetry, this framework has served well. Yeh Chia-ying has convincingly discussed the development of Tu Fu's seven-character regulated-verse poems in terms of these stages. She has illustrated advances in his skill and feeling in each period, advances that well justify her designation of them as stages in his development.[116]

Reservations might nevertheless be noted about this model of Tu Fu's artistic growth. A framework so dependent upon biographical facts lacks sufficient poetry-based evidence by which to make refinements. In fact, in nearly all criticism, the four periods are characterized by biographical information masquerading as thematic analysis (Thatched Hut peace, Thatched Hut difficulties; Hsiang River uncertainty). Clearly, for the poetry of a given period, we need nuanced characterizations that add up to more than a subtle portrait of the poet. The model makes only rough divisions, adequate for the pattern of the whole life but inadequate for understanding poems within any given stage. We have a small number of poems, 130 (less than 10 percent), in the period before the An Lu-shan rebellion; a somewhat larger number in the years from then to 759, when Tu Fu left the Central Plains – and then an unmanageable 70 percent of his poetry in the last two stages. Are we better off, really? The numerical imbalance alone raises doubt. Even the most manageable group of poems, the poems of the pre-755 years, such as "Ballad of Beauties" and "Five Hundred Words Expressing My Feelings on the Way from the Capital to Feng-hsien County," are mostly interpreted in terms of biographical information and as anticipation of the work to come (which, of course, it is).

Tu Fu's style clearly changed over time, and the periodization of his poetry remains the basis by which one may investigate this change and refine the model. My discussion of his use of the structure of juxtaposition relates the changes in its frequency and context to his poetic stages and thus reinforces the validity of the standard divisions.

116. Yeh Chia-ying, "Lun Tu Fu ch'i-lü," in *Chia-ling t'an shih*, pp. 84–117.

On the other hand, not everything in his poetic oeuvre changed. Although he experimented with new uses of the ballad form, he also wrote conventional ballads throughout his life, and his use of the long, journal-like poems also appears to have been constant. In trying to define changes more fully, we should not forget that some aspects of his poetry do not change.

Prosodic forms

Study of Tu Fu's prosodic forms usually is initially very productive, for he employed every prosodic form available to the T'ang poet and, depending on the state in which he found a particular prosodic form, either made outstanding advances or contributed outstanding examples. The prosodic forms that he used are: old-style verse (*ku-shih*), both the five- and seven-character line; regulated verse or recent-style verse (*lü-shih* or *chin-t'i shih*), in both line lengths; the quatrain (*chueh-chü*), in both line lengths; extended regulated verse (*p'ai-lü*), in both line lengths; and the ballad (*yueh-fu*) form, also in both line lengths. This makes a total of ten verse forms. In addition he wrote an irregular version of seven-character regulated verse that became an established variation known as *ao-t'i shih*. Most commentators single out his seven-character regulated verse (*ch'i-lü*) and its variant (*ao-t'i*) as his greatest innovations; to this may be added his work in five-character old-style verse, by his time long a fully established form.

Roughly speaking, the regulated form and the old-style form raise the overall methodological question of how to connect the study of prosodic forms with other issues in the poetry. The study of prosodic form, in particular the study of regulated verse, has obvious approaches and guarantees at least some results. However, prosodic studies have tended to take place in isolation. It has proved difficult to state, except in the most preliminary way, what functions each form served for Tu Fu, whether these functions changed over time, and similar questions.[117] By contrast, the analysis of his themes is sure to cut across prosodic categories, but here the problem is that in Tu Fu's work any theme is illustrated by so many poems as to defy organization.

Regulated verse, in particular seven-character regulated verse, has been the most studied of Tu Fu's prosodic forms. This emphasis was encouraged in part by the poet's frequent references to his interest in regulated verse. Effective methods of analysis exist and have been widely applied. Scholarship and connoisseurship between them have provided

117. For a good summary, see Davis, *Tu Fu*, pp. 107–27.

the necessary observations, vocabulary, theory, and history, and knowledge in this area is most concrete, being closely based on examples. The many comments on individual lines and couplets, especially those made in the compilations known generically as "remarks on poetry" (*shih-hua*), has given us a rich technical vocabulary with which to discuss questions of word choice, word position, prosodic requirements, line balance, imagery, feeling, and many other points. One instance of detailed observation is the attention paid to Tu Fu's choice for the final character in odd-numbered, nonrhyming lines. Regulated verse usually employs a level-tone (*p'ing-sheng*) rhyme; hence the nonrhyming lines usually end with an oblique-tone (*tse-sheng*) word. Rather than using one of the three oblique tones at random, Tu Fu rotates among the three tones (rising, leaving, and entering) that make up the category,[118] a prosodically unnecessary but musically pleasing refinement. That one poem by his grandfather Tu Shen-yen employs the same device has also not escaped attention.[119] A corresponding methodology and vocabulary in English criticism are provided by the close-reading methods developed by the New Critics. Modern criticism is thus able to adapt easily to the study of regulated verse. In addition, the history of the seven-character version of regulated verse is simple up to the time of Tu Fu, and his development of the form is also well documented, since it took place within a dramatically few years. These reasons together mean that the finely wrought poem represented by regulated verse has been much studied.

The limitation of investigating regulated verse in isolation lies in the frustration that results from simply analyzing one intricately perfect form of self-expression after another. An artistically perfect poem is easy to study as "the poem itself" but difficult to relate to other issues. For this reason, the approach in this volume does not focus on regulated verse alone but studies it in contexts that yield two highly contrastive conclusions. First, in Chapter 2, I shall argue that Tu Fu's characteristic theme of pity for the suffering of ordinary people has a different character when it occurs in a perfect regulated-verse poem than it does when it occurs in an old-style poem or in a ballad. In the regulated-verse poems that I use as examples, the placement of each line and theme, however heartfelt, is so balanced and right that its beauty tempers feeling. By contrast, in old-style poems and ballads, other conventions than aesthetics prevail. Thus in Chapter 2, regulated verse and old-style verse are antithetical forms when examined in the light of certain themes. The

---

118. Chu I-tsun (1629–1709), *P'u-shu-t'ing chi* 33.10b–12a. Discussed in Yang Lien-sheng's review of William Hung, *Tu Fu*, in *Harvard Journal of Asiatic Studies* 15 (1953), 267–8.
119. Noted in Ho Shu-chen, *Tu Fu wu-yen chin-t'i-shih*, p. 9.

poems discussed in Chapters 3 and 4, however, demonstrate the opposite connection between the two verse forms: here I find that regulated-verse and old-style poems share a distinctive structural feature which I term "juxtaposition." Tu Fu's characteristic themes occur in structurally the same manner, whether in regulated-verse or old-style poems.

The problems encountered in the study of the old-style form, especially the five-character version, are different from those presented by regulated verse. Unlike regulated verse, the old-style form has usually not been treated as a single entity. Consistent with the traditional tendency toward fragmentizing definitions, old-style poetry is usually subdivided into many stylistic categories. The principles of division are at least partially systematic. Two major divisions categorize the poems according to themes or subgenres (travel poems, allegorical poems are examples). Another system is chronological: poems are characterized as "Chien-an style" (after the reign era), or "Ch'i-Liang style" (after the poetry of the Ch'i and Liang dynasties). A related chronological system is eponymous: "Su–Li style," after Li Ling and Su Wu; "Hsieh style," after Hsieh Ling-yun. Anthology-based terms (*Wen-hsuan* style, *Yü-t'ai* style) are also employed. In these methods of organizing the vast number of poems in old-style verse, poetic innovations were recognized by the creation of new categories, rather than by a conceptual reformulation of the whole. Theory and technical vocabulary are thus scarcely developed. Furthermore, since the old-style form appeared simultaneously with lyric poetry (*shih*), additions to the uses and possibilities of the old-style form were inseparable from changes in lyric poetry itself. Until the evolution of regulated verse, old-style poetry *was* lyric poetry. Thus critical interest focused on lyric poetry (*shih*) rather than on its prosodic (old-style) form. Only with the evolution of the contrasting regulated verse was the old-style form conceptualized as a form. But it was a form in only a limited sense, a matter of stating its two simple rules: (1) there must nearly always be an even number of lines; (2) the second line must rhyme.

Tu Fu's 263 poems in the five-character old-style form encompass too many kinds of poems to permit wholly consistent organization. Many of his great poems are written in the five-character old-style form, but it is the content of a poem rather than its prosodic form that tends to receive the critic's attention. A five-character old-style poem has rarely been studied as an example of the use of a prosodic form. Take "Journey North," for example. In discussing this poem, critics have singled out the sincerity of the poet, the boldness of his strictures on those in power, the freshness of his descriptions of landscape and family. These are indeed the achievements of "Journey North," but the question, also interesting, of why Tu Fu used the old-style form remains unanswered in detail. In this study, I define two subgroups of the five-character old-style form that can be usefully analyzed. The poems of Chapter 2 are used to demonstrate the uncertain boundary between the old-style form and the ballad. The tentative overlap found in some poems reveals old-style form and ballad form at an experimental border. In Chapter 3, I suggest that the elastic structure of the old-style form includes various types of structures, including that of juxtaposition. Thus the known versatility of the five-character old-style form is made less amorphous by the creation of two newly defined types within this form.

The legacy of Tu Fu is complex and belongs both to cultural history and to the history of literature. To an unusual degree, his reception has been equated with his achievement, and the explicit unraveling of the two has perhaps required the evolution of a different world from that of China in traditional times. The debt owed to scholars of the past is enormous, but with the creation of realms beyond Confucianism's penetration, the pattern of the past becomes more discernible. It may be true that every era constructs its own version of a heroic figure. It is not, however, the purpose here to make Tu Fu relevant – that can be accomplished, or not, by the poetry itself – but to renew our appreciation of a great and complex talent by reconsidering the contexts of his greatness.

2

Social conscience: Compassion and topicality in the poetry

Tu Fu was forty-four in 755 when the An Lu-shan rebellion began. When he died fifteen years later, political control had nominally returned to imperial hands, but the turmoil set in motion by the rebellion had spawned second- and third-generation rebellions. By then, many of the main leaders on both sides had died, but there was no lack of parties eager to exploit the weaknesses revealed and deepened by the initial rebellion. The unrest spread beyond the Central Plains of An Lu-shan's activities, southward into the Yangtze region and southwest into Szechuan Province. To the native disruptions were added incursions by Uighurs to the northwest and by Tibetans in Szechuan. Even after the surrender of rebel forces in 763, the northeastern provinces essentially retained their independence. For the remaining twelve decades of the dynasty an uneasy balance, with periodic outbreaks of conflict, was maintained among the ambitions of the various parties.

From the evidence of Tu Fu's poems, he either personally experienced or closely followed these developments, at first at the center, in the Central Plains, later on the empire's periphery. At the rebellion's outbreak, Tu Fu was living in the Ch'ang-an region, and thus he witnessed and recorded many of the dramatic crises of the first years. With the prolongation of the conflict, he moved his family to Szechuan (in 759). There he encountered local rebellions and Tibetan invasions, while, as his poems show, he continued to follow the news and rumors from the Central Plains. At his death, in a river town on the Hsiang tributary of the Yangtze, he had just waited out the suppression of an insurrection at T'an-chou and was perhaps altering his plans to contend with yet another local rebellion. Thus, for the remainder of his life, wherever he lived, the consequences of the initial rebellion were evident to him.

61

Tu Fu was forty-four and, it seems, already writing seriously when the empire changed around him. After the onset of the rebellion, his subject matter changed completely as he turned his entire attention to the devastation and suffering that followed. What he saw around him – the lives of his family, neighbors, and strangers – what he heard, and what he hoped for or feared from the progress of various campaigns – these became the most enduring themes of his poetry. A rebellion that turned out to have unlimited consequences was thrust upon him. He was, as Philip Larkin wrote of Wilfred Owen, chained to a historical event. Recording a world that erupted and was destroyed became the work of his life.

It is on this record that Tu Fu's moral authority as a poet is founded. The concerns of this record are widely known and may be summed up as the theme of compassion. It surfaces in the many poems and passages in which Tu Fu feelingly describes the suffering of his countrymen, criticizes the state for its conduct of the war, and calls for the redress of injustice done to the people; it is revealed in poems in which he speaks for the people by voicing their desire for lighter taxes and for peace; it is found in poems where he writes warmly and intimately of his wife, children, relatives, and neighbors. In discussions of his compassion, certain poems and passages are repeatedly cited. The reader will recognize the group when a few representative titles are mentioned: "Journey North," "Ch'iang Village," "Ballad of P'eng-ya," the two sets of poems known as "Three Officials" and "Three Partings," "Ballad of Firewood Carriers," and "Song of My Thatched Roof Torn by Autumn Winds." One might also include some poems that antedate the rebellion, "Ballad of Army Carts," "Ballad of Beauties," and "Five Hundred Words Expressing My Feelings on the Way from the Capital to Feng-hsien." These poems, and their themes, are familiar to even the casual reader of Tu Fu.

Another, equally important, reason for holding Tu Fu in high esteem is his technical achievements. The brilliance and number of his innovations, the intricacies of his diction and grammar, and his mastery of prosodic form have made him the favorite poet of connoisseurs. Over the centuries, collections of comments on poetry came to devote more space to Tu Fu than to any other poet.

Admiration for him has long been based on an appreciation of his double achievement. Wang An-shih, who was among his earliest admirers, lauded him both for his moral seriousness and for the variety and intricacy of his work.[1] But these two components, although always linked

1. Wang An-shih includes Tu Fu among the four poets of his (now lost) *Ssu-chia shih-hsuan*, whose preface praises the dazzling range of his tone. (See Hu Tzu, *T'iao-hsi yü-yin ts'ung-*

as the twin bases for his unparalleled eminence in the tradition of lyric poetry, indeed in the traditional culture as a whole, have seldom been joined together in demonstration. Even the poems on which they rely differ. Comments on his poetic achievements, dwelling on technical subtleties, have usually been illustrated by specific lines and words rather than entire poems. If illustrated by entire poems, the poems are largely drawn from his later periods (chiefly the K'uei-chou years), with an emphasis on the seven-character regulated form and its variant (*ao-t'i*). By contrast, discussions of Tu Fu's moral authority have been based on a different set of poems, in particular those written in the early years of the rebellion, including those just named. Many poems, of course, can serve as examples for both theses, especially since concern for the suffering of others persists throughout Tu Fu's life and is evident also in the later periods of more intricate techniques. Nonetheless, critics have by and large used one set of poems and passages to illustrate his technical achievements and another for his moral achievements. Consequently technical subtlety and moral exemplariness have remained separate aspects of the appreciation of Tu Fu.

There is, however, one area in which the twin bases of his achievement have been linked together: criticism of the poems concerned with the larger issues of the nature and functions of lyric poetry. In this context, Tu Fu is seen as someone who both revived and sustained the most ancient of the purposes of poetry, its moral seriousness. In this view, the never-dormant demand that lyric poetry fulfill a morally worthwhile purpose found its perfect illustration in the body of Tu Fu's poetry as a whole. By the consistency and quality of his example, he permanently rescued lyric poetry from the superficial gracefulness and aestheticism to which, as an indispensable element of official social life, it was always liable. The undeviating, active Confucian sense of responsibility which Tu Fu expressed in his work brought the moral function of lyric poetry to attention in a forceful new way that was, in addition, to have a permanent influence on subsequent poetry. Although three centuries passed before the moral tenor of his writing was appreciated, the force of his example, once established, ensured that poetry could never lightly pass into frivolity for long.

In this chapter I seek to integrate the two components of Tu Fu's reputation in the same group of poems, by uncovering, in precisely that group of poems most frequently cited as evidence of Tu Fu's compassion, evidence of a continuing literary endeavor as well. Usually the

---

hua, ch'ien-chi, 6.37.) In his poem "Portrait of Tu Fu," Wang An-shih focuses his praise on Tu Fu's poverty, dedication, and loyalty (in *Tu Fu chüan*, 1:80).

K'uei-chou poems are evoked as examples of his interest in poetry as poetry. In this chapter I ask whether in these "compassion poems" as well (to use a shorthand term) Tu Fu was trying to solve problems relating to his medium, and, at the same time, wanted to depict the sorrow and suffering that followed upon the rebellion. If this is the case, what were the problems which he encountered? What forms did the problems take, and what were his solutions?

The formulation of these questions is designed to take us beyond the one quality of the compassion poems that is abundantly clear: their moral burden. Tu Fu's appeal, though unheard by his contemporaries, has since been heard by every generation of readers. Yet it is curiously difficult to say anything about this achievement that amounts to more than a restatement of the same basic observation about his compassion. One could say of one poem, "Here Tu Fu shows his burning desire to set to rights the empire," and of another poem, "Here Tu Fu shows his deep sympathy for the common people," and continue in this vein through the many examples in his work. Elaborations upon this basic observation, however, are not easy either to make or to find. It seems that the concept of Tu Fu's moral preeminence, having being established in cultural terms, is of limited usefulness in literary issues. In order to move from a moral to a literary description, one must shift attention from the author to the poetry, but the existing categories of analysis do not allow this. The result is that concepts formed in one sphere are asked to serve in the other. To avoid this conflation, it is proposed here to find a way to join the literary nature of the poems and their moral status in one concept. Before proposing such a tool, it is first necessary to clarify a few concepts.

The first clarification concerns the concept of compassion. Compassion, though surmised from the poems, is a quality of the poet rather than the poems. It is clear, then, that an equivalent concept is required that is equally broad but that is based directly upon the poems. Furthermore, in Tu Fu's case the quality of compassion may be thought of as a component of his social and political concern. In Tu Fu's poems, political criticism and appeals are made in a far from dispassionate way, for emotion rather than reason acts as their driving force. It follows that many of the characteristics of compassion can be explained by its affinity to Tu Fu's political concern. For example, its boundaries in the poems – almost coterminous with the poet's work – are difficult to delimit, since traditionally political views are so broadly construed that all social comments have potentially political implications. And, like the political views, Tu Fu's compassion unifies numerous otherwise disparate poems and themes by centering the focus on the poet. Just as Tu Fu's social and political views are valued not so much for their practical worth as for their evocation of a man of deep moral concern, so it is that the poet as a person, by his abiding compassion, ties together diverse themes under the heading of "compassion." "Compassionate" describes the author very well, and when applied to the poems, it sums up an attitude, a motivation, that is held in common by these poems. The words "attitude" and "motivation," of course, again refer to the author. The need is clear for a concept equivalent to compassion which has an equally unifying capacity but refers directly to the poems.

This equivalent is topicality. That in Tu Fu's poems topicality and compassion are near-equivalent qualities is evident: all the various events and scenes which so arouse the reader's sympathy are topical in nature; the poet has recorded what he has witnessed or heard or experienced. The concept of topicality, however, has an important advantage over that of compassion. It provides an objective way of regarding his particular contribution to poetry, for the recording of topical events is not as fraught with moral values as is the act of bearing witness to suffering. Recasting the concept of compassion as one of topicality enables one to open the discussion to literary issues, for it is then easier to ask related questions: which topical issues are treated? how is the selection made? Other questions of poetic interest follow naturally – questions about the manner of treatment, about how that treatment compares with the poetic tradition which Tu Fu inherited, and about the language and styles which he used to depict his topical subjects. These questions allow access to aspects of the poems that are primarily literary rather than moral.

The questions raised in this manner can be thought of as concerning either content or style. Tu Fu's selection of topics, although highly original, is quite straightforward. (I shall deal with it later in this chapter in the section entitled "Subject Matter.") The greater part of this chapter will explore how Tu Fu approached the seemingly simple stylistic problem of recording what he saw around him. This may appear to be a simple problem, because in these compassion poems his language is generally simple. Nonetheless, no matter how directly he expressed himself, his expression could not be truly direct. The words he used are modified by their organization into poetry, and their organization is modified by the poet's consciousness of the multifarious traditions that govern poetry. To see the effects of those modifications, one must identify and describe the processes of modification. This is especially true when studying a poet like Tu Fu, who, more than most, appeared to write his experiences directly into poetry, seemingly without the veil of literature. In fact, however, in many of the compassion poems Tu Fu related to the reality around him in a formally complicated way. The problem he faced can be framed as one of depiction. We shall see that he tried a variety of partially successful solutions, retaining some and dropping others. Then without being fully resolved, the whole problem of the depiction of topical events as he had first formulated it gradually receded as other interests and obsessions developed.

It is important to begin by looking at the problem of depiction in an overly dry way as a purely technical one. Although in our criticism depiction must ultimately be reconnected with the themes of compassion and morality, to do so too soon will cut off necessary further investigation. For example, Tu Fu has often been praised for the vividness and simplicity with which he conveys scenes of suffering and thus arouses the reader's sympathy. That he conveys such scenes vividly is, of course, beyond question, but it does not necessarily follow that this vividness should immediately be attributed to the poet's moral integrity, exemplified in his compassion. A poem can be completely sincere and compassionate and nonetheless be quite wooden. In a successful poem, the vividness might be attributed to something called "genius" (to be sure an unsatisfactory solution in its own way), but one can see that it does not absolutely have to be attributed to something called "compassion." To take another example, Hu Shih and Hsiao Ti-fei, both writing in modern times, praise Tu Fu for his vividness and attribute it to the simplicity of his language. For Hu Shih, eager to promote the vernacular as the literary medium, this was vernacular language (*paihua*); for Hsiao Ti-fei, enjoined to make a proletariat case for Tu Fu, it was "the language of the people."[2] Both views are partly true. In many poems it is the simple, direct language which renders scenes vivid, and, as Hu Shih and Hsiao Ti-fei have pointed out, there is a parallel between Tu Fu's sympathy for the people and his liking for the people's language. Even so, Tu Fu's approach to recording what he saw was far from simple. Why did he choose a simple language (or vernacular language, or "the people's language")? What does the choice mean? To rush to a conclusion, heaping praise with alacrity on Tu Fu's character and his compassion, will take the reader too quickly past problems in which the poet may have been interested.

Subject matter

The equivalent to compassion, I have suggested, is topicality of subject matter, the recording of what the poet observes. By reexamining in the

2. Hu Shih, *Pai-hua wen-hsueh shih*, p. 344; Hsiao Ti-fei, "Hsueh-hsi jen-min yü-yen te shih-jen Tu Fu" 學習人民語言的詩人杜甫, in *Tu Fu yen-chiu*, pp. 163–75.

light of topicality several points which have frequently been made about
Tu Fu's compassion poems, I shall explore in this section the ways in
which Tu Fu's topicality is unusual and how it inaugurated a great
change for poetry.

The first point concerns the widespread praise for the uniqueness
of Tu Fu's themes. Such admiration has usually been phrased in moral
terms, but the uniqueness of his themes can be translated into literary
terms using the idea of topicality. In literary terms, Tu Fu's use of topical
subject matter expanded the themes of lyric poetry (*shih*) to topics
seldom met with in it before. In his hands, anything which has happened
– whether large or small, portentous or trivial – can become the subject
of poetry. Without firing off any manifestos, Tu Fu simply ignored
conventional conceptions of the topics suitable for poetry and went
ahead and used poetry as the vehicle for all his concerns. Through Tu
Fu, lyric poetry was enormously expanded in range and came to
accommodate many new subjects. His poems may vary in their
effectiveness, but the significant thing is that they exist at all. Such
an attitude toward poetry as an extension of experience was to be taken
many steps farther during the Sung dynasty, when the range of subject
matter was expanded even more and the appreciation of small subjects
came to be handled with a connoisseur's delicacy. "Unlike Tu Fu, other
poets did not realize that everything in this world is poetry" – in this
comment by Chang Chieh, Sung-dynasty recognition of his achievement
is precise.[3]

Another characteristic for which Tu Fu is often praised is the consistency of his moral concern. This point, most famously stated in
the comment by Su Shih quoted earlier, and much repeated, is the idea
that through all Tu Fu's vicissitudes, "not for the space of a meal did he
forget his sovereign."[4] Su Shih's point is easily supported, for although
Tu Fu was not alone in describing the Troubles, he was alone in describing them so untiringly in poetry. Poems by others do exist, but they
make up only a handful. Kao Shih devotes a long passage to the imperial
defeat at Ho-yang in 759 (an event which also stimulated the writing of
Tu Fu's "Three Officials" and "Three Partings"). Ts'en Shen wrote a
poem on the effects of civil disorder after a local insurrection in
Szechuan Province. Yuan Chieh wrote several ballads describing the
suffering he saw as prefect of Tao-chou.[5] The examples of these men

3. Chang Chieh, *Sui-han t'ang shih-hua*, in *Li-tai shih-hua hsu-pien*, 1:464.
4. Su Shih, "Preface for the Collected Poems of Wang Kung," in *Tu Fu chüan*, 1:99.
5. Kao Shih (704–65), "Reply to Secretary P'ei in lieu of a Letter" 酬裴員外以詩代書
   (*Ch'üan T'ang shih* 211.2194). Ts'en Shen (d.770), "Halted in Jung-chou and Lu-chou
   by an Insurrection" 阻戎瀘間羣盜 (*Ch'üan T'ang shih* 198.2047). Yuan Chieh (719–

and others,[6] however, do not diminish the praise for Tu Fu. Theirs are isolated pieces, not to be compared with his lifelong production.

The quantity and consistency of Tu Fu's poems have usually been the grounds for praising his morality. But, one might ask, do they not equally provide a key to how his attitude to poetry was different from that of others? Whereas a handful of poems on this subject sufficed for the others, it did not for Tu Fu. One would certainly hesitate to suggest that he was more profoundly moral than some of his contemporaries. Yuan Chieh, for example, by his defense of Pi-yang in 759, secured fifteen cities from Shih Ssu-ming's forces. In addition, Yuan Chieh's severe standards of moral poetry, evinced in his anthology *Ch'ieh-chung chi*, testify to his character in action and in thought. Another hero of both action and morality was Yen Chen-ch'ing, who, with his brother, organized loyalist resistance in rebel-held territory and served the throne well for the remainder of his long life. Even his death in 785 was the meaningful death in the service of his emperor for which Tu Fu yearned in "Year's End."[7] One must conclude that Tu Fu stands in a different relation to both his subject matter and poetry. The intertwining is complex: it is not an interest in poetry alone or moral government alone that produced Tu Fu's works. To take the example of Yuan Chieh again, his "Hymn on the Renaissance of the Great T'ang"[8] concerns two subjects that appear often in Tu Fu's poems – the rebellion in its early months, and the recovery of the two capitals. Yuan Chieh, however, chose the appropriately solemn and noble form of the hymn, and his work takes its place in the tradition of public hymns that date from *Classic of Poetry*. Yen Chen-ch'ing, in an equally grave and public gesture, wrote out the text of Yuan Chieh's hymn for carving as a stone inscription.[9] Tu Fu did not use so public a forum. Perhaps the reason was not simply his obscurity but that formality on this level was not congenial to him. As far as subject matter is concerned, it appears that for Tu Fu the large and the small, the trivial and the far-reaching, were not dissimilar but part of one continuum. For him, even the large subject of good government could be expressed in arresting, trivial details that were both new to poetry and memorable to the mind. Subjects as far apart as affairs of state and the

72), "Song of Ch'ung-ling" 春陵行 and "Shown to Fellow Officials upon the Retreat of the Bandits" 賊退示官吏 (both *Ch'üan T'ang shih* 241.2704).
6. For a number of other poets who took some note of the Troubles in their writings, see Cherniack, "Three Great Poems by Tu Fu," pp. 112–13.
7. "To meet the needs of the crisis, death would not be fearful," Tu Fu writes in his frustration ("Year's End," 352/21/35, line 7).
8. In *Ch'üan T'ang wen, chüan* 380.
9. The hymn (*sung*) employed the four-syllable line of hymns from *Classic of Poetry*. The inscribed stone is known as the "Mo-ya Tablet."

clothing of his children can fall under the same thought. This is why Tu Fu's themes that express social concern, dull in the recital of literary criticism, are often lively in the reading.

Another unusual quality which has received much attention is the frequency with which he wrote about his domestic arrangements, for his attachment to his family is one of his most attractive personal traits. These poems bring out, even more clearly than the poems on the suffering of common folk, the extent of his ready empathy with others. For the Ch'eng-tu and K'uei-chou years, in particular, so many poems survive that it is possible to weave together from them a picture of his everyday life. In those years, no subject seemed too trivial for Tu Fu to put down in verse. The following clutch of such poems from the K'uei-chou years, often discussed together, illustrates this point:

"Urging Tsung-wen to Put up the Chicken Coop"
"Bound Chickens"
"Getting the Boys to Pick Dark Mushrooms"
"Hsin-hsing Repairs the Bamboo Water Pipes"
"Piping Water"
"On Cutting Trees"
"The Garden"
"Return"
"A Gardener Sends a Present of Melon"
"Shown to the Native Servant A-Tuan"

I quoted earlier the Sung-dynasty comment by Chang Chieh that for Tu Fu, "everything in this world is poetry." The modern critic Jao Tsung-i has made a similar observation, writing that "at that time [while he was in K'uei-chou], there was almost nothing that could not enter Tu Fu's poems, there was almost no subject about which a poem could not be made."[10] Another recent writer, Fang Yü, points out that by this time Tu Fu no longer thought of himself as "writing poetry"; he was simply admonishing the children, advising the servants, thanking neighbors and officials, and so on.[11] All subject matter was possible now, and many subjects were unpremeditated, as suggested by four poems that are simply entitled "On [Current] Events" (即事).[12] The Ch'ing-dynasty scholar Ku Yen-wu, observing that in many Tu Fu's poems the title is taken from the first two characters of the first line, takes this as evidence that the impulse to write preceded a clear sense of purpose. He gives six examples of poems in which the first two characters are used for the title

10. Jao Tsung-i, "Lun Tu Fu K'uei-chou shih," in *Chūgoku bungaku hō* 17 (1962), 108–9.
11. Fang Yü, *K'uei-chou shih*, p. 17, and again on p. 57.
12. The poems are 324/20/8, 365/22/37, 429/28/8, and 457/29/31.

and remarks that this is the sign of a poem based on feeling.[13] (In many poems in *Classic of Poetry*, the title is also supplied by the first two characters, but Tu Fu is not here modeling himself on Classical practice. In this he is unlike, say, T'ao Ch'ien, whose imitations of poems from *Classic of Poetry* begin with the title and continue in meter, language, and stanzaic form.)

Tu Fu's all-inclusiveness became more pronounced over time. It is more noticeable in the K'uei-chou years (766–8) than in the Szechuan days (760–6), and more noticeable in the Szechuan period than before. What needs to be emphasized in connection with the poet's inclusiveness is the change for lyric poetry which this change in his work effected, perhaps without conscious plan. The radical nature of the change for poetry, which is much greater than the change within Tu Fu's own development, has been insufficiently recognized. Having politicized everything and personalized politics, Tu Fu placed all subjects on a continuum and made them all permissible. His inventiveness in this respect has been made to appear orthodox by the Mencian nature of his themes, but his attitude toward poetry is, nonetheless, radical. Tu Fu's poetry greatly increased the range of subjects that might enter poetry and thus increased the psychological range of poetry. Nearly everything that is praised in Tu Fu's compassion is, on this level of analysis, new subject matter.

When one considers that the expansion of subject matter is the basis for so much of Tu Fu's work, it is surprising that it is today the least noticeable of his poetic innovations. Chiefly its moral implications attract attention. The innovation in subject matter was, however, at one time very much noticed and the compassion ignored. Most famously, in the tenth century, the sophisticates of the Hsi-k'un school of poetry, unstirred by the moral weight of Tu Fu's themes, saw only the unsuitability of his new subjects. They felt that these subjects were vulgar, and Yang I in particular disparaged Tu Fu as a mere "village gentleman" 村夫子.[14] His objection was probably to the ordinariness of his subject matter and to a Tu Fu who "never felt this village rustic was foolish" 未覺村野醜 and who said, "I go whenever the farmers invite me" 田父邀皆去.[15] Clearly, Tu Fu's expansion of subject matter was noted – and found

13. His examples are "I Haven't Seen" (381/24/12), "Word Recently Came" (148/11/4), "In the Past" (164/12/1), "Year after Year" (462/30/13), "Since Peace" (150/11/7), and "A Guest From" (225/15/4). See *Jih-chih lu, chüan* 21. Quoted by Hsiao Ti-fei, *Tu Fu yen-chiu*, p. 82.
14. For the opinion of Yang I (972–1020), see Liu Pin, *Chung-shan shih-hua*, in *Li-tai shih-hua*, 1:288.
15. The first quotation is from "Forced to Drink," 134/9/24, line 30; the second is from "Cold Food Festival," 358/22/13, line 5.

reprehensible. By the same token, Han Yü's earlier defense of Tu Fu as aesthetically successful implies that some traits in Tu Fu's work – perhaps his writing about everyday matters – prevented Han Yü's favorable view from prevailing.[16] It was not until the apotheosis of Tu Fu in the Sung era that the homely elements of the compassion themes found a context in which they could be appreciated, and then it was primarily a moral context.

In Sung comments, the simplistic standard of Yang I was replaced by a more sophisticated appreciation of rusticity. The expanded aesthetic is voiced by, for example, Chang Chieh, who wrote, "The world sees only that there are many unrefined [words] in Tu Fu's poetry. It does not know that incorporating unrefined diction into a line is the most difficult of tasks, nor that this [inclusion] is neither clumsy nor uncouth, but an expression of antiquity at its best."[17] One must keep in mind, however, that for a reader like Chang Chieh it is still a moral context which leads the way to a widened aesthetic judgment. The context of his remarks emphasizes the moral valuation of poetry that was expressed by the "Great Preface" and that was, for Chang Chieh, exemplified by *Classic of Poetry*. In *Ts'ang-lang shih-hua*, Yen Yü extends to all High T'ang poets the aesthetics by which roughness becomes an object of delight to the refined: "As for High T'ang poets, their work may appear to show rough spots, but they are not rough; they may appear to be clumsy but are not clumsy."[18]

In Tu Fu's work as a whole, the unforced, unobtrusive introduction of new topics forms part of a larger pattern of a poetic mind ranging freely. Often these subjects are in areas that lie far from the moral compassion that concerns us here. Poems on friends, poems on poems, calligraphy, painting, horses, and eagles, all received repeated attention. Tu Fu was not always the first to introduce a subject, but he wrote on each new subject in such abundance as to leave no doubt that the choice of subject was intentional, not an accident of circumstances. Once introduced, his new subjects came to have the obviousness and inevitability of the inventions of genius. The broadening of subject matter in essence constitutes a redefinition of the proper topics for poetry, and, like all of Tu Fu's innovations, was accomplished without fanfare, without drawing attention, simply by quantity and consistency.

The topicality of Tu Fu's subject matter is different from the contextual, occasional method of composition that is such a notable feature of Chinese lyric poetry. The impromptu impression conveyed by many lyric

16. Han Yü, "For Chang Chi, a Light Poem," in *Tu Fu chüan*, 1:9.
17. *Sui-han t'ang shih-hua*, in *Li-tai shih-hua hsu-pien*, 1:450.
18. *Ts'ang-lang shih-hua* 2.140.

poems results from the fact that composition is usually prompted by a poet's immediate situation. One might argue that this occasional quality of lyric poetry makes it "topical," but in truth the occasions are those of convention – a parting, a meeting, a banquet, a rainfall. In Tu Fu's work, in contrast, many more types of occasions serve to initiate poems than with any poet before him, and in the end this accumulation amounts to a revolution in subject matter. Even conventional occasions include aspects not visible before (as when, on a visit to a friend – a conventional subject – his children run in, curious to know who is their father's guest).[19]

In time, the new subject matter acquired its own iconic status, and imitators of Tu Fu imitated his subject matter (as well as his language). His inventiveness made many moments and tableaux in life visible to others and worthy of being put into poetry. Immediate moments in Tu Fu's poetry become allusions in others. In the eleventh century, when the poet Ch'en Shih-tao parted from his children, he saw them exactly as Tu Fu did his: "My daughter has just begun to plait her hair. ... / She leans on me and won't get up, / Afraid I will go away and leave her."[20]

Discussion of the growth in subject matter may be extended to a consideration of its role in literary theory. Choice of subject matter is related to the definition of genres: kings for tragedies, housemaids for comedy; universal emotions for classicism, personal emotions for romanticism. The rules which specify the language, style, vocabulary and tone appropriate for a genre have as their unspoken condition the correct choice of subject matter. By the same token, the rejection of these rules widens the boundaries of the literary but does not eliminate the issue of subject matter. In Tu Fu's case, the debate about what topics were suitable for expression in a particular literary form was answered by the choice of topical subject matter. Ordinarily the choice of subject is settled without thought, for convention and tradition smoothly channel the topics proper for each genre, while transitions from one era to another are marked by alterations in these assumptions. Without ever having explicitly debated the assumptions (as did, say, both Po Chü-i and Han Yü), Tu Fu transformed the rules of decorum, although his experimental boldness was partially obscured by the orthodoxy of his themes. Perhaps for critics, attributing the new subject matter to compassion served as an explanation for Tu Fu's innovations; and perhaps for Tu Fu

19. "Presented to the Recluse Wei Eighth," 17/1/20.
20. Ch'en Shih-tao (1053–1102), "Parting from My Three Children" 別三子 in *Hou-shan shih-chu*, 1.4b–5b. This is quoted in Yoshikawa Kojiro, *An Introduction to Sung Poetry*, pp. 130–1.

much of this was not a matter for debate, because he was compelled by the urgency of his mission.

Language is, of course, an inseparable part of the classification of subject matter. Because, generally speaking, the new subject matter introduced with Tu Fu's compassion themes is unpretentious, the language and other characteristics that distinguish this group of poems simply follow the descriptive requirements of the subject matter. One of the earliest comments on Tu Fu's poetry, by Yuan Chen, says as much, describing it as written "with compassion and set down directly in the words of his day" 憐渠直道當時語.[21] In the same vein, the Ch'ing commentator Shih Hung-pao makes a list of some fifty colloquialisms in Tu Fu's poetry.[22] The vernacular vocabulary for which Tu Fu is nowadays lauded – for example, his references to widows, dogs, and chickens[23] – is, in this context, a by-product of the humble subject matter. When humble life is introduced naturally, in its own right rather than as motifs in pastoral poetry, the vocabulary is simple and straightforward. What T'ao Ch'ien had done, as a half-involuntary exile to a life among humble neighbors, Tu Fu did in greater quantity and variety. To find the language suitable to a new subject matter, a poet concretely struggles with his presentation. The struggle, however, concerns more than language; it also concerns the subject served by the language. I have not discussed language at length here because modern readers are already so conscious of issues relating to language.

The development of Chinese poetry followed complex principles and distinctions which cannot be briefly stated, but turning points in its development are nonetheless simply indexable by changes in subject matter. The most obvious case is that of "song poetry" (*tz'u*). When the song form initially used by courtesans for love songs was adopted by literati and, in the late Northern Sung period, transformed into a serious, expressive lyric, it was the subject matter that changed entirely (and, necessarily, the language).[24] An enormous change in literati attitudes toward the genre was required, of which the dramatic change in subject matter is the most difficult aspect to explain. The history of lyric

21. Yuan Chen, "Ten Poems in Reply to Poems Received from Hsiao Fu," poem 2, in *Tu Fu chüan*, 1:13.
22. *Tu Fu shih-shuo*, p. 245, "fang-yen" entry.
23. Representative articles are Hsiao Ti-fei, "Hsueh-hsi jen-min yü-yen te shih-jen Tu Fu," see note 3; Li Ju-lun, "Shuo lao-Tu li-yen su-yü ju shih" 説老杜俚言俗語入詩, in *Tu shih lun-kao*, pp. 182–6; and Fu Keng-sheng, "Tu Fu tsai shih-ke li yun-yung jen-min yü-yen te ch'ang-shih" 杜甫在詩歌裏運用人民語言的嘗試, in *Tu Fu shih-lun*, pp. 188–209.
24. See Kang-i Sun Chang, *The Evolution of Chinese "Tz'u" Poetry*, and Ronald C. Egan, "The Problem of the Repute of Tz'u during the Northern Sung," in *Voices of the Song Lyric in China*, pp. 207–25.

(*shih*) poetry does not provide an equally dramatic shift. Even so, the periodic introduction of new subject matter serves as one way to measure stages in the development of lyric poetry as well: the introduction of landscape subjects by Hsieh Ling-yun; the emphasis on the personal world by T'ao Ch'ien; the love preoccupations of poems in the anthology *Yü-t'ai hsin-yung*; the "reintroduction" of seriousness into early T'ang poetry. Here again, historical changes can be described in terms of shifts in subject matter.

One might ask what motivated any introduction of new subject matter. In Tu Fu's case, a fundamental lack of external information leaves this innovation unexplained. New subjects were introduced on a scale so massive (compared to earlier poets) that it is impossible to attribute the innovations to general historical trends, to a gradual change in poetry over the decades, or to the influence of earlier poets or contemporaries. The common explanation stresses Tu Fu's social conscience, but the sources of change do not have to be solely ideological (whether political or aesthetic ideology), or even mainly ideological. One may suppose instead that Tu Fu was an unusually clear-sighted person – that he could see what was right before his eyes – and could therefore revolutionize the nature and content of lyric poetry without stressing his revisionism and without posturing. It may be that the most important ability in a poet is to see something directly. Ruskin named "clear-sightedness," the ability to see "the plain and leafy fact" of a flower, as what distinguished truly great poets such as Homer and Virgil from good but lesser poets such as Wordsworth and Byron.[25] This leaves, at the center of Tu Fu's work, an unexplainable something, which could in principle be partially cleared up were more information available, but which remains, in its resistant residue, after all a part of the mystery of genius.

Critical understanding of the relationship of subject matter to poetry in a given poet's work is built up through cumulative evidence. When there is a substantial change in subject matter, a new kind of poetry results. In the case of the compassion themes in Tu Fu, greater alterations occurred in the nature of old-style poetry than in poems written in regulated verse. Furthermore, in examining the alterations, the useful contrast proves to lie between old-style verse and the ballad form, rather than between the more commonly made contrast of old-style form versus new-style (regulated) form. These are but two signals that old-style poetry was undergoing expansion in the eighth century (Li Po was writing

25. In many places in his writings, Ruskin attributes the distinction between the achievements of poets of the first order and other poets to the faculty of sight. See, for example, his famous discussion of the "pathetic fallacy" in *Modern Painters* III, excerpted in *The Literary Criticism of John Ruskin*, ed. Harold Bloom, pp. 66–7.

his incomparable old-style poems at this time), even though literary history has paid greater attention to the more exciting story of the maturation of the regulated-verse form. The old-style form, elastic in every way, by undergoing a change in subject matter, became a more notable form in the Northern Sung period. One of its beginnings is seen here in Tu Fu's poems.

Realism

From their detailed portrayal of the conditions of life during the Troubles, we may assume that one motive for writing these compassion poems was to make a record of events. How, then, did Tu Fu approach the task of recording? Two styles – I shall term them "realism" and "stylized realism" – can be distinguished in these poems. Realism appears, in certain of its traits, to be original with Tu Fu; stylized realism, of the kind found in ballads (*yueh-fu*), is used by Tu Fu in new circumstances. The first type is analyzed in this section and is seen to be at the heart of many of the poet's most quoted passages; an analysis of stylized realism, in the next section, will reveal some of the formal issues that faced Tu Fu in the task of depiction.

Realism prevails in much of Tu Fu's poetry and is best defined by providing examples. The specific trait which is original with Tu Fu is a kind of realism based on an acute sense of everyday life, very physical and concrete in its expression. Physicality lies at the heart of this realism, and in many of the poems this concreteness extends to a sense of timing as well, an ability to depict the pauses and rhythms of life. The result is that Tu Fu creates, seemingly artlessly and without self-consciousness, a life whose physical reality is easily recognized. This is especially true in his relations with his humble neighbors and with his family.

Stylized realism is in a sense the opposite of realism. As in realism, the scenes described are intended to be actual scenes, or so the reader feels. The language used, however, is neither realistic nor expected to be realistic. A kind of stylized language, derived from the phrasing and other conventions of the ballad form, is adopted, and it is used even when the poems are not in ballad form. Certain discrepancies between intention and result sometimes arise, showing up most visibly, but not exclusively, in problems of interpretation. Analysis will reveal that at issue is the problem of form – notably, how the stylistic distinctions between the old-style form and the ballad form can be blurred. Whereas we might normally associate a straightforward realistic style with the old-style form and a stylized language with the ballad, in many of Tu Fu's poems the situation is not so clear-cut, even on the simplest level of what is happening in a given poem. For example, if a ballad by Tu Fu recounts an actual event, what kinds of pressure toward realism are placed upon a ballad convention such as stylized description? Alternatively, if the conventions of the ballad form dominate a poem which we suppose to be factual, how does that stylization affect our reading? Is its factualness diluted? The relation of the style to the reader's impression of reality is an important issue in itself and in the interpretation of the poetry of Tu Fu. After all, it is as testimony that these poems have become the basis for his reputation for compassion and hence the basis for his moral authority.

In the overall realism that prevails in many of Tu Fu's poems, what seems particularly new and noticeable is his grasp of the concrete and physical. In many passages Tu Fu describes specific, individualized moments in terms of physical actions and shows a keen sense of the rhythm and timing of such actions. The impression is of directness – an unmediated glimpse of daily life and ordinary people. This concreteness and physicality characterize many of Tu Fu's best-known passages. In particular, in his relations with his humble neighbors Tu Fu can create a sense of human intimacy that is peculiarly his. We will begin with a well-known example, the third poem in the set entitled "Ch'iang Village":

Ch'iang Village

The chickens are letting out wild squawks,
And while they still squabble guests arrive –
We chase them into the trees
As a knock comes on the brushwood door:
It is four or five old men,
Come to ask after my long travels.
Each has brought something with him,
And out of their kettles come clear and dark wines. 8
They say, "Please don't mind that the wine is thin,[26]
We have no one to plow the millet fields,
The wars have not yet stopped,
And the young are all fighting in the east."
I ask to sing for these elderly men,
These difficult times – I feel shame before their deep feelings.
The song done, I look to heaven and sigh,
And on all sides the tears flow freely. 16

This poem is the last of a set of three written about a year after the beginning of the rebellion, when both capitals had fallen into rebel

26. Using the variant *mo-tz'u* 莫辭 in *Wen-yuan ying-hua*, rather than *k'u-tz'u* 苦辭.

hands and the imperial cause was at its most precarious. In that year, Tu
Fu, already separated from his family, had managed to make his way to
the court in exile, and there he was rewarded for this act of loyalty with
an office. Shortly afterward he obtained leave to go to his family, then
living in Ch'iang Village. (This is the homecoming recorded in "Journey
North.") Thus, when he rejoined his family they had been separated for
a year with no news of each other. The first poem of this set is quite
somber, describing the trembling disbelief which all felt at the unexpected reunion.

The third "Ch'iang Village" poem is much lighter. The picture of daily
life given in its first eight lines owes little to earlier poems about visitors,
and yet the lines' originality is of a remarkably unstriking kind. The
events noted are so ordinary – here, domestic chaos caused by chickens
– that they are scarcely worth notice. (And it is precisely about domestic
and inconvenient chickens that Tu Fu writes so many memorable
poems.) It is hard to register such moments in life, and even harder to
think of capturing them in poetry. Yet here in the first four lines, in the
inopportune arrival of callers, Tu Fu turns chaos into comedy. Despite
the havoc, the poem's strong structure of four-line segments unfolds the
visit in a well-paced sequence of moods. It begins with the undignified
pandemonium of chasing off chickens; then, in lines 5 through 8, we see
that the unexpected guests are old men – neighbors paying a courtesy
call; next they bring out their gifts, homely gifts which bespeak their
unpretentious selves; in the last section, Tu Fu sings for them, thus
making his own contribution to the visit. With Tu Fu's song, the mood
darkens, and the end is filled with the inexpressible emotions aroused by
his song. The neighbors also feel this; Tu Fu has voiced their feelings,
and we see that his compassion for others is continuous with his feeling
for his family. The development of the visit is human, warm, intimate.
Even sorrow and grief find a place that brings out the warmth of human
life.

Tu Fu's ability to render homely actions unself-consciously is everywhere evident in this group of compassion poems. In another poem
about a visit, this time a visit that he inadvertently makes, more comedy
surfaces. Again it is comedy based on physical motion.

A farmer forced me to drink and praised the censor Wu

Walking in the wake of the spring breezes,
In village after village I saw willows and blossoms.
A farmer, saying it was near Earth Festival,
Had invited me to try his new wine.   4
And now full of wine, he praised the new governor:

Such a one as this, his old eyes had never seen,
And turning, he pointed to his strapping son,
"He was with the crossbow detachment,   8
His name was on the register of the Flying Cavalry,
And he had served for years without rotation,
Then the other day, he was released to come back to farm,
A blessing and a help to his old parents.
Now any order for service, even to the death –
We swear the family will not flee from it.
This year we will have a great Festival –
Will you, sir, stay a while?"   16
He called to his wife to open up the large jar
And helped me to something from a container.
I was touched by this free manner of his –
One knows it is from good government well led.
In his flow of talk, all jumbled and varied,
The governor's name was always on his lips.   22
I had set out on impulse in the morning,
That was early dawn, now it is near dusk.
Long among strangers, I have come to appreciate human
     warmth –
How could I refuse an old neighbor's friendliness?
In a loud voice, he shouted for fruits and chestnuts,
And when I tried to rise, grasped me by the elbow.
His gestures are free and not those of polite society,
But I never felt that this village rustic was foolish.
The moon rose, and still he kept me there,
Vehemently he asked how much wine was left.   32

Like "Ch'iang Village," this poem (written in Ch'eng-tu, probably
in 762), is light in tone. The poem is structured in praise of the poet's
patron in Ch'eng-tu (see the title and lines 5–14, 19–22), but the
old farmer is much the stronger presence. We find in the narration
of the party's progress the same concrete sense of timing and of physical
action as in "Ch'iang Village." Chancing to stop at a farm, Tu Fu is
repeatedly detained by the farmer. When the moon has risen high, we
find him still there, the farmer plying him with more drink. Unlike most
party poems, which end when the party is over, this poem ends in the
middle of the action, with the poet still trying to get away.
The farmer's hospitality is rough and unrefined and is here shown
directly, with no condescension or pastoral touches: as the farmer
drinks, he grows more loquacious; inspired by his own hospitality,
his voice grows louder; he calls for wine and, later, for fruit and chestnuts; he grabs Tu Fu by the elbow to keep him there; more wine comes.

Even the presence of the wife offstage can be felt in the supply of food and wine.

This poem, unlike "Ch'iang Village," does not have a regular structure. For example, the farmer's long speech begins at line 8, a line which, given lyric poetry's basic unit of the couplet, often marks the end of a segment. Furthermore, the description of the visit proper, the physical action, does not begin until the halfway point, at line 17. Within the second half of the poem, the poet's recollection of the walk that took him there and his appreciation of the stranger's warmth that has detained him again comes at the halfway point (lines 23–6, six lines on either side). Although the structure in this second half can be counted in terms of lines, the pacing is beautifully unforced, and the poem's natural punctuation is the hospitality of the unexpected host, not the structural symmetry behind it.

The simple, unaffected language and physical clarity found in "Ch'iang Village" and "Forced to Drink" occur in many passages elsewhere. Tu Fu had an unusual ability to see what was before his eyes. In the best-known of these passages, the behavior of his children is vividly caught. On his return home during the perilous early years of the rebellion, he describes his daughter in smeared makeup and clothes made over from an adult's, the cloth's pattern now upside down. On another return, he describes his son clinging to his knee, afraid to let him go again. Recollecting a journey made by night to seek refuge, Tu Fu understands a child's mentality, how he tries to take part in adult worries and makes trouble instead with his own stubborn plans:

> The boy strained to understand what was going on
> And insisted on looking for bitter pears to eat.[27]

The power of observation remains with Tu Fu throughout his life; living in Szechuan, he watches as his children sleep fretfully:

> After so many years the cotton quilt is cold as iron,
> My dear son, restless in sleep, has torn open the lining.[28]

Traveling with children again, he captures the way they run about, compared to the steady plodding of adults: "The children run into mists, calling aloud." Some years later, in K'uei-chou, when held up by rain, he imagines the comforts of returning home now that his son is old enough to perform some services for him:

27. The references are to "Journey North," lines 67–72 and 83–4, and "Ch'iang Village," poem 2, lines 3–4. The couplet quoted is from "Ballad of P'eng-ya," lines 13–14.
28. "Song of My Thatched Roof Torn by Autumn Winds," lines 13–14.

> I'll have the boy pound me on the back
> And loosen the pins in my hair.[29]

An important component of the vividness of the physical reality is his sense of timing. Like T'ao Ch'ien before him, Tu Fu has worked out the rhythm of a man moving about on his own (or, as in the second example, not moving):

> Morning light enters through the round windows,
> Disheveled, startled, I lie there, in my worn coat,
> I get up, walk a few steps, look at the sky –
> The spring air is warmer, day by day –
> Of a sudden I don't feel so lazy,
> And this morning I comb my hair.[30]

And:

> Dusting off the black leather table,
> Listening to the sounds of fishermen and woodcutters.[31]

It is timing, too, which provides the comedic element of the famous opening of "Song of My Thatched Roof Torn by Autumn Winds." Tu Fu sputters with real rage at the boys who carry off the thatch from his roof, torn loose by a storm, but he knows too the figure of fun he makes, chasing ineffectually after the agile thieves:

> I shout, till my lips are burning, my mouth parched,
> And return, lean on my stick and sigh to myself.[32]

When with another person, too, the poet's sense of rhythm remains acute, as in "Forced to Drink." Another example is from the first poem of the "Ch'iang Village" set. The poet has unexpectedly returned, and in the space of a single line he captures the way the sense of disbelief felt by husband and wife cannot be quieted: "Excitement calmed, still we wipe away tears" 驚定還拭淚. In five characters the emotions turn three times – first the excitement, then the excitement stilled by effort and a passage of time, and then the emotions breaking out afresh. There is also the well-known poem "On Hearing of the Recovery of Ho-nan and Ho-pei by Imperial Troops," which is full of excitement and rejoicing released in successive involuntary bursts of activity: the poet hears the news; he must

29. "Retreating from Lang-chou to the Shu Mountains, with my Wife and Children," 400/25/31, poem 3, line 4; and "Stopped by Rain, Unable to Return to the Orange Grove in West Nang," 172/12/8, lines 31–2.
30. The opening lines of "Seeking out Ts'iu Chi and Li Feng on the Last Day of the Month" (61/4/3), written in 756 or 757.
31. "Stopped by Rain, Unable to Return to the Orange Grove in West Nang," lines 29–30.
32. Lines 9–10. Hu Shih cites this poem in his interesting remarks on Tu Fu's sense of humor. See his *Pai-hua wen-hsueh-shih*, pp. 241–3.

do something; he rolls up the scrolls he has been reading; it is not enough; he turns to look at his wife and children; he feels light-headed; he wants to burst loose, to sing, to drink; a journey home, yes, that's it; and so excited is he that the journey is already begun in his mind and the route traced.

Tu Fu also renders humble objects and actions especially vividly: the look and feel of fruits and crops; the localized havoc of chickens; the taste of cold noodles. One critic lists a thesaurus of thirteen different varieties of weeping described by Tu Fu.[33] Such attentiveness, such responsiveness to physical movement brought an extraordinary level of realism to lyric poetry.

The quality of observation which lies behind such detailed realism has been noted before. It is, for example, at the center of what the Japanese scholar Yoshikawa Kōjiro has called Tu Fu's "minuteness," his ability to pick out the precise detail that gives us the whole. Yoshikawa's examples of minuteness include the passages about the children (the girl with the tattered skirt in an upside-down pattern), but his point about minuteness, the sharply observed detail, covers a larger scope and includes many more examples than physical concreteness. He includes examples drawn from the movements of nature, not just of men – light moving over the water, dew forming on a leaf. Yoshikawa stresses that Tu Fu improves on the mere recording of details from nature, and he gives as an example the way Tu Fu describes, not moonlight, but moonlight that falls at a certain angle upon the poet's knee.[34]

Yoshikawa is certainly right that a gift for unstrained observation underlies many of his varied examples from Tu Fu's poetry. Such observation derives from a larger attitude of attentiveness to the outward world. In the same vein, the Ming-dynasty work *T'ang yin kuei-ch'ien* points out that Tu Fu is fond of using such words as *tzu* 自, *shou* 受, *chin* 進, *tou* 逗, *fu* 府, and *tsuo* 坐,[35] words that show the dynamic relationships of objects to one another (with most of the examples again drawn from nature scenes). The portrayal of physical rhythm and concrete details constitutes one facet of this quality of direct observation. Realism of this kind – undistorted by convention, almost unformed by convention – provides such a clear sense of Tu Fu's abilities and inclinations that we

33. Hsiao Ti-fei, "Tu Fu tso-p'in te jen-min hsing" 杜甫作品的人民性, in *Tu Fu yen-chiu*, p. 71.
34. Yoshikawa Kōjiro, "Tu Fu's Poetics and Poetry: Farewell Lecture at Kyoto University [1967]." Published in English in *Yoshikawa Kōjiro zenshū*, 22:554–21. The moonlight example is given on page 549 and is from the poem "Thoughts" 寫懷, poem 2 (190/13/19), lines 1–2.
35. Hu Chen-heng (1569–1644), *T'ang yin kuei-ch'ien*, chüan 11, first entry.

may initially wonder why he would need to resort (as our prejudices may have it) to stylized realism.

Stylized realism

The second noticeable trait in the compassion poems is in one respect the opposite of realism: events that probably did occur are described in language that is not realistic, nor expected to be realistic. People, actions, scenes, speeches are rendered, but the description, although not untrue to reality, gives the impression of types, rather than of physical concreteness. Not surprisingly, this stylized realism is most often seen in Tu Fu's ballads, but if its only occurrence is in ballads, this would not be of great interest. After all, in ballads we expect to see stylization, whether in subject matter, sentiment, or rhetoric. Rather, what is of interest here is that stylized realism is used to depict actual events as well as the more usual set action typical of the ballad form. Moreover, stylized realism is not confined to ballads but is also used in old-style poems. The effects of stylized realism differ according to the prosodic form in which it occurs. If used in a ballad, Tu Fu's innovation, in literary terms, was the introduction of topical relevance: that is, the transformation of the ballad into a vehicle for criticism *and* representation. But because of the nature of the ballad tradition, this was not a simple matter of inserting contemporary references, for the specificity of history struggles against the generalizing tendency of the traditional ballad.

Even before we examine in detail the use of stylized realism, however, we can anticipate some of the stylistic complexities unhinted at in the common version of Tu Fu's reputation for compassion. Here, in the simultaneous use of more than one kind of verisimilitude, we already have a hint that Tu Fu did not consistently have the same direct relationship with the world he wanted to depict. Even though the praise for his compassion is often made in uniform terms, the circumstances that aroused his compassion are not all represented in the same way, even within the same poem. The use of stylized realism in new contexts is another area where Tu Fu was innovative and experimental.

To illustrate the combined use of realism and stylized realism, we can refer again to poem 3 of the "Ch'iang Village" set and to "Forced to Drink." Sandwiched between the particularized, physical descriptions are brief and easily overlooked passages of stylized realism. In "Ch'iang Village," this occurs when the visiting neighbors apologize for the present they have brought (lines 9–12):

They say, "Please don't mind that the wine is thin,
We have no one to plow the millet fields,
The wars have not yet stopped,
And the young are all fighting in the east."

In "Forced to Drink," the farmer speaks of his son in a stylized manner (lines 8–12):

"He was with the crossbow detachment,
His name was on the register of the Flying Cavalry,
And he had served for years without rotation,
Then the other day, he was released to come back to farm,
A blessing and a help to his old parents."

The words of the farmer and of the village elders have a familiar sound: they resemble lines from ballads, which often describe the failure of crops or the conscription of men. The generic nature of these words contrasts sharply with their particularized setting. The sentiments expressed here most likely were uttered; something along those lines was indeed said: the village men did excuse the present they brought, and the farmer did have a son taken by the army. But the words as reported resemble the stylized words of Han-era ballads about soldiering ("Ts'ung chün hsing" 從軍行). The lines surrounding these passages could not be more realistic, but in the speech of the villagers, the influence of the ballad form temporarily prevails over the otherwise generally direct or realistic tone. Tu Fu has in essence briefly borrowed the voice of the ballad bystander and momentarily shifts from a realistic to a stylized language.

These two examples prompt a more general search for sections of stylized language interpolated into otherwise realistic descriptions. Examples soon turn up. In the poem "Orange Grove" (183/13/6), for example, the style shifts several times. This is a thirty-two line poem in the old-style form, and its first half (not translated here) describes Tu Fu's return to his orange grove in Nang-hsi from the town of K'uei-chou. The next morning the poet walks through the neighboring village, and this is when a village elder approaches him with the villagers' case:

The next morning I walked through the neighboring village,
With an elderly man whom I knew well.
"With times precarious and taxes so many,
I will not ask you for the coarse rice."[36]
We walked together in the fields of bean,

36. This line 脫粟為爾揮 is interpreted in widely different ways by commentators. P'u Ch'i-lung takes it to be Tu Fu's words: that to relieve the farmers Tu Fu has waived his right to some grain due him (*Tu Tu hsin-chieh*, p. 178). He points to a similar situation

Their autumn flowering dense and mixed.
"These plump beans we will not be able to eat,
All are to be sent to market and on to the royal coffers,
Gone to meet the expenses of the armies,
Such is our plight under the government's hand."

(In the remaining six lines, the desperate farmer kneels to ask for advice, to which Tu Fu gives only a lame reply.) In this passage, straightforward narrative is intermixed with the appeals of the farmer, which are couched in the timeless and always relevant appeal of the ballad style.

As a poetic language, stylized realism may appear unremarkable; if so, this is because the typical ballad style is easily recognized, even though the ballad form itself is a large, unwieldy category not susceptible to easy definition.[37] In Tu Fu's work, however, the familiar stylized realism occurs in several new environments, which, if examined carefully, in fact turn it into something unfamiliar. When stylized realism is employed in old-style poems, as in the three examples just given, few problems in interpretation occur (although there still remains the question of why it is used). But when it is retained in ballads, with realistic language mixed in and, so far as we can guess, topicality of reference intended as well – in such cases, the discrepancy between styles can provide an insight into the poetic problems Tu Fu was facing.

Let us first look at stylized realism when it is used in a conventional, unproblematic way, that is to say, in the traditional ballad, of which Tu Fu also wrote many. The poem that follows is taken from "Frontier Poems, First Set" (84/5/15). Probably written in the early 750s, these are among Tu Fu's earliest surviving poems. In this set, the lot of a soldier conscripted to fight in the frontier battles of the 750s is described through the soldier's eyes, and the expansionist policies of the time are criticized. The first poem follows:

With heavy hearts we quit our village home,
To go to far, far Turfan River.
There is a set term for service,
Deserters will be punished with death.

in another poem, where Tu Fu plans to distribute some of his own harvest and asks, "Is it to seek a name as a compassionate village? It is out of pity for this upside-down world" ("Now that it's autumn," 178/31/1, lines 29–30). The translation here follows P'u's interpretation. The *Chiu-chia* edition suggests the farmer is speaking: "Although the farmers were in difficulties over the taxes, they were still able to offer some hospitality to their guest, hence the description of 'a reliable elder' in the previous line" (182/13/6, lines 19–20). Ch'iu Chao-ao says that *er* ("you") refers to the tax collector, and that the farmer is readying his coarse grain for the taxes (*Tu shih hsiang-chu*, 19.1668).

37. Joseph Allen (*In the Voice of Others*, pp. 37–64) examines critically a number of the common assumptions that guide attempts at definition of *yueh-fu*, for which he does not use the word "ballad."

The emperor's land is already vast,
What use is there in extending its boundaries?
Parted forever from our parents' love,
Swallowing our sobs, we shoulder our weapons and march on.

This is the ballad as Tu Fu inherited it, and this poem, like other border poems that were so popular in the High T'ang period, conforms closely to the model of the Han-dynasty ballad. Through a progression of scenes, the set of nine poems describes various aspects of a soldier's life from the soldier's viewpoint. Little in the poems implies their topicality, other than the reference to the Turfan frontier (line 2). That the exact contemporary reference is not known is unimportant (although it is hotly debated),[38] nor is it important that the explicit criticism is limited to one couplet (lines 5–6) in the entire set. The poet's criticism is implied in the very act of writing. This, and his sympathy for the conscript, are part of the ballad tradition. The poem, standing squarely in that tradition, presents no problems in interpretation.

This formally unexceptional ballad provides us with a starting point for discussing Tu Fu's use of stylized realism in the many ballads that, from other indications, appear to be about events witnessed by or heard of by the poet. It is widely agreed that the use of the ballad to describe specific events began with Tu Fu. As early as the Sung dynasty, Ts'ai Ch'i noted Tu Fu's use of contemporary events in ballads as an innovation.[39] The Ch'ing commentator P'u Ch'i-lung writes of "Ballad of Army Carts": "This is a new style in ballads and should be considered the true line of ballads. During the Ch'i and Liang dynasties, the interest had been in imitating the ancients of Han and Wei, not in expressing remonstrance."[40] Yang Lun likewise contrasts Tu Fu's ballads with the imitative Six Dynasties ballads: "Tu Fu alone took what he felt and saw at the time – the tragedy of the state, the pity of the suffering – and without self-consciousness took them as subjects, freeing himself from the restrictions of his predecessors."[41]

Though these comments recognize Tu Fu's revival of the ballads, the fact that a literary problem is introduced by this new, topical ballad was overlooked. The problem arises from the necessity for the poet to introduce clues that indicate that a specific rather than a generic event is being described. This could be done in a number of ways. The use of

38. Most commentators vote for Ko-shu Han's campaigns against the Turfan, although P'u Ch'i-ling, for one, sensibly points out that campaigns in the far west had a long history and there is no need to forcibly pin it on Ko-shu Han (*Tu Tu hsin-chieh*, p. 6).
39. Ts'ai Ch'i, *Ts'ai K'uan-fu shih-hua*, in *Sung shih-hua chi-i*, 2:379.
40. P'u Ch'i-lung, *Tu Tu hsin-chieh*, p. 225.
41. Yang Lun, *Tu shih ching-ch'üan*, p. 225; said of "Three Officials" and "Three Partings."

realistic description is one, or the poet may specifically identify the contemporary event by, for example, using enough proper nouns. Although both of these may seem like simple changes, the literary consequences are complex. For one thing, realistic touches tend to produce problems in interpretation; in addition, there are hints that Tu Fu felt matters had not been satisfactorily resolved. Then, too, it is difficult to alter the generic nature of the ballad form to depict specific events without completely altering its stylized version of reality – that is, without writing lyric poetry. On the other hand, if stylistic limits for the language are observed, how can the reader know the poem refers to a specific actual event? The obvious answer is that other clues must be provided. In practice, however, a poem's factual basis is not so easily signaled.

Let us take some examples of this mixture of signals. The first, the well-known "Ballad of Army Carts," presents no problems of interpretation. Here the specificity of the event is conveyed, convincingly, by the same kind of realism found in "Ch'iang Village" and "Forced to Drink," that is, by vivid physical actions. As the conscripts are marched off and their families pull on them to hold them back, their actions reveal their feelings so clearly that the reader feels the scene before him. The picture is given in the famous opening of the poem:

> Carts rattle along, horses whinny,
> Conscripts – each with bow and arrows at his waist,
> Fathers, mothers, wives, and children run alongside to see them off,
> Dust obscures Hsien-yang Bridge,
> They pull at the conscripts' clothes, stamp their feet, and block the
>   way, weeping,
> Their weeping rises straight up to the skies above.

In this passage, as well as in the remainder of the poem, no contemporary proper nouns are used (except for "Hsien-yang Bridge"); the campaign for which the conscription is made is not named, and we cannot finally determine whether Tu Fu had witnessed such a conscription. Nevertheless the specificity, the physicalness of the opening lines persuade the reader that Tu Fu had actually witnessed a conscription. (The poem is customarily dated to the time of a conscription for the Turkestan campaigns of 750.[42]) And so the poem has been read over the centuries. However, the balance of the poem, which is much the larger part (27 lines), does not continue the extraordinary vividness of its

---

42. Ch'ien Ch'ien-i insists that "Ballad of Army Carts" describes conscriptions for the suppression of Nanchao, in Yunnan to the south (*Ch'ien chu Tu shih* 1.10), but disagreement over this point does not affect the reading.

opening. Instead it contains a description of the cruelties of the soldier's life, put in the mouth of a ballad bystander and stylized in the ballad manner. The long ballad-style part is nonspecific to the occasion, for it could have been about any soldier's life; it is carried forward chiefly by the momentum of the wonderful opening. The contemporary situation is alluded to only once, when the Han emperor Wu's expansionist campaigns (an allegorical reference to Hsuan-tsung's) are criticized. Given the purely ballad section alone, without the opening, the reader could have formed no sense of the poem's topicality. He could have been reading "Frontier Poems," and "Ballad of Army Carts" surely would not have become as famous as it is.

"Ballad of Army Carts" illustrates how Tu Fu uses the ballad form to depict, as the reader believes, particular events. Like the lyric poems "Ch'iang Village" and "Forced to Drink," this ballad contains realistic, particularized description. However, the proportions of realism and stylized realism are reversed: stylized realism predominates, whereas the particularized, physical description forms but a brief initial segment. The realism causes us to think the event did occur, and the stylized realism throws that supposition in doubt. When contradictory stylistic evidence is given, or when there is no supplementary biographical information, then the reader cannot know which convention to follow in interpreting the poem. It happens that in the case of "Army Carts," whether or not Tu Fu actually witnessed the conscription does not much affect one's reading, and so no important conflict arises.

It would seem that when thus laid out, the contending forces in interpretation are clear enough. In practice, however, additional factors from the reading tradition enter into play. The longstanding preference that poems have specific historical references is one such factor. A related one is the preference for allegorical readings, which is another way of producing specific historical references, for allegories often refer to particular cases rather than to concepts alone. In interpretations, these preferences have tended to overwhelm the methodology proposed here, in which as a preliminary step the seemingly factual elements are weighed against the seemingly stylistic elements. The next example illustrates how the reading preference for specificity of reference operates.

In "A Fine Lady," the mixture of contradictory stylistic evidence gives rise to conflicting and ultimately irreconcilable readings. In the poem, the poet meets, under some slender bamboos, a lady of gentle birth and listens to her story. The story is told with certain songlike features which are contradicted by the inclusion of individualizing details. The poem begins in the songlike manner by first introducing the woman ("There

87

is a fine lady of rare beauty" 絕代有佳人) and then having her introduce herself ("She says she comes of a good family" 自雲良家子). She tells the poet that after the Troubles, when her relations lost their offices, she was abandoned by her husband for a new love, and now she stays alive by selling off her jewelry. Her story is not unusual in itself. It is, however, given in a highly circumstantial manner, with many details whose significance is not clear – she is living in Ch'in-chou, on the extreme western edge of the empire (how did she get here?); the setting is out of doors (unusual for a gentlewoman); she pulls at a trellis and plucks some flowers not for her hair; and the poet observes her thin sleeves, inadequate protection against the cold weather. Is this portrait an allegory? That is, did Tu Fu invent this lady for a purpose? Or did he really meet her and is merely telling us her sad story? The many details which Tu Fu supplies argue for depiction; they are not all explicable, however, and abandoned ladies typically tend to allegory. One allegorical interpretation offered is that she stands for a minister who has been cast aside by the emperor; alternatively, Tu Fu is said to be alluding to conflicts at Su-tsung's court between new and old ministers, with the old ministers (the lady) from Hsuan-tsung's reign losing out.[43] If we follow these interpretations, then the lady could not exist. That they disagree about the person whom the lady allegorically represents does not in itself damage the argument for allegory.

Tu Fu's great circumstantiality of description has not been sufficient to overcome the allegorical tradition of lonely women. Indeed, one has the sense that it is the full details of "A Fine Lady" that have, paradoxically, caused commentators to look for allegory. The details are so unconventional and our knowledge of the social history of that era so sparse that it is difficult to believe that Tu Fu has merely recorded her story. Even commentators who favor the view that she was a historical person have had to emphasize the reasonableness of their view ("In the chaos that followed the *t'ien-pao* era, it is reasonable that there would be such a person"[44]). By contrast, when the choice of ballad topic is more conventional, no one doubts for a moment that the cases as reported are at least sociologically factual (for example, the firewood carrier of "Ballad of Firewood Carriers"). Circumstantial richness has, paradoxically, worked in the opposite direction from factuality: anything, however concrete, that cannot be understood can be accounted for by allegory.

43. Ch'en Hang, in his *Shih pi hsing chien* (Preface, 1854), p. 167, gives allegorical equivalences for each element in the poem; he quotes Ch'iu Chao-ao's rejection of allegory only to contradict it. (For the latter, see Ch'iu Chao-ao, *Tu shih hsiang-chu*, 7.555.) The likelihood of an allegorical reading has been revived, somewhat tendentiously, by Fu Keng-sheng in *Tu shih hsi yi*, pp. 134–7.
44. Ch'iu Chao-ao, *Tu shih hsiang-chu* 7.555.

Ironically, although it is likely that Tu Fu has merely faithfully tran-
scribed an out-of-doors meeting, the historical existence of a probably
real person needs to be repeatedly defended because the details of this
meeting stand too far outside the bounds of convention.

The lesson of "A Fine Lady" is that the introduction of elements that
imply a historical reality creates a problem for other portions of the
poem which the poetic tradition holds to be conventional (in this case,
conventionally allegorical). The debates over points of interpretation
often turn on the question of whether something mentioned in the
poem is factual. Being certain whether something happened or not is an
important issue in Chinese poetry, where generally either an event has
occurred or it is allegorical. An underlying difficulty is the reader's
reluctance to accept a new category of subject matter, especially when
only one example exists. There is, in addition, the conflict between the
stylized realism of the genre and the topicality of Tu Fu's subject, for
ballad conventions belie the reality of the subject at the same time as
they help to express the poet's purpose. Thus the apparently simple
innovation of writing on topical subjects creates unresolved tension
between realism and stylized realism.

The mixture of realism and stylized realism varies in kind and proportion in individual poems. In some, the situations remain archetypal,
stylized tableaux, while the language dips occasionally into concrete
realism. The realistic part has the effect of throwing into doubt the
conventional part: is that also real? In most cases, whether a poem's
situation was literally real or not has a less dramatic effect on interpretation than in "A Fine Lady," but the nature of the reader's response is
nonetheless affected.

One might ask whether Tu Fu was aware of these tensions. Why did he
write across conventions in this way? We cannot know with certainty, but
it may be that he was trying to depict his surroundings – in particular the
sufferings of people unknown to him – in the same direct way that he
depicted his family and neighbors, and that the conflicting signals reveal
something about the limitations of the choices he had in handling his
subjects.

Let us take some more examples of the discrepancies that can arise:
the six poems collectively known as "Three Officials" and "Three Partings." Do they depict real people and events? Or are they, or some of
them, closer in style to the "Frontier" poems? Whatever the answer, the
reading is not greatly affected, as it is in "A Fine Lady," but the query
itself illustrates something about Tu Fu's problems of depiction. The two
groups of poems are set in the aftermath of a major campaign undertaken in early 759, in which imperial armies under nine commands were

united in a major assault on rebel forces at Yeh-chou (Hsiang-chou), just north of the Yellow River near Loyang. In the debacle which followed, the imperial side converted an initially advantageous position to an undisciplined rout. Loyang had to be abandoned, and a defensive position was established north of the city, at Ho-yang. Tu Fu, who then held a post at Hua-chou, to the west of Loyang, made a journey in those months to his family home, which was just southeast of Loyang. He was thus in a position personally to witness over a fair amount of territory the effects of the imperial defeat. From the evidence of his poems, including these six, the devastating effects were visible everywhere and were especially poignant in the depopulation of the countryside. It is thus reasonable to suppose that actual events lay behind some of the incidents in these poems.

Although the six poems take their starting point from the major battle of the time and their content from the suffering which ensued, still the stylized effects of ballad conventions predominate over realism. One may expect that when the suffering has been individualized into single affecting cases, as they are here, the result would be one of striking verisimilitude. But in fact Tu Fu's use of direct speech, of question and answer, and of ballad similes all contribute to the ballad manner, and so the protagonist of each poem remains still archetypally "a young bride" or "an old soldier," a case study rather than an individual. A germ of observation of an actual event quite likely lies behind each poem – "The Official at Shih-hao" seems the most specifically observed, and "Parting of Newlyweds" the least – but, despite the customary praise of readers, the freshly described moments, that is, the nonballad moments, in these poems are a mere handful. Little of what the protagonists say and do can be termed unrealistic, but their actions and words draw on a stylized realism whose elements have been shaped by the ballad tradition. Just so had another old soldier returned to find no one remaining in his old village ("Parting from No One"), as did the conscript of the anonymous ballad "At fifteen I entered the army."[45] Just so might a ballad bride address her conscript-husband ("Parting of Newlyweds"). Of the six poems, only "The Official at Shih-hao" contains a story rather than an elaborated talbleau – and it is the one most frequently anthologized.[46]

"The Official at Shih-hao" is circumstantial enough to give the impression of being based on an actual episode. In the poem, an old woman pleads with a conscription officer to spare the remaining mem-

45. In *Yueh-fu shih-chi* 25.365. Translated in Anne Birrell, *Popular Songs and Ballads of Han China*, p. 125.
46. See Ling Tzu-liu, *T'ang-shih hsuan-pen Tu Fu shih*, p. 37, for figures on the frequency of anthologizing.

bers of her family, which had already lost all its young men, but at the end of the poem all are pressed into the army, except for an old man who had earlier fled. As in a lyric poem, the narrator is someone who might be the poet himself (rather than a ballad bystander). Here he is a traveler who is clearly exempt from conscription, as Tu Fu would have been, lodging there for the night by chance. The plot as summarized appears very concrete, as in a lyric (*shih*) poem, but the language is not. The old woman's words, which take up the greater part of the poem, are balladlike.

The Official at Shih-hao

At dusk I stopped at Shih-hao Village –
An official came in the night to seize people.
The old man fled over the wall,
The old woman came out to answer the door.   4
How angry were the shouts of the official,
How broken the cries of the woman.
I heard the woman step forward to entreat him:
"My three boys were all soldiers at Yeh-ch'eng,
The first has sent word –
Two have just died in battle.
The living are just alive,
The dead are gone forever.   12
At home there is no one left,
Only a grandson still unweaned.
His mother still has not gone,
She has no whole skirt to leave the house.
I am an old woman, my strength is gone,
But I ask to follow you, sir, this night to camp,
In obedience to the Ho-yang call for men,
For I can still make the morning meals."   20
The night went on, the voices ceased,
Only the sound of sobbing and stifled gulps.
At day's break I set out on my way,
And take leave only of the old man.   24

This poem, which has not lost its power through familiarity, is the most successful of the six in that it is the most particularized, leaving us convinced that Tu Fu must have witnessed such a scene. Nonetheless, despite its drama and pathos, it lacks the immediacy of the opening lines of "Ballad of Army Carts." The verisimilitude is created by devices rather than vividness. What gives the impression that the poem is an actual record are the demographic details about the family; they are so detailed that one feels they must be real. There are many kinship terms, some used by the poet and some put into the old woman's mouth: old man (*lao-weng*), old woman (*lao-fu*), the sons (*san-nan, yi-nan, erh-nan*), the unweaned grandson (*ju-hsia-sun*), the grandson's mother (*sun-mu*), old woman (*lao-yü*). Using only the old woman's words, the ballad accounts for a complete family and each person's fate. There is an elderly couple (the old man fled at the officer's approach, and the old woman was conscripted that night); their three sons (two of whom died in the recent defeat at Ho-yang); their daughter-in-law (conscripted that night); and the infant (also taken). The semblance of reality stems from the skill with which all this information is conveyed and from the pathos of hearing these words from the old woman. There are also the detailed observations of crying: a shout (*hu*, from the official), crying with sound (*t'i*), sobbing (*ch'i*), and stifled sounds (*yin-yan*). And there is additional shock from the carefully calculated dramatic pause before the curtain line, when the narrator, on resuming his journey, is able to bid farewell only to the old man.

Within the reference frame of topicality, realism is not just a question of language and description. The event recounted must also be real, and it has to convince the reader that it is real. However stylized a ballad might remain in poetic terms, topical relevance injects a cast of realism into the poem's conventions and compels the reader to interpret most of its elements as having had a historical reality. For this reason, the merit of such poems depends to an unusual degree on their factual basis, and the poems are not wholly judgeable on literary qualities alone. In "Three Officials" and "Three Partings," the historicity is made explicit mainly through the use of placenames (Ho-yang, T'ung Pass, Hsin-an), references which provide enough anchor in reality for most readers. One could still hold that Tu Fu invented these elements, rather than observed and recorded them, but it goes against the Chinese tradition of reading to suppose that "The Official at Shih-hao," with its complete and dramatic story, stretching from dusk to dawn, could be totally made up and yet be recounted by a narrator who could be the poet. The other five poems of the set seem more like conventional ballads, slightly modified to have current reference. There is no reason why Tu Fu should not have retold the tale of an old man returned to his deserted village, and so on, but the poems also read well as archetypal situations.

To see the extent to which "The Official at Shih-hao" is a departure, we must consider what the ballad was like, what its possibilities were, when it came into Tu Fu's hands. What was available in the tradition when he began to write his topical ballads? To do this properly we should perhaps first consider what a ballad is, but that is a very vexing question, and in any case definitions have been difficult to sustain, in part because

of such innovations as Tu Fu's. Many attempts have been made to bring
some order to the highly diverse examples that have historically come
under the name of *yueh-fu*. An investigation such as this one may shed
light on some of the difficulties of defining the ballad. In the meantime,
an imprecise definition is employed here: I shall use the term "ballad" to
mean (1) any poem that the poet himself has labeled as a ballad by
giving it a characteristic ballad title or (2) any poem that is included in
the eleventh-century collection *Yueh-fu shih-chi*. As an example of a
balled that has a contemporary reference but is written in a received
tradition, I shall use a poem written by Yuan Chieh, "Song of Ch'ung-
ling," dated 764.[47] It is a ballad written during the first of his two
appointments as prefect (*tz'u-shih*) of Tao-chou, near Ch'ang-sha.
("Ch'ung-ling" is the Han-dynasty name for "Tao-chou.") In the preface
to this poem, Yuan Chieh writes that the population of Tao-chou had
fallen from forty thousand households, before the Troubles, to four
thousand at the time of his appointment, and in the body of the poem
he forthrightly states that the harshness of government tax exactions has
been just as damaging as the banditry which has plagued the region.
Eight lines from the poem describe the devastation of the peasantry:

> After the Troubles small provinces were wiped out,
> The remaining populace all in desperate need,
> Large villages have no more than ten familites left,
> Large clans are dwindled to one survivor.
> Grass roots for the morning meal,
> Tree bark for the evening meal.
> In speaking he struggles for breath,
> The will quick, but the steps stumbling.

Yuan Chieh's purpose is explicit. In case any doubt remains, the poem
ends with a declaration:

> Who is gathering the songs of the land?
> I want to offer up these lines.

Yuan Chieh, blunt in his words and purpose, simply used or, as he saw it,
revived the ballad form as it already existed. It is his approach that seems
more in line with the revival of interest in ballads in the next century by
Po Chü-i and Yuan Chen. His poem shows, on the one hand, that Tu Fu's
compassion for the humble is not unique, and, on the other hand,
throws into relief the uniqueness of Tu Fu's expression of compassion.
Tu Fu's contribution, then, was not a simple one of reviving the ballad as
a vehicle of criticism, as is commonly averred. After all, Yuan Chieh did

47. 舂陵行, in *Ch'uan T'ang shih* 241.2704.

that – and, one might add, to Tu Fu's great appreciation, for in 767 Tu Fu wrote a response to this poem, because, as he says in the preface to his own poem, he was heartened by "the unexpected reappearance of the *pi-fu* [that is, the *Classic of Poetry* style of criticism]."[48] Rather, Tu Fu's contribution was to revive the ballad as a vehicle of social criticism while also rendering his account in a realistic rather than stylized manner. The latter, however, was not a programmatic goal, for Tu Fu wrote many different kinds of ballads.

Some years earlier, in 761 or 762, Tu Fu had himself written a poem in the *pi-fu* style of criticism, "Song of Barley" (130/9/13). He was in Szechuan Province, where men were being conscripted for its defense against raids carried out at harvest time by neighboring peoples: the Tangut, Hu, and Nu-tz'u in 761, and the Tibetans in 762. (The place names in line 3 are all in Liang-chou, which was to the north of Ch'eng-tu and the target of the raids.)

> The barley is withered and the wheat is brown,
> The women weep as they walk and their men are fugitives.
> Chi and Pi to the east, and west to Liang and Yang,
> Whose harvest sickles are these? The Hu and Ch'iang.
> And was it not three thousand men from Shu
> Troops fighting hard across the length of rivers and mountains?
> Oh, if only like birds we had wings,
> To throw ourselves into the white clouds and return home!

This is a "ditty" (*yao* 謠), a deliberate attempt to write in the manner of a song of the type collected from among the people. The opening lines use a song preserved from the Latter Han dynasty: "The wheat is green, the barley withered. / Who is harvesting it? The women and girls. / And the men, where may they be? / Off to the west against the Hu."[49] Like the "Frontier" poems, Tu Fu's poem is a close imitation of the original type, with the words put in the mouth of the conscript. Lacking the factual immediacy of Yuan Chieh's preface, which gave his ballad so much of its power, and lacking Tu Fu's own kind of immediacy, such as is found in the opening lines of "Ballad of Army Carts," "Song of Barley" moves the reader more by the force of tradition than by particularity. The loss of crops is an ever-present theme of ballads, and the individuals have been abstracted as Every Conscript by the ballad form.

48. 不意復見比興體制, preface to his "Matching Prefect Yuan's 'Song of Ch'ung-ling,'" 154/11/15.
49. From *Hsu Han shu*, "Five Elements Treatise," quoted in *Chiu-chia* 130/9/13. Also in *Ku yao yen*, ed. Tu Wen-lan (1815–81), p. 98. Translated in Birrell, *Songs and Ballads*, p. 109.

Tu Fu made a similar descriptive attempt in an earlier pair of poems, "Lament for Ch'en-t'ao" (translated next) and "Lament for Ch'ing-fan." Ch'en-t'ao and Ch'ing-fan are the sites, just west of Ch'ang-an, of two major imperial defeats in late 756. Under the direction of a court official, Fang Kuan, the battles were lost, with a tremendous toll, almost without having been contested ("not a sound of battle," in "Lament for Ch'en-t'ao," line 3). The defeat came while Tu Fu was in rebel-held Ch'ang-an (the "returned" of line 5). In these poems, the seven-character line, with its traditions of rapid narrative and battle themes, carries the reader too swiftly past the tragedy of what must have been a deeply felt defeat. Here is "Lament for Ch'en-t'ao":

> In the first month of winter, sons of good families from ten
> provinces
> Found their blood is become the water of Ch'en-t'ao Marsh.
> In the open wilds under clear skies, not a sound of battle –
> Forty thousand valiant men all perished the same day.
> The barbarians have returned with blood-washed arrows,
> Singing their strange songs and drinking in the market.
> The people of the Capital turn their faces north, weeping,
> Longing day and night for the return of the imperial army.

The tradition of topical ballads in this mode was continued by, among others, Po Chü-i and Yuan Chen, and in the Sung dynasty, by Mei Yao-ch'en. Both Po Chü-i and Yuan Chen left many statements which showed their deliberate and ideological approach, for each sketched a history of the true (that is, socially responsible) tradition within poetry, beginning with *Classic of Poetry* and ending in their own time. Although Tu Fu figures in each man's tradition, they might have traced the line of continuity more directly through Yuan Chieh (who was not mentioned by either man). More than half of Yuan Chieh's surviving poems (out of a total of over one hundred) are in ballad form, and all of them are ballads written with the purpose of supplying the deficiencies in poetry and in policy which he saw about him. Similarly, his anthology *Ch'ieh-chung chi* was conceived of as a program: he included only seven persons and twenty-two poems, all ballads in style and purpose.[50] Tu Fu, by contrast, experimented widely, and consequently his work divides into small groups of poems, which show various traits in various combinations of style and form. Yet it is from Tu Fu's work rather than Yuan Chieh's that Po Chü-i and Yuan Chen created a lineage. Po Chü-i found "Three Officials," "The Pass at Lu-tzu," and "Detention at Fort Hua-men" to be

50. Yuan Chieh's poems are in *Ch'üan T'ang shih, chüan* 240–1. *Ch'ieh-chung chi* is reprinted in *T'ang-jen hsuan T'ang-shih.*

antecedents to his "New Ballads," and Yuan Chen named "Lament for Ch'en-t'ao," "Lament by Serpentine River," "Ballad of Army Carts," and "Ballad of Beauties."[51] To these we may add "Song of Barley," "Lament for Ch'ing-fan," "Ballad of Firewood Carriers," "Song of Boatmen," "Observing Fishermen, a Song" "Observing Fishermen, Another Song." With the exception of "Ballad of Army Carts," "Ballad of Beauties," and "The Official at Shih-hao" (which is one of the set "Three Officials"), the poems named are, in the terms defined here, the less experimental of Tu Fu's poems. They have made one literary leap, to topicality, but the habits of language have remained those of the ballad. The poems which are more strongly marked by experimentation are absent from the line of development. Perhaps this is unsurprising, since the experiments were far from systematic.

These remarks are not made as a criticism of Tu Fu's stylized language. For one thing, realism is not necessarily more effective than stylized realism. The stylized language of ballads carries its own moral freight, and hence, for certain purposes, one could argue that it is more natural to use a stylized language and less natural to use a directly descriptive language. The poetic tradition allows two approaches, hitherto kept separate, but when combined, the discrepancy between the two allows us to see how Tu Fu experimented with the problem of recording the battle-scarred world around him.

We are now in a position to ask two types of questions, depending on whether a given poem is in ballad or old-style form. When it is a lyric poem in the old-style form, we only have to ask, why the interpolation of stylized realism? The relevant distinguishing feature of lyric poetry is that the event in the poem did occur (for if it had not, then allegory, political allegory, would be present). Tu Fu's distinction is that he makes the reality more real, so to speak, by conveying the concreteness of human life and by widening the range of our attention through the unobtrusive invention of subject matter.

When the poem is a ballad, a whole panoply of questions is raised. An event in a ballad not only is archetypal but also tends to "happen" in order to provide information to those above. It provides the knowledge about the realm that a ruler or high official should have and that a responsible official should offer, since the feelings of the people are an

51. "The Pass at Lu-tzu," written at the end of 756, offers advice about military strategy against the rebels (56/3/18) and "Detained at Fort Hua-men," probably 759, offers advice about the management of those uncertain allies, the Uighurs (56/3/17). "Lament by Serpentine River," mentioned by Yuan Chen, is in 43/2/20. Po Chü-i's examples are from his 815 "Letter to Yuan Ninth"; Yuan Chen's examples are from his 812 "Preface to *Ancient Ballads*," in *Tu Fu chüan*, 1:16–18 and 1:13–14 respectively.

index to the condition of the state. For the poet, therefore one goal of depiction is remonstrance; in expectation of this, the reader's attention is focused as much on the implied criticism as on the circumstances presented. Given that the main intent of "Three Officials" and "Three Partings" is interpreted as remonstrance, the novelty of the details tend to be valued for adding poignancy to the poet's appeal to conscience. Their purpose is to act as indicators of Tu Fu's compassion. Thus P'u Ch'i-lung writes of "Official at Hsin-an" that "righteousness walks in the mantle of humane feeling."[52]

When Tu Fu introduces the element of topical relevance into the ballad, he injects a cast of realism into a form which was previously shaped almost entirely by convention. The realism is an extra, so to speak, over and above what is needed for remonstrance. Stylization identifies the ballad, yet the details in Tu Fu's ballads are conviningly historical and specific. In such poems Tu Fu has brought the two forms of old-style poetry and ballad closer to each other. Overall, formal features lead us to make two separate classes of poems out of the cluster of compassion poems. Some of the tension in Tu Fu's compassion poems seems to stem from his attempt to conflate the distinctions – of meter, prosody, and language – between ballads and old-style poetry. "A Fine Lady" and "The Official at Shih-hao" are examples of what happens under this kind of pressure.

Then why not abandon the ballad form? Why not use lyric poetry in its old-style form? An obvious answer is that the ballad tradition offers advantages that are difficult to abandon. For exposing the sufferings inflicted by war, the ballad, with its traditonal themes of war, soldiering, separation, and crop failure, is ready-made for the poet's needs. The reader is already prepared to receive the poet's moral purpose, for the ballad form alerts him to the poem's implicit "criticism of above from below." Furthermore, the convention that the ballad employs the point of view of a common person gives voice to those who are ordinarily voiceless.

It may be, however, that the problem of depiction does not stem mainly from a conflict between old-style poetry and the ballad. The difficulty may not lie in the ballad form but in the fact that the topics which are traditionally treated by ballads are treated only by ballads, and only in a ballad manner. In particular, the ballad form has something of a monopoly on the topic of the ordinary man, especially the ordinary man who is a stranger, not a neighbor. The difficulty seems to lie in dealing with the common man in a believable, or realistic, way. It is not

52. P'u Ch'i-lung, *Tu Tu hsin-chieh*, p. 53.

necessary to write realistically in order to fulfill the purposes of the ballad form. After all, Tu Fu's ballads on K'uei-chou women carrying firewood or Yangtze boathands and fishermen are somewhat impersonal, yet they successfully induce pity in the reader. However, Tu Fu appears to have set himself the goal of individualizing scenes and people. Thus we may interpret the first-person voice of the old soldier, in "Parting from No One," not only as a ballad convention, but also as the poet's attempt to make the ballad convention real, or unconventional. Hence the poem ends with an affecting twist that supplies the title and distinguishes – or individualizes – this old soldier's return from that of other old soldiers. (The old soldier has been gone so long that he knows no one in his home village any more – a traditional motif; thus when reconscripted – and this is the twister – he goes willingly, having no one from whom to part.) Under the self-imposed condition of individualizing persons and scenes, believability becomes a visible problem, not really overcome in "Parting from No One."

In describing the concerns of the common man, there is always the tendency, especially strong in ballads, to look beyond the person depicted in them to the upper folk to whom the exposition is addressed. The problem of believability is most clearly seen in the poems' difficulty with dialogue. The common man, though inarticulate, must be given speech. At best, the words are what he would say if he could. But the direct speech which often makes up the body of a ballad is not speech from the mouths of humble folk but speech put into the mouths of humble folk. Such speech occurs in both ballads and lyric poetry (the examples of "Ch'iang Village," "Forced to Drink," and "Orange Grove," given earlier, are all lyric poems), but it occurs more in ballads because convention invites it. It is often said that dialogue increases the realism, concreteness, and drama of a poem, but in fact it does none of these things. Direct speech in poetry is full of contradictions. In theory, nothing could be closer to reportage, providing evidence of what the vernacular was in the mid-eighth century. As it actually occurs in poetry, however, direct speech is the most convention-ridden, convention-bound of the mannerisms of poetry. A lengthy check through the concordance to Tu Fu's poems reveals that, in the first place there are very few instances of direct speech longer than a line, and that in the second place, those which are longer adopt a conventional form. Dialogue is almost always an echo of the ballads: note that lapses into ballad style in Tu Fu's lyric poems chiefly occur during dialogue.

A related difficulty lies in the handling of poetic situations in which the speaker is not the poet himself. By convention, this cannot be a lyric poem (*shih*), yet only when the speaker is also the poet can an intimate

98

tone be achieved. Deriving its intimacy from its restriction to the voice of the poet, the lyric poem almost always is restricted in subject to the activities of his public self. The poem's starting point is usually certain moments in his life – an excursion, a climb to a height, a majestic mountain, a parting. The other people that figure in a lyric poem tend to be from the poet's own social group – another official, a recluse (that is, an official in retirement), or sometimes a monk. Such an arrangement does not make the lyric poem amenable to the intimate portrayal of women, farmers, or soldiers, and their portrayal was essentially confined to the ballad. Tu Fu was exceptional in that a few of his poems directly address his wife rather than a social counterpart and consequently have gained him much credit for the tenderness of his feelings.[53] The affectionate poems addressed to his son Tsung-wu are also remarkable. By contrast, the conventions of the ballad allow, indeed require, a speaker who is not a member of the elite, who then recounts, in stylized ballad language, his or her tale for the length of the poem. If the story is not told by the person himself or herself, then a bystander is provided, who briefly addresses the initial speaker and proceeds to tell his or her story. "Have you seen...?", the bystander begins, and launches into a long account. The tale told is usually archetypal in nature.

Judging from Tu Fu's experimentation, he tried to compensate for the existing division of functions by making alterations, sometimes in the ballad, sometimes in lyric poetry. In the ballad "A Fine Lady," he casts a nonconventional speaker: the woman is, unusually, of gentle birth, and her situation is individualized with many details – with the consequence that the meaning is much controverted. In "The Official at Shih-hao" and "Ballad of Army Carts," the narrator is changed to someone who could well be the poet himself, evidently an attempt to personalize the tale to follow. The narrator appears only briefly, however: at the beginning and again at the end in "The Official at Shih-hao"; for six extraordinary lines at the beginning of "Ballad of Army Carts," and not again. The bulk of the narration is still carried by the ballad figure – by the old woman in "The Official at Shih-hao," and by the bystander in the remaining twenty lines of "Ballad of Army Carts" (which tells of a conscript's fate in frontier soldiering) – and the individualization is not fully established.

One might ask, why not abandon the ballad form? Why not just write lyric poetry? Tu Fu did do this, and his lyric poems contain many warm, intimate portraits of the types of people usually found in ballads. We can find many examples of easy intercourse with humble neighbors. "Forced to Drink," ostensibly a compliment to his patron Yen Wu, conveys in its

53. For example, "Moonlit Night," 295/19/6 and "The Moon on the Hundred and Fifth Night," 296/19/11.

main part an affectionate portrait of a rustic farmer. A look at Tu Fu's treatment of the topic of neighbors reveals his light, unpatronizing touch. The poet's attitude and perception are physical and human, providing further examples of his concrete realism. A small sample includes neighbors getting a look at the hubbub next door: "Neighbors – their heads crowd above the wall"; neighbors on his return to the Thatched Hut:

> Village neighbors, happy to have me back,
> Buy wine and bring bottles of them.

and neighbors in day-to-day life at the Thatched Hut:

> If you'll have a cup with the old man next door,
> I'll hail him over the fence, and we'll finish the rest.[54]

In these poems, however, the people are interacting with the poet rather than recounting their own stories, as they would have done in a ballad. When Tu Fu can transform someone into an individual, he does, but the magic of interaction is required. As the poet says in "Cold Food Festival," "I go whenever the farmers invite me." An exception is "Again Presented to Mr. Wu" (434/28/25), where the poet gently describes the timidity of someone who had obviously never approached him. He is reminding Mr. Wu to be charitable to an old woman who was taking dates from his trees:

> If she weren't so poor, would she have come to this?
> If only because of her fear, one must be more gentle.

The second line urges on Mr. Wu, not a generalized kindness to the poor, but a specific gentleness that, like the writer's, is called forth by empathizing with the special fears of the woman he sees.

In some cases, the mixture of ingredients is such that one feels that Tu Fu is trying to break through the stylized third-person convention of ballads. The famous set of seven poems in the ballad form written in Ch'in-chou, "Seven Songs, Composed in the Year 759 While Living Temporarily in T'ung-ku County" (94/6/16), may be seen as one such attempt. In this set, the poetic dilemma is reversed. Instead of trying to individualize the descriptions of common folk in ballads, Tu Fu uses the ballad form on an already individualized subject: himself and his family. He had taken his family from the capital area to Ch'in-chou in the far west, apparently with the intention of staying there; they soon moved on

---

54. The lines are from "Ch'iang Village," poem 1, 52/3/8A; "Thatched Hut," 143/10/18; and "A Guest Arrives," 355/21/46.

to Szechuan, however, perhaps owing to the desperate situation described in these poems. The first two poems are translated here:

> A traveler, a traveler, Tzu-mei is his name
> White of hair and disheveled of mien,
> Gathering chestnuts in the footsteps of Chu-kung
> In a mountain valley at day's end and in the year's cold.
> No word from the Central Plains, no way to return,
> Hands and feet frozen, skin and flesh dead,
> Alack, alas! One song, and the song is sad,
> The melancholy wind comes from the skies down for me.

> A long-handled hoe of white ash, of white ash,
> My life depends on you for its life –
> No sprouts on the yellow turnips, the mountain snow lies thick,
> I tug at my short clothing, but the shins are still bare,
> And now with you I come back empty-handed,
> The boy cries and the girls wail, the four walls are still.
> Alack, alas! the second song, and the song just begins,
> The village shows its pity for me.

Of the remaining poems in the set, the third concerns the poet's brothers and the fourth his sister, followed by three on his own situation. (The middle one is somewhat oblique, a political comment, it seems.) The stylistic echoes that place "Seven Songs of T'ung-ku" in a non-*shih* tradition are prominent. Three of the poems (the first, third, and fourth) begin with an archaized line reminiscent of song. Poem 1 opens identically to poem 284 in *Classic of Poetry*: 有客有客; and poems 3 and 4 begin similarly: 有弟有弟 and 有妹有妹.[55] The last couplet of each poem also forms a repeating pattern, enumerating the poem's place in the set and producing the predictable repetition of the song lyric.[56] Other stylistic echoes that contribute to an old-fashioned, songlike effect are the use of the seven-character line, the use of the *sao* 騷 filler word *hsi* 兮, and many choices of diction. These song features seem to objectify – and hence to broaden – our sense of the poet's plight by placing a unique individual's suffering in a visible poetic tradition

55. The pre-Sui work *Sou shen hou-chi*, *chüan* 1, quotes a song which begins with the same construction: 有鳥有鳥. Also in *Ku yao yen*, ed. Tu Wen-lan, p. 765.
56. The pattern of the final couplets (the enumeration and the lament) is the same as the pattern that ends each of the "Eighteen Stanzas of a Hu Pipe" 胡笳十八拍, attributed to the third-century Ts'ai Yen and purportedly a record of her years as a captive of the Hsiung-nu and her return to China when ransomed by Ts'ao Ts'ao. "Eighteen Stanzas," however, dates its earliest textual appearance only to the eleventh century (in *Yueh-fu shih chi*), and the relationship between the two sets of poems remains a matter of conjecture.

(whereas lyric poetry, being the more usual personal expressive form, might be considered invisible).

The situation recounted is grim and specific enough: chestnuts their only food, the bitter cold, the desperate want, being refugees at the edge of empire. It is, however, the factual details (one might say the details from lyric poetry) rather than the stylized song traits that make clear the family's bleak situation. In the second poem is a couplet much like Tu Fu's other intimate descriptions of his children: "I come back empty-handed, / The boy cries and the girls wail, the four walls are still." Other details, while specific enough, lack the physical vividness noted earlier. They are chiefly nouns – "chestnuts," "hoe," "short clothing" – and are accompanied by the predictable verbs – "gathering chestnusts," "tug at short clothing." And in the final poem, the reference to a chance to socialize with a scholar could have been from lyric poetry:

> In the mountains is a Confucian scholar I knew of old,
> We talked of old days, melancholy over our former ambitions.

It is hard to know what to make of this set of poems. It is a great experiment, but it is difficult to measure its success, for one gropes for criteria by which to decide. It is, one might say, unique, and therefore impossible to judge. If we follow Tu Fu's hint – he never wrote in this manner again – we might say that he was dissatisfied with it in some way. That "Seven Songs of T'ung-ku" was an experiment we may feel confident, for it dates from his extremely productive month and a half in Ch'in-chou, when he wrote an extraordinary eighty poems. Why he was dissatisfied (if we may suppose it to be dissatisfaction) with this set of poems is unclear. Looked at biographically, his situation was never again so hopeless until the very last year of his life, but this form did not make a reappearance at that time. The dilemma lies in the integration of the song features, which tend to generalize the poet's situation, with the extremely specific content, for the bleakness of the poverty portrayed is highly unusual (at least for a poem written in the first person) until then.

That this set of poems has received lavish praise does not help to resolve the critic's uncertainty, for the praise revolves around the two points we have been examining, without integrating them: Tu Fu's vividness in conveying his desperate situation, and the uniqueness of his expression of it. For example, Chu Hsi (1130–1200), who notes the influences of "Nine Songs" 九歌, "Four Sorrows" 四愁, and "Eighteen Stanzas of a Hu Pipe" 胡笳十八拍, says that Tu Fu nonetheless created his own style.[57] That the set is unique we can also see from the imitations

57. Quoted in P'u Ch'i-lung, *Tu Tu hsin-chieh*, p. 265.

it attracted. Wen T'ien-hsiang in the thirteenth century and Ch'en Tzu-lung in the seventeenth produced the most famous imitations, written when they, like Tu Fu, found themselves in great personal and political distress. Wen T'ien-hsiang's imitation is closer than Ch'en Tzu-lung's, but from the original both took the form, the style (opening lines, ending, *sao* diction, and so on), and the subject matter (national disintegration and, in the case of Wen T'ien-hsiang, his own and his immediate family's danger).[58] Their choosing to imitate "Seven Songs of T'ung-ku" when in distress confirms its uniqueness, and the closeness with which they followed the original confirms that its uniqueness consists of those elements in combination. These imitations chiefly confirm that the poems are admired as unique specimens.

"Seven Songs of T'ung-ku" takes its place among the examples of this chapter which, when arranged along a line, show that Tu Fu was experimenting with the interaction of form and topical content. The elements in the poems along this line occur in varying proportions: at one end, the generality and impersonality of the "Frontier" poems; next, the introduction of specific, circumstantial details into ballads in various ways (the opening lines of "Ballad of Army Carts"; the demographics of "The Official at Shih-hao"); at the other end, the transformation of the ballad form into a highly personal vehicle ("Seven Songs of T'ung-ku"). The examples discussed in this chapter form a line which, though sometimes untidy, shows Tu Fu varying his approach to the task of depiction. Note, however, that his experiments are not associated with a development over time. That is, Tu Fu does not consistently move away from ballads to the kind of realism associated with, say, "Ch'iang Village." Although he experimented, he did so without a particular goal in mind. Many of his formats he did not return to – that of "Seven Songs of T'ung-ku," for example, as well as of "Three Officials"; but he did repeat the more standard ballad form of "Ballad of Firewood Carriers." The conflict does not ever resolve itself in Tu Fu's poems. However, one outcome that did emerge over time should be discussed.

What happened over time was that the conflict receded. Prolonged descriptions of objective suffering decreased. Did Tu Fu lose interest? Even a cursory glance at the late poetry shows that this was not the case. Rather, his topicality altered and was internalized, and, freed of

---

58. Ch'iu Chao-ao (*Tu shih hsiang-chu* 8.700) mentions that many poets of the Sung and Yuan dynasties imitated "Seven Songs of T'ung-ku," but that Wen T'ien-hsiang's imitation was the finest. He goes on to compare Tu Fu's circumstances with those of Wen T'ien-hsiang and concludes that Wen's were worse. Wen T'ien-hsiang's six poems, entitled simply "Six Songs" 六歌, are found in *Wen-shan hsien-sheng ch'üan-chi* 14.508. Ch'en Tzu-lung's imitation is entitled "At Year's End, an Imitation of Tzu-mei's 'Seven Songs of T'ung-ku'" and is found in *Ch'en Tzu-lung shih chi* 10.309–11.

specificity in this different way, it recurred ever more often. It became both more fragmentary and more pervasive. Themes amalgamated and became broader. The cluster that had consisted of the people's suffering, family concerns, and policy recommendations also came in later years to include reminiscence, homesickness, longing for the emperor, the rise and fall of fortunes, time, and eternity. Direct description persisted into Tu Fu's last poems, but the themes became more internalized, more part of his personality. This is most clear when the elements of the conflict are transferred to the regulated-verse form, where reality tends to be entirely filtered through the mind and is experienced or recalled as images. Depiction, that is, gave way to expression and to an interest in expressiveness. Two examples will illustrate these features. The first is "White Emperor City" (459/30/2):

> From within White Emperor City clouds issue from its gates,
> Down on White Emperor City the rain basin overturns –
> High river, narrow gorges: thunders locked in battle,
> Ancient trees, black vines, sun and moon darkened.
> The battle horse is not as eager as the homing horse,
> Of a thousand families, a hundred are alive today,
> How sorrowful the widow, stripped of everything,
> Bitter cries on the autumn plains, ah, from what village?[59]

The prosodic form is seven-character regulated verse, in the *ao-t'i* variant; the first four lines, as Ch'iu Chao-ao remarks, resemble a ballad in their flow, and it is the ending, as P'u Ch'i-lung remarks, that shows Tu Fu in his characteristic colors.[60] But in this poem, the people's suffering and the poet's compassion have been integrated, in mood and in placement, with the scenery, especially in the last line. In that line, the wails of suffering are located on the autumn plains, of which at that moment we first gain a sweeping perspective. And the final query, "from what village?", rises from the landscape, consigned to time. The scenery in turn is integrated into the seven-character regulated form, loosened here in its *ao-t'i* variant, but nonetheless existing against a grid of exacting rules. In other words, when the depiction of sorrow occurs in regulated verse, as it often does in Tu Fu's late years, the sorrow tends to be integrated into the landscape and provides, aesthetically speaking, the meaning and poignancy of the landscape.

59. 459/30/2. Ch'iu Chao-ao suggests that "from what village?" means that the cries can be heard from every village (*Tu shih hsiang-chu* 15.1350–1). This is certainly more likely than that they can be heard from only one village, but surely, artistically speaking, the cries are meant to be representative – and single in source.
60. Ch'iu Chao-ao, *Tu shih hsiang-chu* 15.1350, and P'u Ch'i-lung, *Tu Tu hsin-chieh*, p. 645.

The second example is "Night at the Pavilion" (498/31/43), also a seven-character regulated verse:

> At year's end nature's forces cut short the last light,
> Here at sky's edge, frost and snow, then a cold, clear night.
> Drums and bugles of the fifth watch sound sad and strong,
> Starry River's image in the Three Gorges tosses and shines.
> In the wilds, weeping rises from a thousand homes, tidings of war,
> Aborigine songs rise here and there from fisherman or woodcutter.
> Sleeping Dragon and Leaping Horse – they ended too in the
>   yellow earth;
> This world, news from home – idle to sigh over them.[61]

In this regulated verse, the human points of the landscape (lines 5 and 6) also contain the sole topical reference ("tidings of war"). As in "White Emperor City," a single line (line 5) provides both the explicit statement of emotion ("weeping rises from a thousand homes") and also the view from a height that typically imbues a landscape with its poignancy (view from a height implied in "rises"). In the final line, human suffering is obliquely reprised; this time it diminishes, viewed against the scale of eternity. Sorrow here forms part of an unbroken image surface and in that sense is subordinated to the complex aesthetic and expressive motives of the poem.

To say that the compassion is aestheticized is perhaps too detached a view, given the realness of the suffering which Tu Fu had witnessed. It might be better to summarize this change by saying that the Troubles, originally a subject, became an obsession. Internalized, they stirred in Tu Fu upon any kind of stimulus; nothing could be described without veering off into a reference to them. Moral concern, compassion, topicality: the manifestation of these constant qualities changed over time and between genres in Tu Fu's poetry.

In discussing the issues of compassion and topicality, we have found that although Tu Fu's innovations in lyric poetry, *shih*, were great, they require comparatively little comment, whereas the alterations in the ballad have required an investigation into the nature and range of the ballad form and of depiction. We might now ask what this has to do with Tu Fu's famous compassion. At the risk of sounding analytic in the face of this profound quality, I think that we can first put Tu Fu's achieve-

---

61. In line 1, I have used Hawke's translation of "nature's forces" for *yin-yang* (*A Little Primer of Tu Fu*, p. 183). In line 5, I use the variant "thousand homes" 千家 rather than "some homes" 幾家, and in the next line I use the variant *ji-ch'u* 幾處 ("here and there").

ment in terms of style, for it is the style which convinces the reader that the poet is truly bearing witness to suffering, and it is the reader's conviction of this which makes the themes forceful in the reader's mind. In the end, in reading literature, there is always some level on which one has to begin to compare it with knowledge gained from one's own experience. The willingness to do so, and the willingness to allow the literature to expand and deepen those experiences, benefit the reader and reflect back on the literature. In the case of Tu Fu's compassion themes, the reactions of readers through the centuries, as well as our modern experience, show that in literature the dedicated depiction of human misery is no less timeless than the exploration of the human psyche. Today, when our experiences of misery tend to be simultaneously more distant and, through the images of film, more immediate, Tu Fu remains an icon of conscience whose exceptional attention to ordinary people has made their sufferings more visible.

3
Juxtaposition I:
A structural principle

This chapter and the next constitute a single project with two related purposes. Chapter 3 identifies a poetic criterion – a structural principle – by which to define a meaningful set of poems within Tu Fu's work, and Chapter 4 uses this set of poems to explore some connections between Tu Fu's poetry and his life. That there is an intimate connection between the poetry and the life seems the most obvious feature of his work: his poems, whatever else they do, manifestly provide a detailed chronicle of his life and of the historic events he had witnessed. The reader learns more about Tu Fu from his poetry than is possible for any poet up to his time. The relation of a poetry of such content to the life is intimate, direct, and informative to a degree unique to him.

The richness of this material has had a far-reaching effect on the focus of scholarship and hence on our present ability to approach the study of Tu Fu's poetry, including the tasks posed in this chapter. To reprise briefly, the tendency in scholarship has been for nearly all discussions of Tu Fu's poems to end up in biography. This tendency is understandable in view of the personal tone of his poems, but it has been unintentionally one-sided. The biographical inclination has been most notable in the grouping of the poems into categories for study. For reasons owing both to Tu Fu's poetry and to traditional perceptions of lyric poetry, the classifications have been primarily biographical. Consequently, critical analyses have been carried on within divisions created by biography rather than by poetry. Of course some important classifications, such as periodization, can only be based on biography. Others, however, although they may begin as something else, end up as biographical categories in another guise. Tu Fu's friends, his patrons, his kinsmen; his travels, his homes, his offices – this is only a sample of the common topics of study which, whatever intentions may have been, end up telling us rather more about the poet than the poetry.

Even groups of poems seemingly sorted according to poetic criteria have in practice been analyzed along biographical lines. The study of prosodic forms constitutes the most prominent example. The long old-style poems are primarily journal-like and poems of reminiscence, and thus their analysis easily becomes the study of Tu Fu's actions and frames of mind. Analyses of ballads lead on to an analysis of Tu Fu's social protest and political sympathies. Information about him in the poems is so plentiful, and much of it is so intriguingly piecemeal, that one is always led on to uncover more about the poet. By contrast, categories that commonly produce more purely poetic criticism (for example, study of seven-character regulated verse or seven-character quatrains) tend to be difficult to connect to the rest of Tu Fu studies.

Studies that end up in biography in effect proceed as though the poems directly provide information about various aspects of their author. They assume that the relation of poet to poetry is simple and direct. In one important respect, this assumption is valid, for Tu Fu's poetry seems always to represent its author in some direct way. Tu Fu does present the many spheres of his life in an unambiguous manner. That is to say, although the degree of artifice associated with his use of poetry varies, Tu Fu does not modulate his tone or phrasing so as to cause the reader to divorce Tu Fu's views or moods from the poem's. In this Tu Fu takes many steps farther the admonition of the lyric tradition that the voice of the poet speak sincerely through the poem. For the reader, Tu Fu exists as a person exactly because of a stronger connection between the life and the poetry than can be found in the work of any of his contemporaries.

The direct relation between poet and poetry, of course, favors biographical approaches. When the medium of poetry is considered not to distort, the reliability of the information imparted by the poems leads to corresponding neglect of the poetry. The commonplace of Western literary theory that the poetic medium alters the nature of our information is usually not considered, even hypothetically, in Tu Fu criticism. Even when this view is taken into account, it usually evinces itself by the critic's cautiousness in making generalizations. Rather than providing insights, the discriminations of theory tend only to place restrictions upon the use of information gained from the poems. Seldom is the opposite possibility explored: that the poetic medium might be exploited for additional information about Tu Fu, that separate evaluation of the poetry might produce corroborating evidence concerning the poet rather than imposing restrictions.

These two chapters seek incidentally to strengthen the poetic dimensions of Tu Fu studies without denying the validity of biographical studies. By identifying a poetic trait that can be used to isolate a meaningful group of poems, I hope to add to the repertoire of poetic criteria that can create fruitful subdivisions within Tu Fu's work. Certainly, to grasp the achievement of an imposing poet such as Tu Fu, whose collected works number fourteen hundred poems, subdivisions are needed, and in fact much methodology in Tu Fu studies can be understood as a search for useful categories. The next chapter uses the group of poems identified here to study a connection between the poetry and the life. This undertaking incidentally seeks to emphasize the broader usefulness of poetic traits – to show that a better understanding of the poetry can lead back to knowledge of the poet, that poetic insights need not be solely technical. Tu Fu's familiar traits can be shown to be firmly grounded in particular poems. The poems which fall outside the classification of this chapter are then illuminated by their contrast with this group.

The relation between the life and the poetry for which I shall argue will be unexpected, if judged by the rich field of Western literary theory. Developments there, in sum, cause one to insert a wedge between the author and his work. They show that the work of art acquires a life separate from its author and possesses its own logic and meaning; or they show the ways in which the author is, a priori, an unreliable guide to his own meaning. By contrast, the set of poems isolated in this chapter confirms the familiar picture of Tu Fu, a picture that is in turn based on the assumption that the persona is the poet, and that the poet is the poem's speaker. Indeed, if anything, these poems show Tu Fu more concerned with what he wants to say than with how he says it, so that in these poems the needs of the persona partially supplant the interests of the poet.

Juxtaposition defined

The approach used here isolates a group of poems by identifying a poetic structure that they share, a feature that I shall call "juxtaposition." Juxtaposition in Tu Fu's poetry has been noticed before, in that some of its effects have been (negatively) appraised by commentators, but the common structure which produces these effects has not been singled out nor a name supplied. This section defines the characteristics of juxtaposition; the next section, headed "Examples," illustrates its usefulness in the reading of both familiar and unfamiliar poems; in the final section of this chapter, this class of poems is analyzed in poetic terms, as a question of structure.

Structure initially appears to be solely a poetic issue, discussable within the confines of literary debate. One might well ask how issues of personality or other extrapoetic factors can enter into it. Our starting point is the observation that in certain poems structural problems arise that have always been explained through biography; critics have supplied an explanation concerning the poet rather than the poem. I shall argue that although a biographical explanation undoubtedly exists, and may even be primary, a poetic dimension also deserves notice. The early provision of a (convincing) biographical solution has obscured the usefulness of investigating poetic aspects of the problem.

The dimensions of the issue can be most quickly established by examining particular cases. I shall use one long old-style poem and three regulated poems to illustrate the occurrence of this structure and critical responses to it in both long poems and short ones. Let us begin with the old-style poem:[1]

Seeking out Ts'ui Chi and Li Feng on the Last Day of the Month

Morning light enters the round windows,
Disheveled, startled, I lie there, in my worn coat,
I get up, walk a few steps, look at the skies –
The spring air is warmer, day by day –   4
Of a sudden I don't feel so lazy,
And this morning I comb my hair,
Go out the door – no carriage waits for me –
I walk alone, savoring the freedom.   8
Leaning on my stick, this sense of abandon returns,
I have been absolved of the duties of office.
I came late to friendship with Ts'ui and Li,
But our hearts are as one: true, rare companions.   12
Visits back and forth, companionable wine,
In both homes I stay for long periods;
Happy to find friends in this kindly village,
On this lucky day I linger on.   16
The garden of Master Li is growing wild,
The ancient bamboo finely detailed.
The guest looks upon the sweeping that welcomes him,
And at frequent intervals we drink to each other.   20
At Lord Ts'ui's, even as we approach the feast,
He is anxious that no cup be empty.
I do not know whether among the gentlemen of the world

---

1. The Ts'ui Chi and Li Feng of the title are not otherwise known.

Any other are of such forthrightness.   24
The sprouts of grass show their green,
The sounds of bees course in the warmth.
Then: there lie farm tools rusting –
When will arms and men be at rest?   28
The Ko-t'ien emperor of High Antiquity
Did not pass on the imperial concern,
And today men of Juan Chi's kind
Soak themselves in drink to stay alive.   32
The great phoenix – soaring is his flight
And the whale has gobbled up the Nine Provinces.
And so the axis of the earth tilts,
And the hundred rivers flow out of their courses.   36
To sing, to release it in song –
If tears came, they could not be stopped,
In this unstrained wine there is a secret principle,
Among its uses, solace in an uncertain world.   40

In this poem, written in 756 or 757,[2] the poet has decided, on impulse, to visit some friends; while he is there, sitting at ease, the sight of farm tools left in the open and rusting reminds him of the rebellion that is raging; the wine he is drinking turns into Juan Chi's wine, that is, wine drunk by men out of office, useless to state and ruler; the poet feels deep despair, and on this note the poem ends. As thus summarized, the poem appears to develop naturally, but the smooth paraphrase is deceptive. The poem is quite odd, for if one looks at the first eight or ten lines and then at the last dozen lines, they seem not to be from the same poem. The beginning is happy and light; the ending is somber and distraught. From a pleasant narrative about getting up on a nice day, visiting friends and drinking with them, the poem has changed into a dark, agitated series of half thoughts about decline and neglect. The language changes from a simple description of actions, scenery, and thoughts to cryptic allegorical and symbolic allusions (the phoenix, the whale, the axis of the earth, the hundred rivers, lines 33–6).

The break occurs at line 27. After a couplet which describes the warm day, the new grass and buzzing bees (lines 25–6), the poet looks around him – and suddenly the whole mood of the poem changes. With line 27, his eyes light on the rusting farm tools, and the sluice gates to what is to become his permanent grief open. The chance sight reminds the poet of the rebellion just begun, and the remaining twelve lines of the poem

2. The years 756 and 757 are the only choices, because by 758 the two capitals had been recovered, and phrases such as "the whale has gobbled up the Nine Provinces" (line 34) and "the axis of the earth tilts" (line 35) would not have been used. This is the reasoning of Lu Yuan-ch'ang, quoted in Ch'iu Chao-ao, *Tu shih hsiang-chu* 4.296.

show a kind of agitated sorrow that turns first to one thought, then to another. The poem finally ends, because it has to; to dwell any longer on these thoughts would open an irresistible torrent of sorrow. Thus the poet switches to another medium to stave off his sorrow ("to sing, to release it in song," line 37), and so ends the poem.

Clearly it is necessary to deal in some manner with two halves of a poem so different in mood and language. What is there in the first part, one asks, which might lead the reader, on subsequent readings, to accept the onrush of feeling in the second part? The final fourteen lines are emotionally too full and prolonged to be set in motion by a stimulus (the sight of the plow) so briefly mentioned and so quickly left behind. The reader's natural response to this problem is to make an attempt at reconciliation, and reconciliation is in fact the most commonly sought solution.

One such reconciliation was given by the commentator P'u Ch'i-lung, who explained the poem's pronounced contrasts by saying that the poet sets out carefree and arrives careworn, that he tries to use wine to soothe his cares and finds that wine has focused them instead.[3] This is sensitive, and true too. But it should be noticed that P'u Ch'i-lung has framed his answer in terms of the psychology of the poet. The question "Why does the poem evolve like this?" has been answered by "Because of the despondency into which the poet has fallen." As the Troubles widen and deepen through the 760s, this is to become a common answer concerning the development of Tu Fu's poems. Such an answer is sometimes extended to "thus we see the sense of social responsibility which Tu Fu feels at all times." In this way Tu Fu's famous reputation for social concern both confirms and is confirmed by each succeeding poem. An explanation like P'u Ch'i-lung's takes the contrast between the beginning and the ending of the poem to be one of a progression of moods, that is, changes in the psychology of the poet are directly recorded in his poem. Although such an explanation must indeed be part of the answer, a cluster of poetic or aesthetic problems remains: why does the poem develop this way? is disjunction to be accepted? is reconciliation the proper reader response? The biographical context can be only part of the answer.

At this point, basically two choices are available. One can attempt, upon encountering each such problem, to construct for the poem a scenario in which the progression of emotion and events is continuous enough to satisfy. Such a solution is essentially both ad hoc and ad

3. P'u Ch'i-lung, *Tu Tu hsin-chieh*, p. 24.

hominem. Alternatively, one can posit the existence of a principle which can be extended to the reading of an entire group of poems. The principle proposed here is the concept of juxtaposition, which permits us to define the inconsistency in the poem as an issue of structure. The inconsistency in mood, and the concomitant changes in style, language, diction, and mode of progression, all point to a question of structure. In essence, another kind of poem has replaced the one with which the poet began. The imbalance that comes from the two parts cobbled together can fairly be considered a structural issue.

"Seeking out Ts'ui Chi and Li Feng" might seem to present an isolated problem, or at least a problem limited to Tu Fu's old-style poems, since this form allows an author to ramble on indefinitely. But similar inconsistencies occur in some of Tu Fu's short poems as well, where they have already been noticed and criticized. Among these, disjunctions within regulated-verse poems, especially, have drawn comment, possibly because the form is so elaborately symmetrical that disjunctions are all the more noticeable there. In the regulated-verse poems, the criticisms focus on inconsistency of tone, but the problem can be usefully reframed as one of structure. Three of the regulated-verse poems criticized in this way are among Tu Fu's most acclaimed works. These poems are said to descend too quickly from the sublime to the pathetic. They begin with a physical vista of profound grandeur but in the second half (or in the last couplet, or the last line), they recount something trivial: the poet's hair is thinning, or he has had to stop drinking. In such shifts, the figure of the poet cannot help appearing ridiculous. Is this intentional? Many otherwise admiring critics have found it hard to overlook such anticlimatic endings. Let us examine the disjunctions in three poems: "Climbing Yueh-yang Tower," "Climbing to a Height," and "Spring Prospect."

In "Climbing Yueh-yang Tower" (541/35/4), the first four lines magnificently convey the immensity of nature – but the last four dwell on Tu Fu's own worries (no word from his family; tears flow as he leans weakly against the railing).

> I had heard of the waters of Tung-t'ing,
> And today I climb up Yueh-yang Tower –
> Wu and Ch'u divide to east and south,
> Here is suspended the cosmos day and night.
> From friends and family, not a word,
> Old and ill, only my solitary boat;
> War horses are north of the passes,
> I lean on the railing, tears flowing.

Huang Sheng (1622–ca. 1696) found "the change in scope extremely sudden from the broadness of thought in the scenery to the desolation of his self-description." "Quite unexpected," he added, "is the appearance of the words 'From friends and family, not a word.'"[4] Huang's comments are not meant critically, but Wang Fu-chih (1619–92) is more negative. He objected in particular to the last line, holding that "the excellence of the poem ends with the seventh line."[5]

"Climbing to a Height" (411/26/39), probably written at K'uei-chou,[6] begins with a "threnody for dying nature"[7] – and ends anticlimactically with Tu Fu's complaining about his hair turning white and about being forced by his bad health to give up drinking.

> Strong winds, high skies, gibbons cry mournfully,
> A clear islet, white sand, birds circling about,
> To the horizon, leaves of trees come falling down,
> Endlessly long, the River tumbles, tumbles on.
> Ten thousand miles in melancholy autumn, this eternal traveler,
> Ill all the years of my life, I ascend this terrace alone.
> Hardships and sorrows have turned these temples to frost,
> I am discouraged, had to stop drinking dark wine.

The whole of the second half, dwelling on the poet's travails, seems puny against the great sweep of the scenery, and the last line in particular seems trivializing. Although Hu Ying-lin (1551–1602) considered the poem the most excellent among seven-character regulated-verse poems of all time, he also raised the question of the ending as "a bit weak compared to the bold and majestic movement of the first six lines, . . . appearing to switch into another mode."[8]

In "Spring Prospect" (295/19/9), a much earlier poem, written in the spring of 757, while the poet lived in rebel-held Ch'ang-an, a similar incongruence appears.

> The state has fallen, mountains and rivers endure,
> Spring in the city, grasses and trees grow thick,
> I am moved by the times, flowers bring on tears,
> My sorrow at separation, birds startle the heart.
> Beacon fires have burned for three months on end,
> A letter from home would be worth its weight in gold.

4. Huang Sheng, *Tu kung-pu shih shuo* 5.19a.
5. Wang Fu-chih, *T'ang-shih p'ing-hsuan* 3.18a.
6. Originally classified with the Ch'eng-tu poems (for example, in the *Chiu-chia* edition), the poem has been shifted to the K'uei-chou locale, to the stretch of the Yangtze which is the habitat of gibbons (mentioned in line 1). See Ch'iu Chao-ao *Tu shih hsiang-chu*, 20.1766, for the reclassification, and Gulik, *The Gibbon in China*, p. 106, for a map showing the historical ranges of the gibbon.
7. Hawkes's phrase, *A Little Primer of Tu Fu*, p. 204.
8. *Shih sou, nei pien*, 5.95–6.

My white hairs even shorter now from tugging
Soon will not take even a hatpin.

The critic this time is a modern one. David Hawkes notes that a "sudden shifting of mood . . . takes place in the poem after line 6. The sombre anguish of the first part ends, as the tragic figure of the opening lines turns into a comic old man going bald on top."[9]

These criticisms all agree that the tone has changed drastically and without justification from grand to pitiable. In addition, Hawkes rightly points out that "Tu Fu does this sort of thing so often that one must look for something other than mere neurotic self-pity if one is to reach any sort of understanding with him at all."[10] Because these are well-known criticisms of famous poems, many defenses have been constructed. In general, however, the defenses only consist of an assertion to the contrary, an assertion that the two halves of the poems *do* work well together. Hu Ying-lin, for example, whose query about the ending of "Climbing to a Height" is quoted earlier, quiets his uncertainty by deciding that "it is only by this kind of desolate, passive ending that the boundless sorrow of the poet can continue beyond the poem's words." Among modern critics, Fang Yü states of "Climbing to a Height" that the shift is not abrupt, and Chien En-ting states of "Climbing Yueh-yang Tower" that the sweeping immensity of nature in the first half makes the friendless, letterless poet of the second half even more pitiable.[11] Such responses bring the debate down to one of contrary assertions. Hawkes is a notable exception, since he discusses each of these poems and in each case has attempted to reconcile the parts by offering a theory about Tu Fu and the way his poems work. Because his suggestions are specific, they offer the reader a basis for further discussion.

For "Climbing Yueh-yang Tower," Hawkes suggests that "the comparatively more trivial fifth line . . . is due to the rapidity with which one mood succeeds another in the course of the poem. . . . The result of compressing so many mental happenings into so exiguous a form is that the actual wording of the poem becomes a kind of shorthand from which the poet's full meaning has to be reconstructed." For the poem "Climbing to a Height," Hawkes suggests that the ending is not due to "mere neurotic self-pity" but that "Tu Fu's famous compassion in fact includes himself, viewed quite objectively and almost as an afterthought." The final image in "Spring Prospect" Hawkes explains as "a

9. Hawkes, *A Little Primer of Tu Fu*, p. 46.
10. Ibid., p. 204.
11. Hu Ying-lin, *Shih sou, nei-pien*, 5.96; Fang Yü, *K'uei-chou shih*, p. 134; and Chien En-ting, *Ch'ing-ch'u Tu-shih-hsueh yen-chiu*, p. 196.

note of playful self-mockery which is nevertheless infinitely pathetic."[12] In the terms of this chapter, Hawkes has supplied two kinds of answers. The first type concerns the poet's state of mind. The solution that Hawkes suggests for two of the poems is that Tu Fu's compassion includes himself ("Climbing to a Height"), and that there is a note of playful self-mockery in his portrayal of himself ("Spring Prospect"). As in "Seeking out Ts'ui Chi and Li Feng," inconsistency is resolved by an appeal to the kind of person the poet is, or to the mood or situation in which he finds himself. Hawkes's second type of explanation is stated in terms of structure, although the structure he has in mind is that of regulated verse. Hawkes suggests that regulated verse is an exiguous form which produces a shorthand style of communication ("Climbing Yueh-yang Tower").

The poems already examined suggest that the disjoint structure is a characteristic of many of Tu Fu's poems. Therefore the first requirement is to recognize that this problem forms one of a perhaps large category, not one that simply arises in individual poems as the poet's mood dictates. As we shall see shortly, a large group of Tu Fu's poems end very differently from the way they begin; in fact, portions of a given poem can vary so much as to appear to be from different poems. Since a large sample exists, disjunction can be defined and its component traits investigated. In this way explanations grounded in the poet's personality may be deferred until the other half – the issue of structure – is sufficiently understood.

The structural principle of juxtaposition may be defined by its characteristic traits. Juxtaposition is a poetic structure in which two different topics are placed side by side. No transition is made between the topics; no preparation indicates a pending change in topic. In addition, the topics which are juxtaposed in general are drawn from two specific categories: something before the poet's eyes is placed next to something in his mind's eye. Thus the juxtaposition of topics is also a juxtaposition of worlds: exterior versus interior, immediate versus associational. What is before the poet's eyes takes in all the occasions and settings on which Tu Fu writes poems. Thus description of scenery or family usually makes up this part of the poem, and its nature is vivid, specific and physical, often pleasant. What recurs to the poet's mind's eye is, from very early on, one of two topics: the Troubles and himself. These two topics often overlap, for the Troubles is shorthand for a large number of phenomena, and Tu Fu, in dwelling on his own situation, often is simply focusing the rebellion's effects on the case he knows best. Rebellion and self are

12. Hawkes, *A Little Primer of Tu Fu*, pp. 207, 204 and 46 respectively.

thus often in effect one subject. In poems structured by juxtaposition, the poem jumps from an external, immediate scene to an internal, distant, but more urgent concern, and it does so in an abrupt, unpredictable way.

The juxtaposition of topics is often accompanied by changes in language, style, and tone. The disjunctive structure of the poems is paralleled by a disjoint alteration of style: diction, figures, and grammar change their kinds and levels. The two styles then exist side by side without blending. In any given poem, whatever the style adopted for the visible topic, when the topic shifts to the interior topic, a different language and tone take over. With this theory of juxtaposition, the choices of diction and such, which is all the time being made in individual lines, can be elevated to more than just local significance: it enables each choice to take its place as part of a larger pattern, which then provides a model of one way Tu Fu's poetry achieves its effects.

The Japanese scholar Hirose Tansō (1782–1856) noticed the structure in Tu Fu's poems that I term "juxtaposition." In discussing two poems which show this trait of abruptness, "Daytime Dream" and "White Emperor City," he said:

The first half of "Daytime Dream" describes a dream of spring, the second half, his feelings in this war-torn world; the first half of "White Emperor City" describes a rainstorm, the second half, his feelings in this war-torn world. In both, the halves are unconnected. Many of Tu Fu's other poems are also like this. Nowadays, people, by trying to force a reconciliation between the two halves, misunderstand the methods of the past.[13]

Hirose Tansō's answer to a poetic criticism of the two poems was put in poetic terms. This critic (and Jao Tsung-i, who quoted Hirose) saw clearly that criticism about tone in fact concerns an issue of structure. Furthermore, by stating that "many of Tu Fu's other poems are also like this," Hirose clearly perceived that the principle of structure encompasses a larger class of poems than those under discussion. The juxtaposition thesis of this chapter most closely resembles Hirose Tansō's observation that structure in Tu Fu's poems often consists of two unblended styles, and that consistency of a certain (and sometimes desirable) kind is thus precluded.

The juxtaposition proposed here is not the same as the changes in topic that one would naturally expect to find in a long poem, where the logic of the development may prepare the reader. Nor is it a sudden

13. Hirose Tansō, *Tansō shiwa*, p. 18. The two poems mentioned, "Daytime Dream" (423/27/36) and "White Emperor City" (459/30/2), are translated and discussed later in the present chapter under "Examples" and in Chapter 2, respectively. Hirose's comment is quoted by Jao Tsung-i, "Lun Tu Fu K'uei-chou shih," p. 116.

change which, deliberately employed, can be appreciated for its brilliant rhetorical effect. It comes close, perhaps, to what Stephen Owen calls, using quotation marks, the "shifting style" of Tu Fu, which he characterizes as showing "rapid stylistic and thematic shifts." It is not argued here, however, that the rapid shifts "join to represent a problem or experience in several dimensions" or that they produce "new aesthetic values" that successfully displaced older values.[14] Rather, the changes involved in juxtaposition are unexpected and are also inexplicable after the fact. Furthermore, juxtaposition is not proposed as the only structure to be found in a poem. Each poem generally demonstrates, in addition to juxtaposition, an individually justifiable evolution and often a larger structure that is prosodically determined. But juxtaposition occurs as a large division upon which the individual structural needs of the particular poem are organized in a more local manner. It is literally a division: the local structure that is built up within this major division is of the more usual kind, conforming as circumstances require to the demands of the content.

Defining juxtaposition as a stylistic trait logically exempts the critic from justifying or reconciling the disparate parts of a poem.[15] Asserting that unconnectedness is a characteristic of Tu Fu's style in effect sets a limit on possible interpretations of the poems. The change in tone is a given, to be accepted rather than explained or rationalized. Otherwise one can only find the poem deeply flawed, as indeed the critics quoted earlier do.

To define structure as juxtaposition means that disjunction rather than coherence is the first principle of what might still be termed the unity of such a poem. The theory is not designed to reconcile the conflicting elements of a poem by appealing to a specially tailored meaning of "unity." In this the proposal resembles the theories of poststructuralism, which reject coherence in a work (or at least reject easy coherence) in favor of instability. More important, it means the inapplicability of analytic concepts such as paradox and ambiguity, favored by New Criticism. These favorite terms, which aim to join together conflicting elements in a dynamic tension, more readily suit the controlled deployment of complexities in the last great poems of Tu Fu, such as "Autumn Meditations," than they do most of the examples in this chapter.

14. Stephen Owen, *The Great Age of Chinese Poetry*, p. 184. Owen uses the term "shifting style," in quotation marks, in the analysis of poems by Tu Fu on pp. 192, 194, and 198.
15. In the same manner, Hawkes's comment on the poem "Climbing Yueh-yang Tower," quoted earlier, simply admits that no extenuating circumstances can be found by the critic ("the comparatively more trivial fifth line . . . is due to the rapidity with which one mood succeeds another in the course of the poem").

It may seem perverse to propose what is essentially a lack of structure as a structural principle, but juxtaposition applies only to a subset of Tu Fu's poems. Tu Fu wrote many poems, especially in regulated verse, in which all the elements combine in perfect harmony. In many of his late poems in regulated verse, prosody lays down a grid of pleasing symmetry, and a poem unfolds its fullness in a patterned, mutually reinforcing manner. The poet reveals himself only in the context of the complexities of the whole, his feelings skillfully matched to its objective correlative. Such a poem, however, does not give the reader as ready a chance to consider issues of the poet's personality. The personal and poetic aspects tend to be well blended within a tight structure. Poems of this kind can be analyzed by techniques that are already familiar and do not require a new methodology. By contrast, juxtaposition isolates from the mass of Tu Fu's poems those whose structures are unwieldy, and it is these poems, rather than the seamless poems, which prove to be revealing of personal aspects of Tu Fu. (In any case, as will be seen, disjunction in fact infiltrates many of the late regulated-verse poems: indeed, five have been cited so far.) To take one point in anticipation of later discussion, the juxtaposition of topics enables us to deal with nonpoetic issues such as Tu Fu's reputation for political concern, and ultimately it enables us to see something of the personality in which such political concern is rooted.

With juxtaposition defined, let us see how it functions in the reading of the four poems considered so far. In "Seeking out Ts'ui Chi and Li Feng," the topic changes at line 27 from description to reaction, from the scene before Tu Fu's eyes to a troubled stream of thoughts about the empire. A stimulus is present (the rusting farm implements), but it is inconspicuous in comparison with the reaction. Before the poet spots the plow, he has taken up a lot of time to give a setting and a mood of unhurried leisure. The opening of the poem is quiet and full of rediscovery: every little item noted is an added pleasure. The light wakes the poet up; he has been feeling low, but this morning suddenly seems a new beginning, and he reacquaints himself with the world. It takes an expansive eight lines to get him out-of-doors; when, on the spur of the moment, he decides on a visit, the impulsiveness is consistent with the mood. Twice he says he is free to follow his slightest inclination: "of a sudden" (*hsing lai* 興來, line 5) gets him tidied up to go out; "a sense of abandon" (*tzu yi* 恣意, line 9) prompts a visit to friends. The actual visit is described only indirectly: after some complimentary lines on his friends, we find Tu Fu already in the garden, "lingering on" (line 16) and basking in the warm sun (line 26). Up to this point, the poem has been a perfect illustration of the hospitably lax structure of old-style prosody.

Juxtaposed against the unhurried ease are the last fourteen lines, which are agitated and full of incomplete thoughts, thoughts that are incomplete because they cannot be completed. The emperor is – the thought can barely be touched on – imperfect (lines 29–30); men like Tu Fu's hosts and like himself are out of office (lines 31–2). Now Tu Fu's thoughts are disconnected and receive only one line or even just half a line each. The state – chaos (line 33); the rebels – insatiability (one line, line 34); the world – nature reversed (couplet, lines 35–6). The poet's thoughts are jumbled and random, for sequential reasoning can only lead to more despair. Confronted by the great crisis of the rebellion, the poet jumps in an agitated manner from one point to another.

This juxtaposition of very different moods and subject matter is reflected in the language as well. The beginning uses a relaxed, imagistically simple, and narratively continuous style. Allusions are employed, but they are also simple and fit smoothly into the poem, working as borrowed vocabulary that adds a nice sheen of companionship from history to the poet's new day. In saying of himself, "of a sudden I don't feel so lazy and . . . comb my hair" (lines 5–6), the poet recalls the eccentricity of Hsi K'ang, of the Seven Sages of the Bamboo Grove, who was lazy and did not wash. With the break at line 27, however, the poet suddenly introduces a tense, allusive series of broken half thoughts couched in the incoherent animal and avian imagery and the mythic geography typical of political allegory.

Juxtaposition in the three regulated-verse poems works in a similar manner, within a smaller compass. Having been identified by the criticism quoted earlier and now provided with a context, these incongruities can no longer be glossed over or be defended merely by making an assertion to the contrary. We see now that the incongruities are characterized by final lines whose highly personalized tone is unanticipated. Even within the context of a second half which focuses upon the poet himself, the endings seem excessively personal. Here again are the final couplets:

> From friends and family, not a word,
> Old and ill, only my solitary boat,
> War horses are north of the passes,
> I lean on the railing, tears flowing.
> ("Climbing Yueh-yang Tower")

> Hardships and sorrows have turned these temples to frost,
> I am discouraged, had to stop drinking dark wine.
> ("Climbing to a Height")

> Beacon fires have burned for three months on end,
> A letter from home would be worth its weight in gold.
> My white hairs even shorter now from tugging
> Soon will not take even a hatpin.
>
> ("Spring Prospect")

All three poems end with a focus on details (tears at that moment, his weak health, his thinning hair) in a way that provides no potential for a larger significance. The endings contrast sharply with the landscape descriptions which begin each poem and which in each case heighten and enlarge a momentary experience. The endings also contrast sharply with the physical realism that in other poems renders such homely details as thinning hair memorable by their vivid solidity. Here, although the observation is detailed, it is so tightly focused as to leave no room even for the reader's concurrence.

Examples

This section provides more examples of juxtaposition to show that it is not a phenomenon of a few selected poems. Some of the examples are among the most familiar of Tu Fu's poems. In these, the analysis introduced by the concept of juxtaposition places their customary reception in a new light. The reader may notice that it is easier to accept disjunction in the less well-known poems, possibly because their interpretation has not yet been fixed. This section is limited to illustrating juxtaposition through examples. The implications are discussed subsequently. In the next section of this chapter, I compare juxtaposition as a poetic trait with other structures that have previously been identified in Tu Fu's poems. In Chapter 4 I examine the connections between the life and the poetry that are revealed by poems structured by juxtaposition.

The first example is so familiar that its juxtaposition is easily overlooked. "Journey North" (47/3/3) records a journey Tu Fu took in 757 to rejoin his family, then living in Ch'iang Village.[16] ("Seeking out Ts'ui Chi and Li Feng on the Last Day of the Month," if dated to 757, would have been written the same year, after the poet's return.) The year before he undertook this journey was an eventful one for himself and for the dynasty. In that year Tu Fu had lived in rebel-held Ch'ang-an, then

---

16. As befits such a well-known poem, "Journey North" has been translated many times. Among the translations are Hung, *Tu Fu*, pp. 115–18; Davis, *Tu Fu*, pp. 57–9 and 129–31; Owen, *The Great Age of Chinese Poetry*, pp. 195–6; Cherniack, "Three Great Poems by Tu Fu," pp. 162–5 (Cherniack also discusses the structure of "Journey North" on pp. 177–90); and David Hinton, *The Selected Poems of Tu Fu*, pp. 31–3.

made his way to Su-tsung's court in exile, and now he was taking a leave of absence from the court to make the journey here recorded. The times were filled with military crises, and the fortunes of the imperial side were at a low point, with both capitals still held by the rebels. The structure of this very long poem (140 lines) initially arises from the biographical situation and seems naturally determined by its subject. The first section explains the discouraging circumstances of the trip (16 lines); then a long part describes the difficult journey itself (40 lines); and this is followed by the famous and poignant scene of his arrival home as he takes stock and surveys the condition of every family member (36 lines).

The topic for the remaining 48 lines of the poem, however, is unexpected. In these lines, Tu Fu, surrounded by the happy hubbub of his family, mentally removes himself and reverts to a prolonged consideration of the military situation. This situation had, in the opening section of the poem, served as an explanation for the trip; in the narrative of the journey which followed, it had served as a background for the desolate scenes the poet encountered (he also saw some spectacular scenery, free of man's imprint). Now Tu Fu is reunited with his family, but at this point (line 93) his thoughts turn away from them. Suddenly he thinks instead of the world outside his family. The change is abrupt, obscured only by the poem's familiarity. The couplet (lines 91–2) which precedes this final section does not prepare the reader for the change. It shows the poet beginning to settle in, to realize he is home, and so to begin to take on family worries again. He says:

> Newly home, for the moment at peace;
> Our livelihood – we haven't spoken of that yet.   92

This couplet could have served as the ending of "Journey North." Befitting the poem's journal-like content, the couplet would have summed up a warm homecoming and would also have referred in an open-ended manner to the uncertainty of the future. Alternatively, the couplet could have served as a transition to what it hints at – worries about the family's future. What does follow, however, is quite different. For 48 lines, Tu Fu reviews the military situation, the wisdom of forming an alliance with the Uighurs, the strategic choices available to the emperor, the recent turmoil, and his hopes for the future, all soon to become familiar in his poetry.

As with the earlier examples, one could explain the new topic by the psychology of the situation. With the rebellion at a critical point, it is natural for someone who is home again to wander in thought to a situation that he has, after all, not successfully left behind. Such an observation would be undeniably true, but again it focuses on the poet and assigns to the poem only a passive role as record. Alternatively, one might argue that in poetic terms each of the sections has its own mood and that this political concern is but the mood of the last section. But the fact is that here we have 48 lines that could easily have made a completely separate poem. Furthermore, these 48 lines have their own subdivisions of topics and development: a division is customarily made at line 120, marking the end of Tu Fu's military advice and the beginning of his hopes for the restoration of imperial rule. That continuity is lacking between these 48 lines and the preceding 92 lines is implicit in the weakness of the transitions suggested by commentators. P'u Ch'i-lung improbably located the transition in lines 89–90, that is, in the couplet before the transition couplet. P'u picked up the sentiment suggested by line 89's "I remember my worries while among the rebels" and said it introduces the final long section.[17] The proposal is plausible only until one sees that the line in question is firmly bound to its sequel in the couplet, which concerns the children, "And happily suffer their clamoring voices." More subtly, Yang Lun suggested a connection with line 93, "His Majesty is still amidst the swirling dust [of rebellion]." He contrasts the emperor "still" in difficulties with the poet at peace "for the moment" in line 91. "An astounding change in pace," Yang comments.[18]

In "Journey North," when we turn to the poetic manifestation of Tu Fu's social concern, the abrupt juxtaposition of styles is also apparent. Before and after line 92, the poem shows different kinds of logic in structure and development. In the first three sections, the narrative of the journey and arrival home is quite straightforward. Although many different poetic devices are employed and each section is differently treated (the second section, the actual journey, is a tour de force of journey landscape description, and the return home is the kind of intimate, freshly observed family scene at which Tu Fu excels), nevertheless on the whole the poem is impelled forward by the narration of events. However, once he is home the poet turns from the immediate, visible scene around him to internal, distant concerns. Not only is the content now different, but the language has also changed. As in "Seeking out Ts'ui Chi and Li Feng," many thoughts are not quite completed, evidently because they cannot be followed to their logical conclusions. The poet devotes twelve lines (97–108) to the uncertain wisdom of enlisting as allies the Uighurs, with their vast cavalry, to help defeat the rebels. But typically, neither the exact reference nor the exact meaning is quite clear:

17. P'u Ch'i-lung, *Tu Tu hsin-chieh*, p. 42.
18. Yang Lun, *Tu shih ching-ch'üan* 4.161.

> Of those, fewer is better,
> All sides bow to their courage and determination. 104

We see here instead the euphemistic language characteristic of hesitant criticism and unsolicited advice. The wisdom of the alliance was debated from the beginning, but this too cannot be stated directly:

> The ruler is inclined to wait and see,
> In court discussion there is hesitancy. 108

(In the event, the emperor did employ the Uighurs to assist in the recapture of the capitals, an assault that took place some months later.)

As one might expect, the final section somewhat resembles the poem's opening, which concerns the political situation at the time when Tu Fu took his leave of absence from the court. It is possible, therefore, to argue that the poem has returned to its initial topic. Yang Lun is one commentator who did, remarking that Tu Fu steps from family to country as he has earlier stepped from country to family and praising "Journey North" for its grandeur in ending as it had begun, with the enterprise of empire.[19] The poem, however, is not nearly as symmetrical as Yang's remarks imply. The function of the first section within the poem is clear: Tu Fu hesitates over whether to leave his post at such a crucial juncture. After much debate with himself, he does leave and so sets in motion the next parts of the poem. By contrast, poetically speaking, the function of the final section is not clear.

What I call the disjunction in "Journey North" has been noted before, but, unlike that in the three regulated-verse poems discussed earlier, it has been noticed in the context of praise rather than criticism. This seems to be because the subject abruptly introduced is the public-spirited topic we have learned to expect from Tu Fu. The 48-line passage which ends "Journey North" is cited as an illustration of how Tu Fu, even in the most extreme circumstances and even when he is happy in his family's safety, turns his thoughts immediately and inevitably to the state and to other people's troubles. Yang Lun writes, "He is beset by hardships himself, yet he does not put aside concern for policies of state and the livelihood of the people. Only someone who wished to emulate the ancient worthies Chi and Ch'i [as Tu Fu said of himself in "Five Hundred Words"] could be like this."[20] Translators, perhaps less sure of finding fervent appreciation like Yang Lun's among the English-reading public, sometimes silently omit this final passage.

19. Ibid. 4.161 and 4.163.
20. Ibid. 3.111.

The next example of disjunction also occurs in a familiar poem, "Song of My Thatched Roof Torn by Autumn Winds." In Chapter 2, I discussed the first section of this poem as an example of Tu Fu's concrete realism. In particular, the physical humor which he brought to many poems permeates his description of the boys who make off with the thatch from his roof, of his futile chase after them, and of his helpless rage. (We see also the truth of Hawkes's comment, made of "Spring Prospect," that Tu Fu can show a playful self-mockery.[21]) For the poem's structure of juxtaposition, we focus on the famous ending:

> Where shall I find a mansion of a million rooms?
> To shelter every poor gentleman in the world that all may be happy,
> Unshaken in wind and rain, fast as a mountain.
> Oh when will such a house spring up before my eyes!   22
> Then if my hut alone were fallen and I froze to death,
>   I should be content.   23

This wish – impassioned, altruistic, but nonetheless centered on himself – is completely different from the humor of the first sixteen lines, which is physical, dispassionate, and what is most different, not self-pitying. As with "Journey North," the complete and abrupt change in subject matter and tone is easy to overlook both because the entire poem is so familiar and because the sentiment of what follows has been the object of so much praise.

One might argue that the couplet before this outburst forms a kind of transition, but this is true in only a limited way. The couplet preceding says:

> Since the rebellion I have not slept well:
> Soaked through the long night, when will dawn come?   18

The couplet acts as a kind of transition, in that its mood belongs neither to the preceding active chasing and fuming nor to the grand vision which follows. The mood of this couplet is quiet and also a little restless. One could argue that it suitably closes the first section of the poem, which has begun, after line 10, to calm down. The poet has given up chasing after the boys, night has fallen, and he is watching his children sleep under a now-leaky roof. In the night, his mood turns reflective, and this is when he thinks to himself:

> Since the rebellion I have not slept well:
> Soaked through the long night, when will dawn come?   18

21. Hawkes, *A Little Primer of Tu Fu*, p. 46.

In the quiet, the poet is able to step back to allude more generally to a turn of fate that has brought him to a cold thatched hut in Szechuan. This couplet, tinged with self-pity, is a kind of closure. But is it also a transition? The couplet is then unexpectedly succeeded by the poet's "magnificent outcry"[22] against fate, his passionate evocation of other men in desperate straits.

If the couplet is a transition, then what the transition leads to is a surprise, if this word can be used of such a familiar poem. The splendor lies, as the commentator Chiang Juo-liu has remarked, in the shaking off of self-absorption for a larger cause.[23] This excellent description shows that on a poetic level juxtaposition can be very effective. Indeed, the suddenness of the poet's plea appears to play an active part in the recurring pleasure felt by readers. The disjunction seems to have the effect of making the reader's discovery of Tu Fu's generosity especially intense. Wang An-shih thought so highly of it that in his "Portrait of Tu Fu," a near-quotation of the poem's final two lines stand as the impassioned climax of his intense tribute to Tu Fu.[24]

The disjunction in "Song of My Thatched Roof" is all the more reinforced by the completeness of the vision which expresses the poet's altruism: an imagined mansion, one thousand rooms, warmth, complete security from the buffetings of weather and fate. The fully developed metaphor for utopia, rarely encountered in lyric poetry, increases the sense of a break. The last section is exceptional in prosodic terms as well. It consists of five lines, an odd number and highly unusual, especially for Tu Fu, who prefers the prevailing symmetry of lyric poetry. In addition, the line lengths are irregular in this last segment. Hitherto, the lines have all been seven characters long (save for line 6), but the last five lines are (respectively) seven, nine, seven, eleven, and nine characters in length and impressive, Li Po–like in vigor and control.

The coda of "Song of My Thatched Roof" can be interestingly differentiated from the ending of "Five Hundred Words Expressing My Feelings on the Way from the Capital to Feng-hsien County." Written on the eve of the rebellion, only two years – and a lifetime – earlier, this is also one of Tu Fu's best-known poems. Like "Song of My Thatched Roof," "Five Hundred Words" ends with an altruistic attention to the hardships of others, turning away from, this time, the poet's grief. Like "Journey

22. A. R. Davis's words in his *Tu Fu*, p. 80.
23. Chiang Juo-liu, quoted in Yang Lun, *Tu shih ching-ch'üan* 8.314. "Juo-liu" is the style (*tzu*) of someone whom Yang Lun quotes frequently but does not otherwise identify. Chou Ts'ai-ch'üan has identified him as one Chiang Chin-shih, whose commentaries on Tu Fu, *Tu shih pien-tz'u* 杜詩編次, he has uncovered in the library of Hangchow University. See Chou's *Tu chi shu lu*, pp. 542–3.
24. In *Tu Fu chüan*, 1:80.

North," "Five Hundred Words" covers a journey undertaken to rejoin his
family. The last twenty lines of this one hundred–line poem recount the
ending of his journey. Here the poet tells us for the first time that he had
earlier left his family in Feng-hsien, "an unfamiliar district" (line 81), and
that he is now rejoining them "to share their hunger and thirst" (line
84). His arrival home follows immediately after this four-line exposition
and takes place simultaneously with his learning of a family sorrow:

> On entering I hear wails and cries –
> My young son, starved, has already died. 86

Tu Fu is grief-stricken and, understandably, reproaches himself (lines
87–90). His sorrow is compounded by the irony that his son's death was
not the result of famine but of poverty (lines 91–2). At this point comes
the section comparable in altruism, but not on other points, to "Song of
My Thatched Roof." Turning away from his own grief, Tu Fu remembers
the many people who are even more unfortunate than he, and he
concludes the poem with thoughts of others:

> I am exempt for life from taxes,
> My name is not among those conscripted,
> Yet my path is so bitter,
> The common people must be even more sorrowful. 96
> I think of those who have lost their livelihood,
> Of the soldiers at distant borders,
> And my worries reach an extreme, level with Chung-nan
>   Mountain,
> Surging up, not to be gathered in. 100

This reflection, as large-hearted and rightly lauded as the coda of "Song
of My Thatched Roof," is more unusual than unexpected. Although the
progression of the poet's thoughts takes an unpredicted turn, they
remain consecutive, and the language remains expository. The
unpredictability that characterizes juxtaposition is absent in this passage
ending "Five Hundred Words."

These analyses should clarify the process by which juxtaposition is
discerned in a poem and the contribution that it can make to the
reading of poems. Since disjunctive poems form a large category, they
deserve separate consideration and explanation. As noted earlier, David
Hawkes has rightly pointed out that "Tu Fu does this sort of thing so
often that one must look for something other than mere neurotic self-
pity if one is to reach any sort of understanding with him at all."[25] In the
remainder of this section, I shall analyze (at less length) some further

25. Hawkes, *A Little Primer of Tu Fu*, p. 204.

examples in order to prove that juxtaposition occurs in both short and long poems. In general, the short poem will be represented by regulated verse and the long poem by old-style verse, even thougth it is certainly true that many old-style poems are brief and that the extended regulated-verse form (*p'ai-lü*) is lengthy. Taken together, the examples support the thesis that Tu Fu commonly composed in this disjunctive manner.

It is interesting to note that once one begins to look for juxtaposition among Tu Fu's poems in the regulated-verse form, disjunctive poems can be found as often as well-made poems. The examples examined here should remind readers of many other similarly structured poems. Our first example is "An Old Country Man," written in 760:[26]

> An old country man by a bamboo hedge at river's bend,
> The brushwood door, crooked, opens onto the River.
> The nets of fishermen are gathered to be let down into the clear pool,
> The boats of merchants come upriver following the evening rays.
> The long road here – a heavy heart grieves over Sword Pass:
> For what purpose does a single cloud linger by Lute Terrace?
> Imperial generals have not yet reported the recapture of the
>   eastern capital,
> By the city gates,[27] autumn comes on, painted horns lament.

In the first four lines, Tu Fu sketches a scene whose serenity and unhurried air are unblemished as the poet looks out upon the river at dusk. The second half is quite different. Lute Terrace, which lies to the north of the Thatched Hut, is associated with Ssu-ma Hsiang-ju, the great literary figure of the Former Han dynasty and native of Ch'eng-tu. The "single cloud" which lingers by Lute Terrace is Tu Fu. The poet asks himself how he came to be here, in Ssu-ma Hsiang-ju's faraway homeland. The uncertainty in this couplet, the regret over circumstances that have brought him so far, these feelings are quite absent from the presentation of the scene of the first half. If the second half of the poem had continued in a peaceful vein, the reader would not have been surprised. Nothing about the landscape as presented would cause the poet to turn, in the second half, to painful thoughts of the north, of Lo-yang and home. If the scene had been set thus,

26. 346/21/17; the poem is approximately dated by the reference in line 7 to Loyang being in rebel hands; Loyang fell for the second time in 759 and was not recaptured until the end of 760.
27. *Ch'eng-ch'ueh* means "palace gates," but the palace gates are not those of Ch'ang-an. Tu Fu's notation explains that he uses this term of Ch'eng-tu, which received the title "Southern Capital" in 757, when Emperor Hsuan-tsung sought refuge in the city. The translation uses "city gates," in order not to mislead by the word "palace."

> Rain sounds now for two nights,
> Cold weather tasks, the plangent winds of autumn . . .[28]

then certainly the reader would have expected some echoing restiveness in the observing poet's heart. To create a connection, we may speculate that the beauty of Shu (in lines 1–4) cannot long distract the poet from his grief. P'u Ch'i-lung's sensitive response reasons along such lines. He says that the first gazing yields the beauty of nature, while prolonged gazing moves the already grieved heart.[29] His comment has caught the kind of person Tu Fu likely is: his long-standing grief frequently overtakes him, whatever the situation he is in. But the "already grieved heart" is nowhere visible in the first half. P'u's comment may double as an explanation of the aesthetics of landscape poetry, for indeed a scene may release its latent meaning for the poet only over time, after "prolonged gazing." The continuities suggested here, however, are brought to the poem only by a reader able, from other information, to bridge the gap between a first half consisting of nature description and a second half that is not predicated upon the first.

Another regulated-verse poem, "Evening Sunlight" (433/28/22), is structured the same way: the first half describes scenery which does not anticipate the feelings that surface in the second half.

> North of the palace of the king of Ch'u it is just dusk,
> West of White Emperor City the passing rain leaves its marks;
> Evening sunlight enters the River, reflecting the stone cliffs,
> Returning clouds embrace the trees, hiding the mountain village.
> In my declining years, with ailing lungs, I can only lie pillowed,
> In this remote land, when in poor spirits, I close my doors early,
> One cannot stay long in the chaos of leopards and tigers –
> Truly in the south there is a soul still unsummoned.

The first half shows the sky clearing in the dusk after a rain, a frequent scene in nature description by this time: one would not be surprised to find it in Wang Wei. In the second half, the poet departs from nature description as written in his time and dwells upon his illness, the war-torn times, and his inability to return to the Central Plains. The departure is typical of Tu Fu. "Evening Sunlight" (and "An Old Country Man," quoted earlier) illustrate a common regulated-verse structure in Tu Fu, in which a poem begins with what is before the poet's eyes and opens up to a subject that is on the poet's mind, typically his own illnesses and longings. Because this progression is familiar to readers, it has not been

28. "Rain in the Village," 475/30/42, lines 1–2.
29. P'u Ch'i-lung, *Tu Tu hsin-chieh*, p. 617.

seriously studied. Even less has it been noticed that within the basic pattern a disjunctive variant exists in which the association between the two parts, whether mental or metaphoric, is not provided.

The disjunctive and nondisjunctive variants of the pattern may be seen by comparison with another poem, identically entitled "Evening Sunlight" (511/32/27). This one, by contrast, begins and ends in the same mode of quiet observation. Also in regulated-verse form, this "Evening Sunlight" is in a five-character line length.

> Evening sunlight opens up Wu Gorge,
> Making the chilly sky half visible.
> In its low site, Fish Return is dark,
> Not obscured is solitary White Salt Peak.
> The reedy shores are like autumn water,
> And Pine-gate Gorge seems a picture.
> Cows and sheep know their herders
> And come to their calls at dusk.

It seems that in the narrow Yangtze Gorges, at day's end, the evening sunlight finally is angled in such a way as to bring back some light to the inhabitants. Delicate touches in each line show the poet working at an effect more thoughtful than the bucolic. As Ch'iu Chao-ao points out, the whole poem is structured on a theme of partial visibility.[30] The motif begins explicitly in line 2, with the sky said to be half visible (*pan yu wu* 半有無). It is continued in line 3 where the city of Fish Return (K'uei-chou)[31] is half invisible ("dark"), while White Salt Peak of line 4, across the Yangtze from K'uei-chou, is half visible. The indistinct reeds of line 5 and the picturelike Pine Gate Gorge continue the emphasis on the observer's trying to bring into focus what he is seeing. The scene thus sketched is not simply clever but also captures the quality in the last light of day that throws a shimmer of uncertainty over everything and makes seeing difficult. In this poem, then, unlike the other "Evening Sunlight," the sudden reappearance of the sun at the end of the day brings before one a lovely scene where "prolonged gazing" moves the poet's desire to describe and where his "already grieved heart" is nowhere in evidence.

The final regulated-verse poem examined here is "Daytime Dream" (423/27/36). This poem is interesting in that it presents some ambiguity as to whether the structure is one of juxtaposition.[32] A convincing

---

30. Ch'iu Chao-ao, *Tu shih hsiang-chu*, 20.1738–9.
31. So called because it marked the point at which fish swimming upstream turned back.
32. "Daytime Dream" is one of the poems that Hirose Tansō cites as an example of Tu Fu's typically disjunctive style (*Tansō shiwa*, p. 18). He does not, however, elaborate on his meaning.

reading can be made that the poem changes abruptly and without preparation at the halfway point; and an almost equally convincing reading can be made that it does not do so, that the two halves complement each other nicely:

In the second month, sleeping a lot, all sleepy and dazed,
Are the nights not shorter? – asleep at midday.
With warm air of plum blossoms, eyes grow drunk,
At sun's set by the spring sandbar, dreams lead one away.
The gate and path to my old home lie beneath brambles and thorns,
Ruler and officials in the Central Plains lie by wolves and tigers.
When, when, may one attend to farming, the fighting ended,
And the whole world be without officials seeking money?

The events in the poem seem clear enough. In the first four lines, the poet is drugged by spring: he is sleepy all the time, or asleep at midday, or befuddled by the warmth and blossoms, and we find that by sunset he has succumbed and is led into dreams. The next four lines show, presumably, his dreaming and then his waking: the poem's title, after all, is "Daytime Dream." In lines 5 and 6, the poet's troubles – his homesickness, the empire's danger – come to him unbidden in his dream. In the last couplet the poet, caught in that vulnerable moment of just awakening, feels anew the heartbreaking truth that he lives in a world of war and tax officials and no peace for farming. One reading of the last couplet suggests a more complex time frame for it: that the poet also dreamed of a happy utopia of farming, and that the reader learns of this dream when the poet wakes up to find it an illusion.[33]

The question is whether the somnolent spring day of the first half and the troubles and anguish of the second half are sufficiently integrated. The strongest argument for coherence focuses on the title. In a poem on dreams, especially one employing the contradiction of daytime dreams, one would expect paradoxes of waking dreams and dreamlike reality, of waking reverie followed by awoken seeing. These paradoxes could be used to make interconnections between the poem's parts. The reading suggested by Fang Yü plays on these possibilities. She writes,

On the surface the poem is about a dream on a spring day; underneath are the poet's deepest wishes. The lovely utopia where people "attend to farming, fighting is ended, and the whole world [is] without officials" – all this is placed after the interrogative "when?". Like a brief dream on a spring day, it is gone when one awakes. By contrast, "thorns and brambles" and "wolves and tigers" are not restricted to the imaginings of a dream but are reality in this world. Real and

33. Fang Yü, *K'uei-chou shih*, pp. 77–8.

imagined, dream and reality are beautifully blended in the title of "Daytime Dream."[34]

Now for a disjunctive reading. The title creates the expectation of a dream, but what kind of dream can follow the thick, indolent spring of lines 1 through 4? That spring day is its own daytime dream, with the poet struggling all day to stay awake. These first four lines are light. Tu Fu has fun with all the repetitions and synonyms of "asleep" and shows mischief in the depiction of himself drowning in the synesthesia of spring. After four such lines, the troubled dream that overtakes him is unexpected, juxtaposed. One might argue that although indolent spring is all around, when the poet lets down his guard what surfaces is his "accumulated longing"[35] for home, a longing deeper even than scented spring. This is a believable explanation of the poem's development, but one must note that it is rooted in the psychology of the poet. In addition, we have to ask whether there is a poetic as well as a personal connection between the two halves. It may be that the troubled dream and the troubled awakening of lines 5 through 8 are meant to give the lie to the lazy, sensuous spring day so well evoked in lines 1 through 4, but there is no hint of such an intention.

It is worth noting that another characteristic of juxtaposition is found here, a change in language between the two halves of the poem. The wordplay and the skillful handling of time in the first half are succeeded in lines 5 and 6 by standard phrases about desolation and political villainy ("brambles and thorns," "wolves and tigers") and, in lines 7 and 8, by prepositional language and a run-on line.

The final example of disjunction in the short poem will be a poem that is not in regulated-verse form, "Ballad of One Hundred Accumulated Worries" (111/7/15). Generally dated to 761 (from line 5, which gives his age), the twelve-line poem describes first the poet's youthful rompings, then the bitter poverty that overtook him at this time in the Thatched Hut period. Attempts to unify the poem in a number of ways each proves unsatisfactory. In the end, no adequate connection can be found between the poem's two sets of striking images. Initially it appears that the poem can be paraphrased as a pair of contrasting portraits between his happy youth (six lines) and his present circumstances (six lines). The contrast, however, seems involuntary and produces no interesting connections. Furthermore, the poem's rhyme scheme divides it into three sections of four lines each, thus definitively voiding the poss-

---

34. Ibid.
35. "The accumulated longing for his home in the Central Plains is transformed into the dream"; Wu Chien-ssu, quoted in Ch'iu Chao-ao, *Tu shih hsiang-chu* 18.1603.

ibility of a contrast, or at least a contrast consisting of six lines each. In turn, the rhyme scheme presents a new problem: it creates a middle set of four lines which is evidently intended as a transition between the past and present.

The poem opens with four lines of lively images of Tu Fu as a youngster. We see him at age fifteen, brown and healthy as a calf, climbing trees a thousand times a day for their pears and dates. The rarity of this type of information and the unexpectedness of the energetic youth double the reader's appreciation.[36] ("Wanderings of My Prime" contains the only other portrait of Tu Fu as a youth, and there he is, predictably, memorizing poems and composing reams of verse at a tender age.[37]) Thus the poem opens with an attractive, quotable, and dramatic segment that quite rivals what one presumes, from the title, to be the intended topic.

The last four lines show the dire poverty of Tu Fu and his family in the present. I quote them with the two preceding lines, for together they provide a fuller portrait of the family's circumstances:

> With forced cheer I offer pleasant words to those on whom I call,
> With sorrow I see a hundred worries accumulate over our livelihood.
> Coming home, the four walls are bare as ever,
> My old wife sees that my expression is as before.
> My spoiled children do not know their manners,
> Seeking food they cry out in petulance, crying east of the door.[38]

These lines paint a heart-wrenching picture of poverty in which each family member suffers. Tu Fu must go out and humble himself before the indifferent potential patrons on whom he calls, cosmeticizing his importunings with an acceptably cheerful demeanor. On his return, his wife silently reads his failure in his face, providing a poignant glimpse of the woman as mediator between the hungry family and the failed breadwinner, trying to comfort both sides without the means to do so. The hungry, crying children are the only ones who can give voice to the distress that all feel.

The contrast between the youthful scampering about and the present desperation is jarring because its purpose is not discoverable. Indeed two commentators find readings that unify the poem by continuity rather than by contrasts. Chao Tz'u-kung in the *Chiu-chia* edition proposes that the title means to apply to Tu Fu's entire life, for worries have been

---

36. And alarm some readers, who are hard put to justify such behavior in someone who is of an age to be seriously studying (see comment in *Chiu-chia* 111/7/15, after line 1).
37. "Wanderings of My Prime," 169/12/7, lines 1–8.
38. Kitchens are sited to the east (Ch'iu Chao-ao, *Tu shih hsiang-chu* 10.843, where he notes, "the word 'east' is not used just to fill the rhyme").

accumulating since he came into this life. P'u Ch'i-lung also joins past and present, suggesting that the memories of youth include searching for food in the courtyard's trees, while the present lacks food altogether, with both halves focused on the searching.[39] The readings seem implicitly to acknowledge a problem in connecting the two parts of the poem.

What of the four middle lines? Clearly they are intended as transition. But they constitute an awkward, unsuccessful one. The lines begin with a charming expression of the poet's surprise at how quickly the years have passed and end with a bitter self-portrait. In the first of these lines, the energetic youth is visible in the old man still vigorous enough to poke fun at himself:

> And suddenly, today, I am already fifty,
> I sit or lie down a lot and stand or walk very little.

In the next lines, however, old age becomes something very different from merely sitting down a lot:

> With forced cheer I offer pleasant words to those on whom I call,
> With sorrow I see a hundred worries accumulate over our livelihood.

In its tone and sense, the first couplet of this middle section belongs to the liveliness of the first four lines, whereas the second couplet belongs to the hopelessness of the last four lines. The amusing self-portrait of lines 5 and 6 brings up to date the cheerful memories of lines 1 through 4, whereas lines 7 through 12 finally take up the "Accumulated One Hundred Worries" of the title, even using the title phrase in line 8. Although each couplet resembles its neighbor on the other side, the rhyme scheme binds them to each other. The four lines seem intended as a bridge to force a connection and soften the juxtaposition. What connection is created, however, is uncertain.

We now turn to examining juxtaposition in long poems. Juxtaposition is more difficult to identify in long poems than in regulated-verse poems, since, as the analysis of "Journey North" showed, they are often quite loosely structured in the first place. The examples here, all dating from the K'uei-chou period, illustrate some of the ways in which juxtaposition is manifested in poems longer than eight to twelve lines. We discuss first two poems of medium length, "Orange Grove" (32 lines) and "Climbing to the Height behind Nang at Dusk" (20 lines), and then the eight memorial poems that form a set entitled "Eight Laments."

39. Chao Tz'u-kung in *Chiu-chia* 111/7/15, under the title. P'u Ch'i-lung, *Tu Tu hsin-chieh*, p. 272.

In "Orange Grove" (182/13/6), the juxtaposition is obvious. The "grove" of the title is an orchard that Tu Fu bought in West Nang in 767, together with some land for farming. This poem is usually read for its wealth of biographical information: we learn that he dislikes the position he held at K'uei-chou and that he is happy to be going home, and we learn something of his life as a farm owner and about the tax burdens of the peasants. The break in this poem occurs at the halfway point, after line 16, in a highly unusual fashion which we have not yet encountered. The first half is a conventional journey poem. The poet leaves his boat, crosses a ridge, and, since he is happily on his way home through scenery made especially pleasant by his destination, he contrasts his content in his poverty with the strifes of wealth and station in the town he has just left behind him. This half is clearly about going home. The second half, lines 17 through 32, is entirely different. These lines narrate the events of the next morning, when Tu Fu walks about his fields. The farmers who accompany tell him of the government's confiscatory purchasing policy (a segment discussed in Chapter 2); one farmer kneels to ask his advice, and the poet, feeling helpless, makes a feeble reply about loyalty and not fleeing the land.

Such a next-morning scene has gone very far from the happy homebound journey of the day before. Even if the morning's walk had not been so saddening, it is quite unusual to find a poem which covers two strikingly different narratives that, moreover, belong to two separate days. The briefest of transitions in the form of a time lapse is provided in line 17 – "next morning" – but lines 1 through 16 and lines 17 through 32 could easily have made two separate poems. Indeed, if it were not for the phrase "next morning," one might suspect that a textual error had joined two different poems together. Perhaps the title of "Orange Grove" is intended to unite the two subjects as two faces of landowner-ship, but this seems an unconvincing unity. One commentator seems to imply that the poem departs from its title deliberately, for he remarks that "Orange Grove" does not return to the orange grove of its title, just as another poem, "Stopped by Rain, Unable to Return to the Orange Grove in West Nang," does not.[40] The disjunction is so striking that a deliberate change in topic may well have been intentional, but what is its purpose? This is not clear.

Our next example, "Climbing to the Height behind Nang at Dusk" (197/13/34), is reminiscent of "Seeking out Ts'ui Chi and Li Feng." Like that poem, this one begins with the poet acting on the spur of the

---

40. Lu Yuan-ch'ang, quoted in Ch'iu Chao-ao, *Tu shih hsiang-chu* 19.1669.

moment and ends with the poet overwhelmed by feelings which come faster than their exposition. The poet undertakes, on impulse, a climb on horseback. Ch'iu Chao-ao points out that he does so to relieve a sense of restlessness (the *ku chi* 故臍 of line 1, "I deliberately climb").[41] Except for this one hint, however, the tone is, if anything, one of a sense of relief as the poet attains a height and, finding himself in the open, sees a "lively," "vigorous" scene before him. Here are the first eight lines of the poem:

> I climb the lofty bank of Nang
> To be away from the dense cliffs,
> I open my chest, expansive in the wilderness,
> And tie the horse, blossoms in the woods shaking.   4
> The parapets of K'uei-chou are white as clouds,
> In the hills, no boundary ridges in the wheat,[42]
> With evening, the spring air is more lively,
> The river's flow is calm but vigorous.   8

In the next lines, the poet's thoughts travel away from the scene before him. It is, of course, conventional (and probably psychologically accurate) for a climb to a height to produce far-reaching thoughts. But while one does expect reflective thoughts, Tu Fu's turn out to be disjointed and quite unrelated to the view before him. His habitual interrelated worries, all of which he mentions on this occasion, come to the fore again: the rebellion (line 10), the poeple's suffering (line 11), the emperor's longing for peace (line 12), his own illnesses and former office (lines 15–16), the lack of wise officials (lines 17–20), and the gloomy prognosis (lines 21–4). These concerns press on the poet so strongly that even in the last line he is unable to recover the ease of his original response to the view.

Line 9 – "The round of seasons entwines my thoughts" – does acknowledge the change in tone of what follows but cannot explain it except in the most general way: the poet has been in K'uei-chou for a year now and some kind of stocktaking occurs to him. This is a common sequence with Tu Fu: he climbs to a height, becomes aware of the passage of time, and laments that he cannot escape his circumstances and return north.[43] The poetic question is how the development of this sequence is carried out. Unusually, while the development is disjunctive in this poem, the disjunction is somewhat retrieved in the final four lines (lines 21–4):

41. Ch'iu Chao-ao, *Tu shih hsiang-chu* 18.1619.
42. "No boundary ridges": because the individual fields are scattered over the hillsides, further demarkation is not needed (ibid. 18.1619).
43. For example, in "Climbing the Hill in the Back of the Garden," 161/11/25.

> Ch'u stars, the southern sky is black,
> A Shu moon, fog to the west is heavy.
> When can I follow the birds in flight?
> So close to fears and dread.

Although, like the preceding lines, these couplets are anguished, they do return the reader to the physical world rather than leave him entirely in the world of the poet's mental wanderings. In Ch'iu Chao-ao's description, "scene and feeling are brought to a conclusion."[44] The first two of these lines represent an especially fine recovery. It is the night sky, which has come on unseen while the poet has been lost in his reveries, that brings him back to the world around him, but it does so without confronting him with the earlier pretty sight of parapets white as clouds and wheat fields nestled in the hills. Rather, the sky's darkness and the fog's denseness delicately indicate the unknown that the future holds for the poet. His wish then for an impossible flight seems all the sadder.

My final example is a lengthy one, consisting of the eight poems of the set known as "Eight Laments." This group of poems, which, at forty to eighty-six lines, are long even for Tu Fu, commemorates eight men of the poet's time. Three were friends from Ch'ang-an days, and two were patrons (one in Ch'ang-an and one in Szechuan). In addition, three men who were not personally known to Tu Fu are included: two generals prominent in the fight against the rebels, Wang Ssu-li and Li Kuang-pi, and Chang Chiu-ling (678–740), chief minister in the early part of Hsuan-tsung's reign. In each poem, an abrupt juxtaposition of topics and moods occurs near the end, and the disjoint part that follows, ranging from six to fourteen lines in length, effects closure. In the main part of each poem, the structure is by and large chronological, with the exposition touching upon the major events in the subject's life. Because these are predominantly political events, they early establish a serious and gravely passionate tone. The tone is typified by Tu Fu's account of General Li Kuang-pi's successful defense of T'ai-yuan early in the rebellion. Control of T'ai-yuan ensured the security of the emperor's court in exile in the Ordos. The tone is patriotically partisan:

> When the Hu horsemen attacked our city
> There was worry and fear, but their intent was thwarted.
> The people felt as calm as Mount T'ai,
> For Chi-pei had been cut off at its right flank.
>
> (Poem 2, lines 3–6)

In a different setting, but in an equally grave and serious manner, Tu Fu describes the brief tenure at court of the great literary figure Li Yung:

44. Ch'iu Chao-ao, *Tu shih hsiang-chu* 8.1620.

> Li argued the rights and wrongs of the decision of the Court of Imperial
>   Sacrifices;
> He challenged the power of the two Changs to their faces.
> Upon the customs of a degenerate time blew a chill wind
> Which cleared the autumn sky.
>
> (Poem 5, lines 41–4)

Extended exposition of this type dominates in each poem.

Subjective emotion breaks out in each poem only near the end, when the poet's own feelings become the focus of the account, displacing the man commemorated:

> Who is it, so utterly exhausted?
> My tears fall, in the gorges of Pa-tung.
> (Poem 2, lines 39–40)

> A lifetime, now one alive, one dead –
> All alone, on whom can I rely?
> (Poem 7, lines 59–60)

In such lines, exposition gives way to feeling. A speaker for whom every emotion is intense suddenly takes over from what had been a disinterested, albeit committed, narrator. That narrator used a tone closely identified with Tu Fu, an undoubting kind of intensity about public events. Emotions are implicitly present, but they are impersonal or civic passions, stemming from a consuming desire to put things right. By contrast, in each poem the emotion of the final juxtaposed section is both unbridled and imagistic.

One might argue that the final section demonstrates in a different way the significance of these eight men to Tu Fu. This is true, of course. The final section does serve a function; indeed, it has more than one function, for it also serves as an extended closural process for each of the lengthy poems. For our purposes here, we may simply note that the final segments differ completely and unexpectedly in language and tone from what preceded. The juxtaposition of these unblended styles contributes to the typical impression given by "Eight Laments" and by others of Tu Fu's late poems that they are, on the one hand, solemn and earnest and, on the other hand, impassioned and overwrought.

"Eight Laments" presents an unusual situation, because juxtaposition occurs in every single poem in the set. Juxtaposition therefore is predictable here, once the pattern is perceived, but within the confines of a given poem the ending is still characterized by abruptness and still deserves the designation of juxtaposition. In fact, we can turn the argument around and say that juxtaposition is confirmed here as a recurring pattern. It would seem that more than chance enters into its use.

The examples analyzed so far present a variety of ways in which juxtaposition occurs. Taken together, they show that certain poems require an analysis that does not rely on a conventional sense of unity. For these poems, the lack of the concept of juxtaposition has prevented more than ad hoc interpretations. The reader makes individual adjustments that are generally uneasy and tentative, circling around the incongruence that persists when neither mode dominates or absorbs the other. The uneasiness sometimes present in the interpretations of all of these poems can be traced to uneasiness with the abrupt changes from one style to another, one mode of thought to another, one realm of thought to another. The inclination has been to conclude that Tu Fu failed aesthetically in not keeping a sense of proportion, especially when the poem ends, as it often does, with the focus exclusively on the poet. Whether the concept of juxtaposition can alleviate a reader's doubts may depend on the reader. Juxtaposition, however, does provide the perspective that such endings form a large category and must be responded to according to a principle, rather than just ad hoc. Juxtaposition, it seems, is more of a feature than theory has hitherto recognized. Certain questions naturally follow. What is the function of disjunctive structure? More specifically, what is its function for the poet and in the poem? These questions are taken up next.

Juxtaposition and other structures

Juxtaposition constitutes an addition to concepts of poetic structure that are already used in literary criticism. Since it bears some resemblance to several of these structures, themselves rather different from each other, the idea of juxtaposition can be clarified by a comparison with each of these concepts in turn. The comparisons undertaken here cannot hope to be comprehensive, but since the question of structure is all-important in the study of poetry and poems, it deserves to be reopened in Tu Fu's work in connection with juxtaposition.

The term "structure" designates the relation of the parts of a poem to the whole. The criteria by which division into parts is made are, in general, either formal or nonformal.[45] Formal divisions are made by prosody, which creates divisions that are regular and predictable. In the case of lyric poetry (*shih*), prosody specifies structure with exactness in regulated verse and only in a general way in old-style verse. As for nonformal divisions, their existence reflects the fact that however closely

---

45. "Formal" and "nonformal" are the initial division employed by the *Princeton Encyclopedia of Poetry and Poetics*, s.v. "structure."

prescribed by formal rules, much variation is still possible in the relation of the parts to the whole.

The structure of individual poems is less schematic or predictable than is the structure provided by prosody. At one extreme, it could be argued that a poem's nonformal structure develops according to the material, and that therefore a unique solution is devised for each poem. Especially in the old-style poems, the absence of detailed rules displaces most of the burden of organization onto the individual poem, and we find that quite varied factors determine the structure of old-style poems. Ideally, given the unrestricted length of the form, each poem may move at its own rate, constrained only by the needs of the material. The nonformal structure thus arrived at would be what the New Critics called "organic" and what Yang Lun praised, in connection with long poems, as "the natural unfolding of the lines."[46] Even regulated verse is capable of much variety in organization. Despite the strictness of its prosodic rules, regulated-verse poems that differ markedly in structure are easy to find. A convenient example of this contrast is provided by "On Hearing of the Recovery of Ho-nan and Ho-pei by Imperial Troops" and "Autumn Meditations." The eight lines of the former poem are, unusually, not based on images. Instead they form a continuous narrative which, in the style of some modern sonnets, renders its prosodic conformity all but invisible. By contrast, the organization of each poem of the set entitled "Autumn Meditations" is based on the smallest unit that is prosodically meaningful, a unit consisting of two characters that are tonally opposed. In this structure, the two-character units accrue unit by unit, all the while forming multiple connections with other units in the same line, as well as units in the pairing line, and between couplets. The effect is retardation, density, clotting. The pace is the opposite of the joyful rapidity that characterizes "The Recovery of Ho-nan and Ho-pei."

Juxtaposition belongs, of course, among the nonformal structures. I would further suggest that juxtaposition constitutes an identifying characteristic of Tu Fu's poetry. It occupies an intermediate level of generality, in that it is neither as comprehensively applicable as prosodic rules nor as uniquely determined as the structure of individual poems. The effect of juxtaposition upon structure varies according to the poem's prosodic form. In old-style verse, which is almost without prescribed structure, the problem is to show that a particular break is more disjunctive than is usual even within the hospitable environs of this prosodic form. In regulated verse, by contrast, where elaborate symmetries are already determined by prosodic rules, juxtaposition is

46. Yang Lun, "General Rules," *Tu shih ching-ch'üan*, p. 13.

readily conceived of as disruptive. Indeed, criticisms of certain of the regulated-verse poems can alert one to the presence of juxtaposition. Juxtaposition in regulated verse tends to be one organizational device in an armory of often overlapping devices. Unlike the other structures available, however, juxtaposition results in discontinuity rather than in the reinforcement of interconnections.

In the remainder of this section, I shall compare juxtaposition with six structural concepts that have often been used in the analysis of Tu Fu's poems: (1) segmentation; (2) ordered and "loose" structure; (3) "prose as poetry"; (4) the title as an organizing device; (5) "a sudden change in the brush's direction"; and (6) the pairing of feeling and scenery (*ch'ing* 情 and *ching* 景). We shall examine each in turn.

Segmentation

The most extensive evidence of critical thinking about nonformal structure in Tu Fu's poems is found in the analyses of individual poems in editions of Tu Fu. In particular, over the centuries, commentators gradually came to the conclusion that in order to grasp the essential meaning of a poem, they needed to show its development and to do that they needed to determine the divisions between sections (*fen tuan* 分段). For long poems, a change in rhyme category always constituted one (incomplete) guide, but short poems too have their developments, which are not flagged by changes in rhyme. Less passive interpretation was desirable.

Systematic awareness of structure was slow in developing. Sections were not marked off or discussed in the extant earliest editions of the complete works of Tu Fu, which date from the Southern Sung period. Examination of Sung editions that were available to me shows that the 1181 *Chiu-chia* edition (the text for the modern *Concordance*) is typical in annotating lines without commenting on their unfolding development. It was not until the Ming dynasty that editions which marked off divisions made their appearance. The earliest of the complete Ming editions, Shan Fu's *Tu Fu yü-te* (preface dated 1382), was such an edition. Shan Fu singled out for praise an earlier editor, Fan P'eng, who made a selected edition of Tu Fu poems (311 poems, printed in 1328) and set a precedent with his structural analysis. Fan's work, no longer extant, was influential in the Ming dynasty,[47] as can be seen in Shan Fu's testimonial. "When I first read Tu Fu's poems," he wrote in the Preface to his *Tu Fu*

---

47. See Chou Ts'ai-ch'üan, *Tu chi shu lu*, pp. 282–3. Fan P'eng's selection is known by the title *Tu Tzu-mei shih p'i-hsuan* and some variations thereof. For its influence in the Ming dynasty, see Chou Ts'ai-ch'üan, p. 283.

yü-te, "I was at quite a loss about their essential meaning." He went on to describe his growing disappointment with one particular annotated edition of Tu Fu and then said that it was not until he saw Fan P'eng's commentary, with its sectional markings, that understanding dawned. For his own work, therefore, Shan Fu also "marked off sections in order to make apparent the nature of the poem's vital meaning."[48]

Concurrence on this point, however, was slow in crystallizing. Neither of the two most important editions of the early Ch'ing dynasty – Ch'ien Ch'ien-i's (1667) or Chu Ho-ling's (ca. 1667) – took any notice of poem division. At about the same time, Chin Sheng-t'an (1608–61) in his *Ts'ai-tzu Tu shih chieh* experimented with dividing every poem with metronomic regularity into sections of four lines each, which he termed *fen-chieh* 分解. Conducting each piece of exegesis within the bounds of these four lines, he analyzed in this manner some two hundred of Tu Fu's poems.[49]

Soon after this time, however, in the K'ang-hsi era (1662–1721), structurally analytic editions multiplied, as did other types of editions. Wu Chien-ssu in his 1672 *Tu shih lun-wen* divided every poem into sections and provided extensive guidance to each of the structural levels of "the poem, the line, and the word."[50] Chang Yuan, who otherwise relied on the historical notes of Ch'ien Ch'ien-i and Chu Ho-ling, felt that his particular contribution was to add sectional divisions that explained a poem's intent. "Without a frame, structure cannot be understood," he wrote. In fact, in his 1705 *Tu shih hui-ts'ui*, three decades in the making, Chang claimed the newness of the enterprise, pointing out the error of his predecessors in "proceeding to analysis without this fundamental step."[51] While the claim of originality cannot be substantiated, the sectioning of long poems certainly was Chang Yuan's main contribution, made the more valuable by his provision of an interpretation at the end of each section.[52] In the K'ang-hsi era, other such

48. Shan Fu, Preface, *Tu Fu yü-te*, 1:1–2. The edition is discussed in Chou Ts'ai-ch'üan's *Tu chi shu lu*, pp. 124–7, where the preface is excerpted.
49. Chin Sheng-t'an's *Ts'ai-tzu Tu shih chieh*, published posthumously by his kinsman Chin Ch'ang from surviving manuscripts held in various hands. For a survey of the criticism of Chin Sheng-t'an's use of *fen-chieh*, see Wu Hung-i, *Ch'ing-tai shih-hsüeh ch'u-t'an*, pp. 158–63.
50. 章法, 句法, 字法. Wu Chien-ssu, "General Principles," *Tu shih lun-wen*, 1:124–55. See also Chou Ts'ai-ch'üan, *Tu chi shu lu*, pp. 177–80, where he remarks on the influence of Wu's analyses on later Ch'ing commentaries. Ch'iu Chao-ao's *Tu shih hsiang-chu*, for example, quotes extensively from Wu.
51. Both quotations from *Tu shih hui-ts'ui*, Preface, 2b.
52. Chien En-ting points out that despite Chang Yuan's claim to originality, Shan Fu preceded him (see Chien's *Ch'ing-ch'u Tu-shih-hsüeh yen-chiu*, pp. 251–2). Chou Ts'ai-ch'üan summarizes Chang Yuan's influence in his *Tu chi shu lu*, p. 217.

editions appear in sufficient numbers to show that generally speaking, a consensus had developed about the need for structural divisions.

As in other areas, on segmentation Ch'iu Chao-ao's edition (1703) acts as both the culmination of earlier editions and the point of departure for later corrections. In line with his nearly varorium-style annotations, Ch'iu recognized the importance of completeness and consistency, and so he provided a structural analysis of every single poem in the oeuvre. One outstanding modification of Ch'iu's proposals will be mentioned here. This is P'u Ch'i-lung's edition. In *Tu Tu hsin-chieh* (1724), P'u Ch'i-lung used Ch'iu Chao-ao's divisions as his starting point and rethought with great sensitivity the development of every poem. His many fine explications constitute our best poem-by-poem study of structure in Tu Fu.

Systematic segmentation is obviously a necessary first step in literary criticism, for it constitutes agreement that the whole is analyzable into its parts and that it must be so analyzed. It then becomes possible to focus critical debate on specific proposed divisions and related analyses, and thus to provide concrete grounds both for agreement and for differences of opinion. Dissent from the entire project also becomes possible. Yang Lun, for one, criticized Ch'iu Chao-ao's approach and averred, somewhat unconvincingly one may think, that subdivision was quite unnecessary: long poems develop along lines dictated internally, and subdivision in short poems is usually forced and awkward, he felt.[53]

Once the analysis of poems into their constituent parts became routine, sufficient information accumulates to permit us to detect recurring types of relationships among the parts. The structures discussed in the following sections can be regarded as examples of some recurring connections.

Ordered and "loose" structures

A number of descriptive labels commonly used in Tu Fu commentaries and criticism may be interpreted as roughly designating two opposing types of structure. One structure results in a poem that is tightly knit, a well-wrought thing; the alternative is a poem that is more generously, or loosely, configured. As utilized in practical criticism, there seems no urgency for more precise definition. It is possible, however, to set up "ordered" and "loose" as a pair of polarities in the vocabulary of structure. By formalizing instinctive classification, a next analytic step be-

---

53. Yang Lun, in "General Rules," *Tu shih ching-ch'üan*, p. 13.

comes possible: if there are polarities, there may well be intermediate types. One may then ask whether any intermediate structural types exist among Tu Fu's poems. Generally speaking, juxtaposition should fall closer to "loose" than to "tight," since it proposes that no connection exists between two segments other than their adjacency. However, if the subparts are orderly in their internal development, the poem should show more affinity with other ordered structures. This is the case, for example, with "Song of My Thatched Roof Torn by Autumn Winds," whose two parts show clear internal development in, respectively, action and thought. An understanding of some of the many ways in which a poem can be loosely structured will provide a useful comparison with juxtaposition.

In the purposed polarity of ordered and loose, ordered structure is frequently analyzed. Most often the word *yen-cheng* 嚴整 is used of a poem which is tightly structured and internally referential. Many technical terms exist for the analysis of such a poem. A common set of terms consists of *ch'i* 起, *ch'eng* 承, *chuan* 轉, *ying* 應, used to explain the development of regulated verse. Terms borrowed from the rhetoric of eight-legged essays, such as *chieh* 接, *yü* 頂, *t'i* 提, and *ying-chuan* 應轉 also prove useful, for example, to P'u Ch'i-lung.[54] Some of the other structural concepts – for example, the title as unifying device, the dichotomy of feeling and scenery (*ch'ing* and *ching*) – also tend to be analytic tools better suited for well-wrought poems than for loosely structured ones.

The concept of loose structure in Tu Fu criticism is more problematic. No single word has been used to designate loose structure, and no technical terms have been coined to name its various manifestations. The paucity of satisfactory terms, however, does not mean that the concept is lacking in practical criticism. The mechanism of loosely structured poems is in fact frequently discussed, but the discussions tend to employ metaphors. By and large, these metaphors arise in the course of commentary upon long poems. They are generally ad hoc in nature, and so no metaphor has gained sufficient popularity to acquire the force of a technical term.

Evidently the organization of long poems is implicitly acknowledged to be a problem. (By contrast, orderly structure is almost always illustrated by eight-line regulated verse.) Some critical comments couched in metaphor will illustrate the usual mode of discussion of loose structure:

1. "[A poem's] waves yawn and furl, as on a great river or a lake,

54. As noted in the modern (1961) preface to P'u Ch'i-lung, *Tu Tu hsin-chieh*, p. 2.

where, before one wave has spent itself, the next has arisen. Like the troop deployment of a strategist – just as one thinks it orthodox, it becomes heterodox, just as one thinks it heterodox, it becomes orthodox."[55]

2. "Twisting, turning, interweaving, interrupting, yet wonderfully congruent with nature."[56]

3. "The rhythms of rise and fall, twists and turns – now they seem broken off and now continuous; suddenly they diverge and suddenly join. The waves come layered one upon the other, entirely without seams. Truly it is an outstanding work."[57]

4. "Because of its author's great talent and learning, the poem can twist and turn at will. It will one moment describe the poet himself, and the next describe others; it will one moment speak of scenery and the next of feeling; it will give an account of events and suddenly change to stating general principles, it will one moment describe what is before one and suddenly advert to what is in the past – all this is accomplished seamlessly, the internal references showing method [rather than randomness]."[58]

5. "The work of a great writer [like Tu Fu] is just like the waters of the Yellow River, roiling and surging on, taking in its onrush fishes and dragons, sand and stone."[59]

What do these metaphors imply about the structure of the long poems they describe? First, each attributes a different structure to the poem. The result is a list of possible ways in which long poems are organized. Second, sometimes metaphor follows metaphor, as in the second and fourth quotations. It seems that one metaphor is not sufficient to express the author's idea about something as complex and varied as a long poem's structure. By the same token, sometimes an author's metaphors are not consistent. For example, the first part of quotation 3 implies in "rise and fall, twists and turns" differences that somehow fit together; whereas the second part of the quotation, "waves layered one upon the other," implies a succession of similarities. Third, all the metaphors are intended to attribute continuity to the poems. Even when the comments specifically accommodate the multiple changes in subject matter, as in

55. The Sung-dynasty poet Chiang K'uei (1155–1221), *Pai-shih shih-shuo*, in *Li-tai shih-hua*, 2:682.
56. Wang Ssu-shih, said of "One Hundred Rhymes," in *Tu i* 7.255. Quoted in Ch'iu Chao-ao, *Tu shih hsiang-chu* 19.1716.
57. Lu Shih-ch'ueh, said of "One Hundred Rhymes," quoted in Ch'iu Chao-ao, ibid. 19.1716.
58. Chang Chin (1621–78), said of "One Hundred Rhymes," quoted in Ch'iu Chao-ao, ibid. 19.1716.
59. The Ch'ien-lung Emperor, on "Eight Laments," in *Yü-hsuan T'ang Sung shih-ch'un* 12.4b. Quoted in Ch'en Ch'ang-chü, "Shuo 'Pa-ai shih,'" *Ts'ao t'ang* 8, 2 (1984), 81.

the fourth and fifth quotations, the changes are said to unfold in a continuous, linked manner. The possibility of discontinuity is not entertained. Fourth, the continuity is obtained by a structure commodious enough to accommodate many very different things, whether "fishes and dragons, sand and stone" (the first quotation), or "self, others, scenery, feeling, events, theory, the present, the past" (the last quotation). For these accommodating structures, "looseness" may serve as a single-word summary.

The strengths and weaknesses of metaphoric discussions of structural issues are apparent. Metaphors vividly capture the type of structural unity envisioned, but they lack reference to specific traits in the poems. Although one can imagine that a poem may possess sweeping energy, "like the waters of the Yellow River, roiling and surging on," the difficulty is to find it in "Eight Laments," which is the set of poems under discussion. Almost every commentator makes use of metaphors of this kind – "starting and stopping, interweaving, rising and falling" – to the point where they are cliches. Yet, used unsystematically and without reference to particular lines within a poem, it has not been possible to make their transformation into terms of structural description. This seems curious, for the metaphors surely supply much-needed theories about the connection of the parts to the whole. We might conceive of juxtaposition as "loose structure" of a particular kind, in which successive topics show the loosest of connections and which is not dependent on the length of the poem.

Prose as poetry

The conundrum for critics is that although Tu Fu's long poems are greatly admired, they are undeniably untidy. Attempts to analyze them sometimes end in despair. "Their problem is their length. They would be greatly improved if half their lines had been cut," Yeh Meng-te concludes about the poems of the set "Eight Laments."[60] Such bluntness, however, is rare and, admittedly, it discourages further probing. Among those who have not given up, two constants can be found. One is the opinion that the long poem is uniquely Tu Fu's forte. Early on, Yuan Chen emphasized their sheer length: "the long ones reach a thousand characters [200 lines], and even the shorter ones are several hundred characters long." Other voices concurred: "Tu Fu made his name with the long poem."[61] The second constant is the attempt to pinpoint his achievement in these poems. In general, it seems that their length in itself

60. Yeh Meng-te, *Shih-lin shih-hua*, in *Li-tai shih-hua*, 1:411.
61. Yuan Chen's grave inscription for Tu Fu, in *Tu Fu chuan*, 1:15.

commands respect. Even while proposing to cut "Eight Laments" in half, Yeh Meng-te concedes, "long poems are the most difficult."[62] It is perhaps for this reason that qualities which one would have expected of lyric poems (*shih*) in general were nonetheless singled out for commendation in the long poems. Yuan Chen mentioned Tu Fu's plan of exposition, the sound pattern, the mastery of voice and tone, and prosodic euphony. Wang Ssu-shih mentioned his daringness and diction, writing, "Every line is astonishing; every word is aptly chosen. This is a feat achieved by Tu Fu alone."[63] Apparently there was agreement that length multiplies the usual problems and complicates the poet's ability to sustain the qualities normally demanded.

The nature of long poems in general was explored in another context as well, during the early Ch'ing period, in the context of a debate over what constitutes poeticalness. The debate itself concerned whether feeling (*ch'ing* 情) or exposition (*wen* 文) should dominate in lyric poetry. Many advances in theory were made in the course of this lengthy controversy, for one of its underlying issues was how to conceive of a poem in order to analyze it justly. In an ill-chosen context, a poem might well be misjudged. Because Ch'ing critics identified exposition as the predominant tendency of Sung-dynasty poetry, whereas they felt feeling dominated in T'ang verse, the debate ultimately came down to the question of whether one wished to champion T'ang or Sung style. Discussion of the purpose of poetry and the nature of poetic gifts also entered into the debate. Phrases that recurred in these discussions are "writing prose as poetry" (*i wen wei shih* 以文為詩), "allowing discussion into poetry" (*i-lun ju shih* 以論入詩), and "using rhymed passages for description" (*i yun-yü tzuo hsu-shu* 以韻語作敍述).[64] Befitting his status as cultural icon, Tu Fu's long poems figured on both sides of the issue, providing advocates of prose as poetry with their strongest argument and presenting advocates of poetry as lyricism with their most troublesome refutation.

In this debate, long poems were compared with prose in ways suggesting that the properties of prose (its length, aethetics, content, argumentation, and function) were transferrable to long poems. Poems by Tu Fu often cited in this argument included "Journey North," "Eight Laments," and "Five Hundred Words," works which are patently discursive rather than lyrical (*wen* rather than *ch'ing*). Their innovative content – accounts of contemporary events and extended reflections upon them – further illustrate functions usually assigned to prose genres.

62. Yeh Meng-te, *Shih-lin shih-hua*, in *Li-tai shih-hua*, 1:411.
63. Yuan Chen, in his grave inscription for Tu Fu, in *Tu Fu chüan*, 1:15. Wang Ssu-shih, in *Tu i* 7.255.
64. See the discussion by Chien En-ting in *Ch'ing-ch'u Tu-shih-hsueh yen-chiu*, pp. 65–8.

To admirers of Sung poetry, prose qualities and lyric poetry were not mutually exclusive, and they could point to many irrefutable examples to support their views. "Journey North" was an often-cited one. The poem unarguably contains nonpoetry characteristics: its title alludes to the great Han-dynasty rhapsodies (*fu*) about journeys, which open the anthology *Wen hsuan*; its *Tso chuan*-like opening signals its intention to describe contemporary events and pass judgment on them; and another model, Yü Hsin's sixth-century rhapsody "Lament for the South," had set the precedent of recording the poet's overflowing feelings.[65]

Those who preferred poetry to be devoted to lyrical qualities were faced with the contradiction that a T'ang poet, and Tu Fu at that, wrote many poems that are discursive. Unable to fault Tu Fu, the critics blamed his imitators instead.[66] Unusually, Shih Jun-chang (1619–83) followed his reasoning to its logical conclusion: "Sung poets often imitated Tu Fu and treated poetry as prose. This trend, developing unchecked, resulted in the great deterioration of poetry – it all began with Tu Fu."[67]

The traditional preference for judging in prose terms the very poems that I have previously used to illustrate juxtaposition – "Journey North" and "Eight Laments" – poses an interesting choice. Can the passages that I have designated as disjoint be better explained in *ku-wen* terms? Huang Sheng, in his *Tu kung-pu shih-shuo* (1696), explains the final, juxtaposed section of "Journey North" by referring to the influence of *ku-wen* rhetoric:

The most marvellous passage is the last one. In truth a continuation of the first section on the poet's departure from court, it was held for the last in order to serve as the grand conclusion for the entire piece. This is the structure of *ku-wen*. No one has remarked on this, save for that master of the essay form, Han Yü. But it really should be recognized as the greatest of passages.[68]

Huang Sheng's sense that a piece like "Journey North" needs a grand conclusion is acute. The modern reader would wish that he had cited the parallel constructions from *ku-wen* that he had in mind. In principle, however, his argument may be correct, and one would hope that it could be applied to other poems as well. Analogies between prose and long poems seem potentially a most productive approach to the problem of the long poem. As for "Journey North," the two interpretations of *ku-wen*

65. These traits are listed in Hu Hsiao-shih, "Tu Fu 'Pei cheng' hsiao chien," in *Tu Fu yen-chiu lun-wen chi*, 3:205–18.
66. For example, Wu Ch'iao criticizes Han Yü as a failed imitator of Tu Fu, *Wei-lu shih-hua* 2.11a.
67. In *Huo-chai shih-hua*, 14a. Quoted in Chien En-ting, *Ch'ing-ch'u Tu-shih-hsueh*, p. 68.
68. Huang Sheng, *Tu kung-pu shih shuo* 1.11b.

and juxtaposition are logically exclusive, since the rhetorical finale that Huang Sheng proposes is presumably deliberate whereas juxtaposition is defined as unintentional. For other poems, however, there seems no reason why *ku-wen* analogies and juxtaposition should not coexist as double explanations for certain poems or passages.

Title as organizing device

One traditional method of explication uses the title (or a key work or key image) to trace the source of unity in a poem by Tu Fu. Each part of a poem is said to refer to, reprise, or echo aspects of the title or key words or images. At its best, this method produces convincing readings that both grapple concretely with the poem's layers and at the same time are informative about the larger themes represented by the key words, images, and title. P'u Ch'i-lung is perhaps the most consistent and subtle practitioner of this type of analysis. In his hands, the method proves far from rigid, for his choice of thematic continuities is astute and his analyses are enlightening, especially of long poems, where unity is often problematic. I focus on the use of the title as unifying element, for the analysis of key words or images works analogously. My interest here is in the structure that is ascribed to a poem by this method of analysis.

When the title acts as the reference point for the poem's development, usually the first group of lines is said to take up one part of the title, the next group to echo the next part of the title, and so forth. In this manner coherence is imputed to the poem's structure. The approach has been applied to a wide variety of Tu Fu's poems, some of them carefully structured but others exhibiting disjoint structure. When a poem is already strongly structured, this approach highlights the poem's mutually reinforcing elements. Such a poem hardly requires references to the title to demonstrate unity, but the common practice is still to center the analysis on the title. Not surprisingly, poems in regulated verse tend to predominate in this category.

In loosely structured poems, by contrast, the title plays a larger role, usually as a mnemonic device signaling the direction and intent of the poem. Since the supplier of a title that lists the poem's contents is the poet himself, it seems that he as well as the critic is conscious of a title's usefulness. A typical poem of this type is "On a winter's visit to the Taoist temple at Chin-hua Mountain, I find the ruins of the academy attended by the late Reminder Lord Ch'en."[69] The loosely structured poem de-

---

69. The late Reminder Ch'en is the seventh-century poet and official Ch'en Tzu-ang ("Reminder" is the title of his office.) Chin-hua Mountain is near Tzu-chou, Tu Fu's refuge for a year (762–3) from a local rebellion in Ch'eng-tu.

votes, as Ch'iu Chao-ao notes, four lines to the mountain temple, eight lines to the journey and scenery, and a final four lines to the ruins of the school.[70] The middle eight lines, which return to an earlier part of the day, begin at the foot of the mountain ("I moored the boat by a sheer cliff"), take the poet on his climb upward, and end with his reaching the temple ("Through the mist comes an immortal"). These eight lines add up to a poem in themselves, of the kind typically written on a visit to a temple. The title, however, successfully holds them in place and subordinates them to the journey's chief discovery, the ruins of a school Ch'en Tzu-ang had once attended.

A title may conceal as much as it reveals about a poem's content (and structure). In some disjoint poems, the synoptic nature of the title provides an illusory connection among a poem's disparate parts. It appears that the title attempts to compensate for a structural problem for which it is not equipped. An example is the thirty-line poem from the K'uei-chou period, "Convalescing in the Garden on a Quiet Day, about to Plant Autumn Vegetables, Supervising the Plow Ox, and Writing of What Meets My Eye." From the title, one would expect a poem that explains the poet's recent illness, describes his current farming plans, and contains a catch-all ending of various thoughts under the rubric of "what meets my eye." This one gets, in a way, and Ch'iu Chao-ao, marking off the poem into three parts (eight, ten, and twelve lines each), quite reasonably alloted one segment of the title to each part.[71] But although the poem does fall into three sections, the first section does not quite fit the title, and the final section, for which the reader has had no precise expectations, is quite startling for "what meets my eye." The relation between title and poem is worth examining in detail.

The first part of the poem is not exceptional. The remarkable thing here is the lack of fit between these eight lines and the title. The title speaks of the poet recovering from the last of an illness on a quiet day, but the poem emphasizes the contrast between the jealous protocols of official life and the ease of private life:

> I dislike going into the prefectural office,
> Fearing others think me naive.
> When I return to my thatched world –
> That's where neighbors are never angered.
> Now old and ill, I detest constraints,
> Ceremonial to and fro dims my spirit;
> In a river village, my mind is freed,
> In woods and trees my heart finds its pleasure.

70. Ch'iu Chao-ao, *Tu shih hsiang-chu* 11.946–7.
71. Ibid. 19.1669–70.

Unlike these lines, officialdom is unmentioned in the title. One may suppose, as is usually the case, that the connection is the illness, which provides an excuse for coming home, but the relations among illness, garden, and quiet day are quite different in title and poem. P'u Ch'i-lung points out the similarity in theme to the first half of "Orange Grove," where the poet is delighted to find himself released and on his way home.[72]

The next section, of ten lines, finds Tu Fu very much the farmer. He explains autumn plowing, the benefits of rain, the ox's renewed strength, the acreage planted, the choice of crops, the local weather, and the expectation of self-sufficiency until spring. Knowledgeable, confident, this section resembles other poems from the K'uei-chou period that show Tu Fu personally supervising the farm work.[73] The normalcy of this section – in itself, in relation to the title, and in relation to Tu Fu's other poems on farming – succeeds in erasing the questions raised by the first section.

Then, however, comes the final section. It begins thus:

> There came flying a pair of white cranes,
> Reeds from the mud in their beaks at dusk. 20

So far, all is within expectations, for "what meets my eye" is a pair of cranes with nesting material. But it seems that of one of the pair is injured:

> On the male the left wing trailed,
> His injury showing in the sinews, 22
> With every step came blood,
> Still in shock from the hunting arrow –
> Three steps, six loud cries,
> His spirit broken, suffering unceasing. 26

Is this distressing scene an allegory or an actual incident? The next couplet, by introducing another bird, seems to imply allegory:

> The phoenix paid it no heed,
> It bent its neck plaintively to the heavens. 28

The ballad source for the scene further removes it from reality. Tu Fu has introduced the pair of white cranes using the exact words of an old ballad on white swans: "There came flying a pair of white cranes" here;

72. P'u Ch'i-lung, *Tu Tu hsin-chieh*, p. 179.
73. For poems that show Tu Fu as "gentleman farmer," see four translated in Hung, *Tu Fu*, pp. 244–9. (The titles are briefly discussed on pp. 240–1.) Eight more poems on this subject are listed in Hung, *Notes*, p. 103 (under "Note to poem CCCVIII").

and "There came flying a pair of white swans" in the ballad.[74] The ballad employs the common motif of one swan injured and the other unable to help; injury of one of a pair is seen in this poem too. There is also indirect imitation in the reference to numbers – "Three steps, six loud cries" here; "Five leagues and one looks back, / Six leagues and one has faltered" in the ballad.[75]

Despite the language, the motifs, and the unexpected change in topic, the title claims that Tu Fu actually saw what he described. Nor is there is reason to disbelieve him. Indeed the last couplet, when the poet seems to watch the bird expire, returns to the verisimilitude of lyric (*shih*) poetry:

> Leaning on my staff, I look down on the sandbar,
> For you, an acrid stinging in my nose.   30

"Leaning on my staff" and "For you" are the language of reality, not allegory.

Questions are raised both about the scene itself and about its role in the poem. Of course the scene contains, as Ch'iu Chao-ao commented, a layer of meaning that applies to the poet himself. Ch'iu singled out the image of the wounded crane looking to the heavens for help and compared it with the wanderer's straits.[76] P'u Ch'i-lung came to a similar conclusion. Although he was, he said, initially bewildered by the drift of this section, he concluded that it is a "shadow" (*ying-tzu* 影子), a representation on another plane, of Tu Fu's struggle, amid chaos, to support his family and turn his present attention to farming.[77] Wang Ssu-shih agreed that the poet refers to his own situation and added a comment about its structure. "It is not," he wrote, "completely unrelated to what came before." Rather the poet has created a new form, one to be used by Su Shih in his second "Red Cliff Rhapsody."[78]

Without denying the implicit symbolism of the wounded crane, and accepting the factualness of the incident, one still asks how the scene fits into the same poem as the poet's relief at his return home and his plans for the autumn crop. The death of a crane cannot have been what the reader – or the poet – expected to witness on setting out that day. It may

74. See Ch'iu Chao-ao, *Tu shih hsiang-chu* 19.1670. For "Two White Swans" 雙白鵠, see *Yü-t'ai hsin-yung* 1.15–16.
75. Birrell's translation in *Songs and Ballads*, pp. 53–4, under the title "An Old Ballad, Two White Swans."
76. "In writing of what meets his eye, the poet hints at his own circumstances." Ch'iu Chao-ao goes on to compare the crane's unheard cries to the traveler's unnoticed suffering, *Tu shih hsiang-chu* 19.1670.
77. P'u Ch'i-lung, *Tu Tu hsin-chieh*, p. 179.
78. *Tu i* 9.308.

be that the disjoint structure in "Convalescing in the Garden" is owing to the unguarded approach to composition typical of the K'uei-chou period. Many poems from this period seem to result from the casual pouring out of the poet's daily life into poetry. Huang Sheng implicitly acknowledged that "Convalescing in the Garden" is disjoint by explaining that there are two kinds of poems. In one kind, a single topic is developed in the course of several poems; in the other, several topics are combined into one poem. "Convalescing in the Garden," he said, is an example of the latter.[79] Huang Sheng could not forsake the concept of unity, however. He held that different qualities are prized in each type, and stated that the quality prized in "many topics in one poem" is seamlessness.

The poem asks three quite different responses of the reader, while – and this is the point – the title blandly provides a (one must say it) misleading list of topics. One concludes that the all-inclusive title is designed as a strategy intended to impose unity. Incidentally, it appears that the opposite strategy is taken in the disjoint poem "Orange Grove." That poem is made up of two distinct halves, a journey home and the poet's inspection of his fields the next morning.[80] Rather than join the two halves by a lengthy synoptic title, the chosen title, "Orange Grove," is terse in the extreme. ("Orange Grove" and "Convalescing in the Garden" are usually placed together in Tu Fu editions.)

To conclude: when the structure of a poem is loose, itemization in the title may be the sole means by which to foster a feeling of connection among the parts. In depending on the title, the critic implies that a justifiable structure exists in the poem. An alternative view is that the structure is entirely and only sequential, one thing placed after another. Whether an intellectual reference to the title is sufficient to impose order upon such poems is debatable. It may be that even commentators who rely on this analysis did not feel that titles (or key words or images) could in every case lend or impose structure. Rather, its use may be a way of acknowledging structure's necessity and its sometimes problematic nature, of acknowledging that disjunctive examples require explanation. I have argued here instead for the validity of a structure other than coherence.

A sudden change in the brush's direction

The term "a sudden change in the brush's direction" (*pi-feng yi chuan* 筆鋒一轉) was borrowed from calligraphy and used extensively in literary

79. Huang Sheng, *Tu kung-pu shih shuo* 2.13a.
80. See the discussion under "Examples" in this chapter.

analysis, where it has become something of a dead metaphor. Yet its literal meaning bears closer examination, for in literary analysis the term retains from calligraphy the sense of forcefulness and suddenness. Thus at first sight this term seems to suit precisely the abrupt changes in topic that constitute juxtaposition. Indeed critics often use this term at exactly those points that I have identified as disjunctive. Of the change of subject at line 92 in "Journey North" (from the poet's arrival home to the state of the empire), Chin Sheng-t'an writes, "In suddenly adverting to the emperor, the force of the brush reaches its limit of abruptness." Of the same change of topic, Chiang Juo-liu writes, "Such a sudden stop requires the strength of thousands." Of the poet's vision of a sheltering mansion in "Song of My Thatched Roof Torn by Autumn Winds," P'u Ch'i-lung writes, "In the conclusion, the brush makes a great turn, now seeming to float, then suddenly like the wind."[81] These comments all recognize the abruptness of the changes in topic and praise their forcefulness. When instances here cited as juxtaposition have already attracted so much attention, the reader might well wonder whether they can be defined as poetically unaccountable and whether it is necessary to add another concept to literary criticism.

It is agreed that these junctures are abrupt, whether one calls them juxtaposition or "an abrupt turn of the brush." The question is whether the qualities of forcefulness and deliberate intention contained in the calligraphic metaphor suit the examples of juxtaposition. An important objection to equating this calligraphic term with juxtaposition is the issue of intentionality. The metaphor implies that, like the calligrapher, the poet intentionally effects the turn in topics. Reflection shows, however, that it would be illogical to praise the change in topic in, say, "Song of My Thatched Roof," as intentional. An abrupt change in that poem is made from the poet's own troubles to a generous vision of succouring others – but he surely did not intend to draw attention to his compassion, the favorite conclusion of readers. The same is true of "Journey North," where Tu Fu turns from the happy clamor surrounding his arrival home to a prolonged review of the dangers that still beset the empire. The purpose of the sudden change is unclear, except to readers who see in it another example of Tu Fu's constant loyalty.

"A sudden change in the brush's direction" better applies to the more common rhetorical device of contrast than to juxtaposition. Indeed many instances where this term is used are examples of contrast. Juxtaposition is confusable with contrast because contrast is often an incidental effect of placing two topics side by side. It appears that

81. Chin Sheng-t'an, in *Ts'ai-tzu Tu shih chieh*, p. 53. Chiang Juo-liu, quoted in Yang Lun, *Tu shih ching-ch'üan* 4.161. P'u Ch'i-lung, *Tu Tu hsin-chieh*, p. 270.

since juxtaposition has not been recognized as a separate entity, it has been swept up in the broader wake of contrast. Consequently at this point a useful clarification is to consider how juxtaposition differs from contrast. When do we have juxtaposition, and when do we have contrast?

The most important difference was just mentioned: one can infer that contrast is intentional. Contrast is a juxtaposition of opposites intentionally made and perceived as intentional. Hence contrast can always be explained. Deliberate contrast is, of course, an effective rhetorical device as old as art. It is furthermore a common one in Tu Fu's poems, for a particular reason: the great division in Tu Fu's life, and in the history of the times, was the Troubles, and the stark contrasts between the splendor of Hsuan-tsung's reign and the disintegration of the empire, between the poet's past and his present, between the past recalled and the present endured, these contrasts form the principal lament in many of his poems, especially as the years go on. In many of Tu Fu's poems the contrast is deliberate: it *is* the theme of the poem. One of many examples is a poem from 768 entitled "T'ai-sui Day" (519/33/1, a day which in 768 fell on the third day of the first month).[82] Sixteen lines long, the poem is entirely dedicated to constructing contrasts. The first four state the poet's plight far from home ("Journeying along the banks of Ch'u, old age approaches / Stationary by Mount Wu, another spring"); the next four recollect the rituals of the New Year at court (a procession by officials in ceremonial clothing, the emperor's distribution of gifts to officials); the second half of the poem alternately contrasts here and there, then and now. Contrast is uppermost in the poet's mind. In this poem we find none of the inadvertency of juxtaposition.

Many of the long poems of recapitulation which Tu Fu began to write during the Ch'eng-tu years are structured on a principle of contrast. Two well-known poems, "Thatched Hut" (143/10/18) and "Wanderings of My Prime" (169/12/7), often quoted for their biographical information, are typical in this respect. "Thatched Hut," written in early 764, immediately announces that it will proceed by developing basic contrasts:

> When I left the Thatched Hut,
> Barbarians filled Ch'eng-tu;
> Today, returning to the Thatched Hut,
> I find Ch'eng-tu is without fearfulness.   4

82. T'ai-sui, the planet Jupiter, is associated with the first day of the twenty-eight-day cycle. In the first month of 768 (since Tu Fu describes New Year ceremonies), this occurred on the third day.

A strong narrative structure ("I'll start from the rebellion's beginning," line 5) continues the many contrasts of the poem, between the past of Ch'ang-an and the present of Szechuan, and between the rebellion that caused Tu Fu's departure from Ch'eng-tu and the peace of his present return. A clear division between the present and the past also underlies the progression of "Wanderings of My Prime." The high spirits of the poet's sight-seeing travels in the 730s contrast with the forced peregrinations that were his lot after the outbreak of the An Lu-shan rebellion. The topic takes several turns, as does Tu Fu's life, but in the poem as a whole the encyclopedic overview unifies the contrasts, for the whole remains controlled by the narrative of Tu Fu's wanderings.

The poems of recollection, because they advance chronologically, inevitably embrace the central contrast in Tu Fu's life between then and now, there and here. Juxtaposition contains the same contrasts, but in juxtaposition a different dynamic is at work. There the unintended alternation of contrasting subjects appears to be involuntary: the existing subject is broken into by another, stronger subject, which cannot be held back, indeed whose existence or strength of feeling was not suspected until it broke through. The biographical implications of the two structures differ. Contrast implies intentionality on the poet's part, the carrying through of a plan; juxtaposition suggests the overwhelming of the poet by his subject. Intentionality suggests some kind of poetic strategy, whereas juxtaposition suggests the relinquishment of any plan.

I must concede that a distinction between juxtaposition and contrast that depends on intentionality, whose presence or absence we can only surmise, retains a core of subjective judgment. Where one reader sees juxtaposition, another may see contrast. However, to admit that an element of "subjective" judgment remains merely means that individual judgment cannot be eliminated. A concept of juxtaposition has been made available, and criteria have been stated for distinguishing between contrast and juxtaposition. I do not suggest that poems can be unfailingly assigned to one or the other category.

The pairing of scenery and feeling

Another common traditional analysis of poems draws upon the pairing of feeling and scenery (*ch'ing* 情 and *ching* 景). Both are terms with long, sophisticated histories, but the pair is considered here only in its relation to structure and juxtaposition. Unlike the five concepts already discussed, the *ch'ing/ching* pair applies more readily to regulated verse than to old-style verse.

Although conceptually subtle, indeed often vague, in practice the pairing of scene and feeling comes down to saying a small number of things about poems. One is that "the first half describes scenery, the second half feeling." This is in truth the structure of many of Tu Fu's poems written in regulated verse. Ch'iu Chao-ao is especially fond of this formulation and analyzes nearly all of the regulated-verse poems as divided into two sets of four lines, the first four containing a description of scenery and the second four expressing the feeling it aroused. Ch'iu Chao-ao uses this analytic model even when it is quite forced, for which he has often been criticized. A typical example is "River Village in the Ninth Month," in which lines 5 and 6, contrary to Ch'iu's suggested bisection, are primarily descriptive.[83] Another way of putting the scenery–feeling connection is Huang Sheng's, who writes, "First scenery, then feeling, this is the constant format of Tu Fu's poetry."[84] When scene and feeling are fully integrated in a poem, a common comment is, "Every line sings of the scenery, and every line bespeaks feeling."

To commentators, the pairing of scene and feeling is not directly connected with the issue of structure but rather concerns responsiveness and the psychology of response. One feeling often elicited on contemplating scenery is regret: in a common phrase, "contact with the scene brings on sorrow" (*ch'u-ching kan-shang* 觸景感傷 or *ch'u-ching shang huai* 觸景傷懷). This stimulus–response model underlies comments concerning the scene and feeling of a poem. In lyric poetry, especially in regulated verse, scene always elicits feeling. A poem that begins by contemplating scenery necessarily progresses to a response which is personal. In this aesthetic, a role for the poet is built in, from which biographical interpretation is but a short step.

If we focus on the structure entailed by the pairing of scene and feeling, rather than on the psychology of response, then we can distinguish at least two types of poems in which scene is succeeded by feeling. These are, as might be expected by now, the disjunctive poem and the well-integrated poem. In poems that are disjunctive, the disjunction marks scene off from feeling; there is no connection between the two, and the pair is dichotomized. This demarcation is seen in all the regulated-verse poems discussed so far as showing juxtaposition. The common division of a poem into two sets of four lines neither entails nor eliminates the possibility of juxtaposition. The crucial issue is whether something in the description of the scene adequately foreshadows the feeling that follows. The judgment must be made made case by case.

---

83. Ch'iu Chao-ao, *Tu shih hsiang-chu* 20.1778. The couplet reads "On the table, heavy yellow oranges, / To stabilize the couch, lovely round stones" (500/31/52).
84. Huang Sheng writes this of "Climbing to a Height" (411/26/39), in *Tu kung-pu shih shuo* 9.14b.

Disjunction results when feeling remains feeling and scene remains scene. Such a poem might sketch a scene whose significance is not clear even when the whole poem is revealed, or, as in "Madman," quoted shortly, a scene which becomes puzzling once the whole poem is revealed. The poem is disjoint between the scene presented and the feelings stated.

The reader can test this with two poems, both of which begin with a description of the calm beauty that meets the eye of one living apart from the world. In one poem, the first four lines are followed by four more lines consistent with the peaceful tone, whereas in the other poem the topic abruptly switches to the poet's internal worries. Which is which? The two beginnings follow:

> Poem 1:
> West of Wan-li Bridge stands a thatched house;
> The water of Hundred Flowers Pool is that of Ts'ang-lang.
> Wind cradles the tender bamboo, beautiful and clear
> Rain moistens the red lotus, tender and fragrant.

> Poem 2:
> A farmhouse in the curve of a clear stream,
> Its brushwood gate beside an old road –
> With the growth so thick I can't find the market,
> Away from everything, I don't trouble about my clothes.[85]

Which poem will become disjoint? Based on the first half, prediction is difficult (unless the reader has prior knowledge). As it turns out, it is the first poem, "Madman," that becomes disjoint, and typically, the disjunction occurs at the halfway point. In lines 5 and 6 the poet turns away from the peaceful scene and reveals thoughts of startling bitterness: his now-important friends have dropped him; the hungry faces of his children are a silent reproach. He then recovers some control and calls himself just a madman (as in the title), one who is retired from service to the state (echoed in line 2's allusion to Ts'ang-lang, by whose waters Ch'ü Yuan was advised to resign himself to his ruler's neglect of him). By contrast, the second poem, "A Farmhouse," continues in the same rural vein in its second half, with willows swaying, loquats giving off their fragrance, and cormorants viewed in the setting sun.

Naturally, many poems in regulated verse divide into halves without any disjunction. In the usual model, poems take up emotion explicitly in the second half, whereas scenery dominates in the first half. ("A Farmhouse" is comparatively unusual in that all four lines of the second half are also devoted to scenery.) The two halves, however, need to be

85. The first is "Madman" (343/21/7), the second is "A Farmhouse" (344/21/11).

connected by foreshadowing and internal references. The scenery must generally hint at something that is then made clearer in the second half. A scene that is presented in a highly intense manner –

> Flowers by the high tower pain the traveler's heart,
> Troubles lie everywhere as I climb to this view . . .[86]

– such an opening clearly portends that something will follow.

The title may help in connecting the scene and feeling portions of a poem. In a poem such as the second one of "Grieved by Spring" (424/ 28/23B), the opening four lines focus on spring's slowing evolving beauty, but since the title names grief as the theme, anticipation guides our reading of these lines. When the rest of the poem then turns to an account of the poet's sorrows (lines 5–12), the title has prepared one for the contrast between the renewal represented by spring and the continuation of his worries. The case of "Madman" is quite different. The title provides some anticipatory information, but the lines of the poem nonetheless remain disjunctive. Given the title, one expects a poem that is not wholly serene, for a madman's withdrawal from society and the allusion to Ts'ang-lang are seldom simple acts of resignation. Nearly always is implied some condemnation of the world's folly for not recognizing the speaker's abilities. Nonetheless, the bitterness expressed in the second half of "Madman" outstrips our expectations. We find that while line 2 on the Ts'ang-lang waters now makes sense, lines 3 and 4 no longer fit ("Wind cradles the tender bamboo . . . / Rain moistens the red lotus"). There is no way to adjust the lines' sweet quiet to the outburst of bitterness, injury, and grief. How does this couplet on tender spring coexist with the children's silent, hungry faces? The poem cannot integrate the tone or image of this couplet into the other six lines.

The pairing of feeling and scene assumes that intensity of feeling lies at the heart of writing. Feeling is elicited by something in the outside world, but it is also limited by that something. The poet has to construct a scene of sufficient power to account for the response. Many terms connected with this model of response have an implicit consequence for structure, for it is implied that feeling cannot carry the poet beyond the initially intended themes into a lopsided poem. Responsive emotion (*kan-ying* 感應) is drawn out of one spontaneously, but for the reader, conviction must also be based in a sufficiently delineated scene. In "Madman," as in other of the regulated-verse poems that show juxtaposition, feelings burst out that have no correspondence to the scenery.

Juxtaposition's most perfect opposite is the kind of poem summed up by the familiar dictum, "Feeling in the scenery, scenery in the feeling." In

86. "Climbing the Tower," 353/21/42.

such poems, feeling and scenery form a duality rather than a dichotomy. Although emotion is usually more explicitly stated in the second half, connections between the two halves are constantly made. In the two poems of the set "Autumn Wind" (185/53/10), the scenery of the Yangtze Gorges takes up the first half, and feelings of homesickness and war-weariness follow in the second half. But no line in the first half is concerned solely with scenery, and hence the feelings expressed in the second half are anticipated by those implied in the first half. Readers of poetry in English are accustomed to poems which, like "Autumn Wind," are tightly structured and internally referential – in short, the poems of the New Criticism. Their structural principles are not simpler than those of juxtaposition, but the methodology for understanding them is familiar to us.

The assertion that unconnectedness is one characteristic of Tu Fu's style in effect sets a limit on possible evaluations of juxtaposition poems. On the evidence of the juxtaposition poems, Tu Fu seems not to have held consistently to the ideals of coherence that he exemplified elsewhere to intimidating perfection. If we accept this view, the change in tone when the figure of the poet is introduced must be considered a given, however discordant the alignment of tones might be. Poetically, the discordance can be neither explained nor explained away, although such attempts are frequent. The other logical alternative is to find the poem deeply flawed. This is the choice duly made, for example, by Wang Fu-chih with respect to "Climbing Yueh-yang Tower," when he writes, "the excellence of the poem ends with the seventh line."[87] Because Tu Fu is Tu Fu, however, it is not a choice critics find themselves willingly or frequently making. Thus there are fewer sharp criticisms of Tu Fu's poems than there are juxtaposition poems. It is hoped that the analysis here, by establishing and populating the category of juxtaposition poems, has made acceptance and further discussion possible.

87. Wang Fu-chih, *T'ang-shih p'ing-hsuan* 3.18a.

4
Juxtaposition II:
A biographical analogue

It is possible now to seek a reconnection between the disjunctive parts of a juxtaposition poem. That poems as varied as the examples given in Chapter 3 should share a method of composition suggests that reconciliation of the parts of a poem is not to be obtained in poetic terms. This leaves the alternative that it is to be made through the person of the poet. In other words, reconnection of the parts of a poem is brought about by the same process as in traditional reconciliations, where the development of a poem by Tu Fu is explained in terms of the poet's mood and personality. Earlier I pointed out that traditional explications such as P'u Ch'i-lung's of "Seeking out Ts'ui Chi and Li Feng,"[1] though ostensibly concerned with the poem, are couched in ad hominem terms. It may seem, therefore, that we have merely arrived at the conclusion with which tradition began. The detour has value, though, in that the isolation of disjoint poems will enable us to validate truisms about Tu Fu in a more precise way, rendering them truths as well as truisms. The concept of disjunction makes clear that a poem's continuity in the poet's mind is posited as a theory rather than assumed as a convention. Whether supposition or convention, identical preoccupations are attributed to Tu Fu, but theory supplies in addition a principle that unites a number of diverse issues.

The sheer difficulty of describing the obvious in Tu Fu's poetry tempts us to assume that the task is unnecessary. However, the thoroughness with which Tu Fu's central concerns have infused every aspect of his poetry means that, whatever the critic's interests, yet another consideration of these concerns is unavoidable. Juxtaposition poems constitute a subset in his works which demonstrates, in structural terms, the truth of many generalizations commonly made about his poetry. Even the most cursory reading of the poems will furnish the reader with the familiar Tu

1. P'u Ch'i-lung, *Tu Tu hsin-chieh*, p. 24.

161

Fu themes of social concern, political dedication, and practical worries. The juxtaposition poems confirm this cumulative, general impression in exact terms. The reason is that juxtaposition occurs when the typical Tu Fu themes are isolated both from the external reality that is the usual poetic stimulus and from echoes of interconnections with the rest of the poem. Under this double isolation, the themes, undiluted by either aesthetic or situational considerations, provide a direct insight into the poet. Only in juxtaposition do themes appear primarily as the content of the author's thoughts rather than as motifs worked into the poem's fabric. In this environment, the themes are construable as personal views, unmediated by the usual niceties of poetry, and the isolation – or juxtaposition – becomes informative about Tu Fu's frame of mind. The poems discussed in Chapter 2 as examples of genre experimentation were chosen to show how, in the expression of his compassion, Tu Fu sought to overcome formal differences between the lyric (*shih*) and the ballad (*yueh-fu*). In juxtaposition poems as well, evidence of Tu Fu's soical conscience is everywhere visible, but in formal terms, it is structure rather than genre which the poet adjusts to accommodate its expression.

The comment often made about Tu Fu, that he simply wrote down his feelings directly, is more valid for the juxtaposition poems than for other poems. The abrupt swerve in topic that constitutes juxtaposition interposes the author's feelings with less calculation than do the carefully crafted poems. The poet appears to have felt so strongly that his feelings spilled unprepared into the poem. "In my weakness, grief and sorrow come easily" 我衰易悲傷, he says of himself.[2] The outcome of elements involuntarily linked together in the poet's mind, juxtaposition poems reveal a purer version than is usually available of the perennial problem of the poet's relationship to his work. In these poems, the poet seems to have laid aside some of the requirements of his craft. A direct apprehension of the visible world before him is succeeded by thoughts and feelings inadvertently aroused, but, following their arousal, the poem is not reworked to accommodate the uninvited arrivals. The poem gives the impression of being a by-product of the mental preoccupations of the poet. The interruption of a subject already under way – be it landscape or narrative or exposition – by a subject that needs expression more strongly and urgently – this is, in poetic terms, juxtaposition and, in personal terms, obsession.

That certain themes predominate in Tu Fu's poetry to the point of obsession is in one sense obvious. It is easy to show that over the years Tu

2. Line 29 of thirty-two lines, "Orange Grove," 182/13/6.

Fu became more and more preoccupied with the events of his times. "On this day, there is no end to my thoughts" 此日意無窮, he said of himself.[3] Yet paraphrases of lines such as this merely document the well-known Tu Fu. Less obvious are the varied poetic manifestations of these constant themes. Examining the themes in their structural placement provides a means of grasping their significance in the poetic realm. The juxtaposition of subjects corresponds to the poet's obsessions and, conversely, the obsessions are revealed in the structure. Poetic support is found for the statement that to Tu Fu such disparate subjects as family, self, empire, and fate are equivalent. Appearing as structurally interchangeable items, one or the other occupies the slot that supplants the visible scene or event. The structural interchangeability could be thought of as a version of the interchangeability observable in Tu Fu's parallel couplets. Thus he writes of family members and of the court in parallel positions in a couplet: "Brothers and sisters in my melancholy song, / The court before my inebriated eyes" 弟妹悲歌裏朝庭醉眼中.[4] State, family, self, and other elements, then, although different in public estimation, are equivalent on other levels. To be sure, this is proof of connections that tradition finds unsurprising. The uncovering of these structural analogues provides a reason other than the weight of tradition to explain why the Confucian interpretation of Tu Fu and his work retains validity for modern critics.

Even within the highly self-absorbed poems of Tu Fu, juxtaposition poems are unusually informative about the poet's personality and attitudes. Their structural interruptions reveal the involuntary urgency of the poet's preoccupations. The terms often used to characterize Tu Fu's poetry – "pertinent," "topical," "relevant," "timely" – in truth do not accurately apply to the juxtaposition poems. We find instead that the poet's concerns, though indeed topical, no longer require the stimuli of appropriate events for their arousal. Tu Fu himself knew this. Taking leave of some new acquaintances in T'ung-ku, he says he knows that the emotion he feels is excessive:

> At the road's fork, I part from several men,
> Clasping hands, tears fall once again.
> These are not long or deep friendships,
> But an old and poor man easily feels bereft.[5]

Although it is true that stimuli such as further dislocations, renewed outbreaks of rebellion, and new abuses by officialdom are not lacking, to

3. Line 8 of the eight-line poem "Climbing the City Wall of Tzu-chou on the Ninth of the Ninth," 380/24/7.
4. From ibid.
5. "Departure from T'ung-ku County," 96/6/17, lines 13–16.

a traveler long away from home painful reminders surface everywhere, not just in particular events. In "Living as a Sojourner," Tu Fu writes:

> Everything I see reminds me of my old country –
> Ten years since I've left my home village.[6]

The later poems frequently mention the number of years the poet has been a wanderer. The stability and peace for which Tu Fu longed receded ever farther, while continual uncertainties made everything and anything a stimulus. This is another face of the compassion for which Tu Fu is so noted.

Tu Fu's major themes surface in nearly all his poems. They appear, however, in formally or structurally different ways, testimony again to the many different uses of poetry for Tu Fu. In the great poems most commonly represented by the seven-character regulated verse of the K'uei-chou and Hu-nan periods, the poet's preoccupations are presented in a seamless tapestry of themes, motifs, and symbols that readers have long found aesthetically, emotionally, and intellectually satisfying. In other poems, experimentation with the method of presentation results in poems that are formally intermediate between old-style poetry and ballads. The juxtaposition poems represent yet another manifestation. Here the same themes appear bluntly, involuntarily. Only here are personal feelings disjunctive, and thus here we may most confidently extrapolate from poetic expression to biography.

The topics that are original in poetry with Tu Fu – his concern for the state, his sympathy for others, his devotion to his family – have been examined with several different approaches in these chapters. One final approach, developed here, will enable us to investigate them from a biographical standpoint. We shall begin by observing that a basic tool of the literary critic – thematic analysis – is, in Tu Fu's case, a consistently two-sided phenomenon, with applications in both poetic and biographical realms. The topics that constitute themes in Tu Fu's poetry – rebellion, loss, concern for the state, the desire to return, remembrance of the past – have another existence as specific people, events, and places in his life. Of course critics have always, without much ado, translated themes in the poetry into statements about the poet. But precisely because of the ease of the translation, it needs to be emphasized that Tu Fu's themes do have a dual existence. Tu Fu's poetry is unique in containing themes which pass easily from poetry to life and back again. By contrast, since the dislocations of the Troubles touched everyone, his life was far from unique. The slight, but vital, distinction reserves for

6. 151/11/9, lines 29–30.

poetry some independence from the overwhelming context of the poet's life. At the same time, the overlap between poetic theme and life's events is so far-reaching that its manifold importance deserves repeated exploration. This chapter exploits the semi-independence of the poetry in order to renew connections between the poetry and the life.

Chronology

Let us begin at the beginning, a task which, in the case of juxtaposition, is almost possible. The themes which are abruptly juxtaposed require the events set in motion by the An Lu-shan rebellion, and with the passage of time these themes became more pronounced in Tu Fu's poetry. Yet some of his typical preoccupations, and structures, might have occurred even without the provocation of the Troubles, surfacing simply as an index to the pain, the small defeats, and the major setbacks dealt by life. A poem which predates the An Lu-shan rebellion shows Tu Fu already inclined to allow whatever is on his mind to override the topic with which he began. This is the poem "Song of Lo-yu Park" (26/2/5).

The poem is set in Lo-yu Park ("Delightful Excursions Park"), a favorite destination for aristocrats and high officials on the elaborate outings customary at three intervals in the year.[7] The park lies southeast of Ch'ang-an, on the highest point near the capital, and overlooks many of the city's famed sites. According to his note to the poem, Tu Fu has been invited to "a wine-filled feast [at the park], given by the chief administrator, Ho-lan Yang, on the last day of the month." Thus "Song of Lo-yu Park" is written on a festive outing, and indeed the first twelve of the poem's twenty lines are what one might expect of such an occasion. The boisterous picnickers praise the spectacular view at the picnic spot, they drink wine from long wooden ladles and canter about in high spirits. A group of the picnickers observes another picnic, an imperial one, in Hibiscus Park, just to the west. That picnic proceeds with even greater bustle and luxury. Lo-yu Park, it seems, is full of the gaiety of the prosperous. Then, quite suddenly, at line 13, the mood changes. With no warning, the poet recollects his own situation ("Not yet drunk, I am already melancholy," line 14), and indeed, as he recounts it, his position is a rather sorry one. He has been disappointed in the search for office ("Before this august court, I know this humble scholar is ill-favored," line 17), and he says he has nowhere to go after the festive

7. On the last day of the first month (the occasion of this poem), the third day of the third month (the occasion of "Ballad of Beauties"), and the ninth day of the ninth month (the occasion of "Climbing the City Wall of Tzu-chou"), to name only the poems mentioned in this volume.

day. These reflections bring on a melancholy from which the poet cannot free himself. The picnic presumably continues its merriment nearby, but this the reader cannot tell. The poet continues to dwell on his miseries, and in the poem's last line he is a solitary figure, quite cut off from the sociable setting: "I stand alone in blue space chanting to myself."

This is still an early poem, usually dated 751. We see only the self-absorption, for the themes of rebellion and family are not yet available. The An Lu-shan rebellion, which began about five years later, only gradually revealed itself to be a prolonged and infinitely difficult event. With the Troubles, Tu Fu's preoccupations acquired public objects (the empire, war, the common man's sufferings) and attained, in Confucian terms, heroic stature. But the predisposition was already there. Its expression – the introspective ending, the inward focus, which shuts out the experiential reality with which the poem began – is already to be seen. The shift from the gay party to his own dismal situation occurs at line 13, "I remember merry drinking every year on this day." The line seems to acknowledge the break but nonetheless is not a preparation for it. One might expect melancholy to follow, but not the bleakness that does nor the end of any further reference to the party.

This dwelling on himself – self-commiseration, if not solipsism – is found in another poem of the early, prerebellion period. "Presented to Li Po" was written probably not long after their meeting in 744. Twelve lines in length, it is, in spite of its title, mostly concerned with the poet himself: eight lines are on himself versus four on Li Po. About himself, Tu Fu recounts his disillusionment with the intrigues of political life, his disgust with the ostentation of the rich, his longing for a simpler life, and his reasons for not having withdrawn from the world. Then he briefly offers his good wishes to Li Po. This unusual reversal of emphasis, "detailed about himself, vague about Li Po," as P'u Ch'i-lung observes, deserves attention. P'u deftly suggests that Tu Fu has chosen elements in his life that are consistent with Li Po's situation and that are applicable to Li Po "with but a change of one or two words."[8] As an alternative, one might suggest that the poet's tendency toward self-absorption, even before the Troubles, can be found in "Presented to Li Po" as in "Song of Lo-yu Park."

To return to "Song of Lo-yu Park," a hint of a serious purpose surfaces in the middle part, but it complicates the poem without providing a bridge to the final section. This middle part, lines 7 through 12, describes the imperial picnic in nearly Hibiscus Park. The imperial party,

8. P'u Ch'i-lung, *Tu Tu hsin-chieh*, p. 3.

heralded by drums, makes its way to Hibiscus Park by a covered passage-way that had been built to connect Ta-ming Palace in the Imperial City with the park. At Hibiscus Park, while food speeds from the palace kitchens, dancers and singers add to the day's entertainment. The scene resembles the Yang sisters' outing on the third day of the third month, depicted in "Ballad of Beauties." The latter poem, probably dating from 753, two years after "Song of Lo-yu Park," unmistakably damns the wanton luxury of the imperial favorites, by means of a surfeit of details over eighteen lines, even before the finale portrays Yang Kuo-chung as villainy personified. The imperial picnic is not condemned in these terms in "Song of Lo-yu Park" – at six lines the description is briefer, and the party seems not overly extravagant – but the unbridgeable distance between the observer and the observed possesses the potential for com-ment upon imperial pastimes. It may be that the observer's cooler eye, which cannot be turned upon a feast in which the poet has just drunk wine from ladles and galloped about cheerfully, retrospectively com-ments as well upon the Lo-yu Park merrymaking. This serious note, however, remains only implicit. The darkness of the ending we have is not the surfacing of that thought.

That Tu Fu's tendency to swerve from what is before him to what is in his mind's eye is present early in his work we can see from another early poem, "Five Hundred Words Expressing My Feelings on the Way from the Capital to Feng-hsien County." (In this case, the change in vision occurs without disjunction.) Written on what turned out to be the eve of rebellion, the poet's reproaches of imperial extravagance came to be read as ominous premonitions of the destruction to come. The most often quoted of these reproaches is the vivid contrast between waste at the winter palace and want outside the gates:

> Behind vermilion gates wine and meats decay,
> On the road the bones of the frozen dead.   68

Tu Fu's ringing condemnation is usually read as though the moral force of the contrast stems from its sense of being immediate, observed facts. (The English poetic tradition, by contrast, tends to assume the opposite, that poets create their stirring images.) It comes as a surprise to note about these lines what is seldom mentioned: that Tu Fu's description of luxury behind the palace gates cannot have been, on this occasion, observed in person. Whereas the dead on the road are there to be seen, the details of palace life are presumably closed to him. He is traveling as a private person and is still to take up his first office. The Ch'ing-dynasty scholar Chao I has noted the precedents for Tu Fu's couplet in several early texts, naming *Mencius*, the biography of the Lord of P'ing-yuan in

Shih chi, and *Huai-nan-tzu.*[9] In each of these texts, a contrast is drawn between heedless waste and destitution and, as here, the contrast is intended to shock.

We see that the hoariest truth about Tu Fu – that he bore witness to his times – is not always literally true. Despite this, the reader's faith in the moral force of his descriptions needs not waver. Chao I, for one, goes on to say, "Although this has been described by men in the past, in Tu Fu's hands, the subject jolts the reader's heart and soul as they have never been jolted before."[10] Nonetheless, the couplet's status as imagined scenes requires, on a poetic level, some greater adjustments than on the moral level. The whole of Tu Fu's famous description of heartless enjoyment in the winter palace is worth rereading in this light:

> Goddesses and immortals in the central hall,
> A mistiness wafts about each fair figure,
> Guests are warmed with furs of sable,
> The sound of sad reeds follows the clear strings,　　64
> Guests coaxed with camel-pad broth,
> Winter oranges overlaid by fragrant tangerines –
> Behind vermilion gates wine and meats decay,
> On the road the bones of the frozen dead.　　68

The concept of juxtaposition has a useful role to play in the study of Tu Fu's poetry and its development over time. It draws attention to the fact that the context in which a theme appears constitutes an important piece of information, and it provides us with a way of analyzing contextual information. It is not difficult to identify important themes in Tu Fu; the problem for literary critics is to go beyond enumeration. In the remainder of this section, I shall attempt to do so by selectively analyzing the chronology of Tu Fu's life and works in relation to juxtaposition poems. In particular, I shall use the concept of juxtaposition to sharpen statements commonly made about two periods in his life – that his years in his Thatched Hut were, exceptionally for him, a period of some contentment; and that the two years in K'uei-chou (766–8) marked the height of his powers. Many poems of a predominantly tranquil tone provide evidence for the first conclusion, and magnificent regulated-verse poems in both seven- and five-character line lengths support the latter conclusion. The concept of juxtaposition is used to link certain issues relating to the life and works of these two periods.

Ch'eng-tu partially fulfilled Tu Fu's search for a refuge after four years of warfare in the Central Plains. During those years, pressed by warfare,

---

9. *Ou-pei shih-hua* 2.22.
10. Ibid.

by reversals in his official life, and by family cares, Tu Fu was never able to live anywhere longer than a few months. His initial decision, it appears, consisted simply of quitting the Central Plains, with his actual destination undecided. In his first stop, at Ch'in-chou, to the west of Ch'ang-an, he several times contemplated settling down. He did not do so, however, and went on to Ch'eng-tu. There, soon after his arrival, with the help of gifts from acquaintances and officials, he found a suitable site on Flower-washing Stream and set about building a home. The eponymous Thatched Hut years are divided into two periods, separated by a gap of slightly more than one year. The first period, lasting just less than three years, begins with Tu Fu's arrival in the first month of 760 and ends in late 762, when a local rebellion forced him to flee first to Tzu-chou, and then to Lang-chou, with his family. The second period dates from his return to Ch'eng-tu in early 764, upon the reappointment of his friend Yen Wu to a position in Shu. It ends with his departure for the Yangtze Gorges in the middle of the following year.

In Ch'eng-tu, Tu Fu was, it appears, happy. He did write many poems during his Ch'eng-tu years that were not idyllic. Then, as throughout his life, he wrote poems whose titles indicate his pent-up feelings: "Ch'ien hsing" 遣興, "San ch'ou" 散愁, "Ch'ien ch'ou" 遣愁, and "Shu huai" 述懷.[11] Other poems, chiefly from autumn of his second year in Ch'eng-tu, 761, show that he was much impoverished at this time.[12] In addition, it is always emphasized that even tucked away in his Thatched Hut, Tu Fu did not forget the common man and the peril of the empire, as many poems bear out. These provisos made, the fact remains that an unusual number of poems survive which show a contented Tu Fu. They include, to list just a few, "Enjoying the Rain on a Spring Night," "Early Summer Rain," the poems on visitors ("A Guest Arrives," "Southern Neighbor," "Northern Neighbor," "A Guest Comes"), the poems on farming ("A Farmhouse, " "Farming"), as well as poems such as "A River Village," and "Four Quatrains." Even a potential flood is viewed without alarm ("The River Rises," "Spring Waters"). The simplification of life to his immediate surroundings, the quiet pleasures of domestic life, and "the pleasant atmosphere of cordiality and mutual respect"[13] in his relations with his neighbors – these themes all signal a period of tranquillity. This was the time when he could envision growing old away from home: "A site chosen for my home, to grow old here."[14] When more precise dating is

11. Nineteen titles begin with the verb *ch'ien* 遣, "to give voice to," "to give vent to." "San-ch'ou" is at 410/26/36 and "Shu-huai" at 46/3/1.
12. See poems listed in *Tu Fu nien-p'u*, pp. 131–2. "Madman" and "Ballad of One Hundred Accumulated Worries" date from this period.
13. William Hung, *Tu Fu*, p. 167.
14. 卜宅從茲老, "Farming," 343/21/5, line 5.

not available, editors have generally grouped such poems together under the first Thatched Hut period.[15] An act of editorial convenience, its consequence has been to reinforce the impression that Tu Fu was contented at this time.

Unlike most attempts at defining workable subcategories within Tu Fu's poetry, it happens to be unusually easy to draw sharply delineated boundaries around the pastoral poems of the Thatched Hut years. Nonetheless, critics frequently blur the boundaries by quoting from pastoral and nonpastoral poems alike to support the portrait of a contented Tu Fu. The problem seems to be on the one hand an insufficient appreciation of the usefulness of wholly pastoral poems and on the other hand an uncertainty about the status of partially pastoral poems. The two difficulties may be simultaneously tackled.

It is best to designate as pastoral those poems that convey without inconsistency in tone a sense of having attained safe haven. "The Hut Completed," written to mark the final completion of the Thatched Hut,[16] typically sets such a tone. In this poem, every line breathes contentment with the poet's new home. His pleasure in it extends beyond himself and his family to include the birds around it as well:

> Now pauses a winged crow, leading its several young,
> Back come chattering swallows to pick out a nesting site.[17]

By the definition proposed and by their nature, pastoral poems cannot be disjoint. They represent, thematically speaking, the opposite of obsession. "A River Village" (346/21/15) is another typical pastoral poem:

> In the bend of the clear river's flow lies a village,
> In the long summer of this river village, all is unhurried.
> They fly back and forth, the swallows above the house,
> Dear and close to one another, gulls on the water.
> My old wife draws a chessboard on paper,
> The children beat needles into fishhooks.
> All one needs for the recurrent aches is medicine –
> What more could this simple person desire?

15. For example, the poems just named are all found in *chüan* 21 of the *Chiu-chia* edition of the poems.
16. Additions and improvements to the Thatched Hut after its initial erection took another two years. "The Hut Completed" (344/21/10) is usually assumed to mark its initial completion in the spring of 760, but P'u Ch'i-lung argues that the shade trees and giant bamboos mentioned in lines 3 and 4 could not have attained enough height to cast much shade so soon, and so he places the poem in 762 (*Tu Tu hsin-chieh*, p. 624).
17. "The Hut Completed," lines 5–6.

On this serene day and in this isolated place, the poet accepts the arrangements of fate and feels a rare contentment. He is content with his lot, with his new home, with his nonuseful life. Only the last line, in disavowing any desire for more, hints at a wider world beyond, and this hint helps us to see that the poem is Tu Fu's way of drawing a circle around his family to keep the world outside.

Pastoral poems testify to the peace of mind which life in the Thatched Hut secured for Tu Fu. Yet in the context both of this period and of Tu Fu's whole life, these poems are exceptional rather than typical. In excluding the world of troubles, the poems exclude the topical subjects that are most typical of Tu Fu. After all, the overwhelming evidence is that "not for the space of a meal did he forget his sovereign." It is as exceptions that the poems shed an interesting light on Tu Fu's years in Ch'eng-tu, and it is as exceptions that they shed an interesting light on the topicality of his usual subjects. In the latter case, their usefulness lies, as we shall see, in the fact that the contrast with juxtaposition poems is not total.

Pastoral and disjoint poems share an uncomplicated opening. "A River Village," for example, opens with scenery and, as in juxtaposition poems, the scenery is free of suggestions of any tension to come. In pastoral poems, however, this serenity is predictive in that the remaining lines maintain a tranquil tone consistent with the opening. In disjoint poems, by contrast, the poet's mind flies unprovoked to quite different thoughts, remote from the scene before him. "An Old Country Man" and "Madman," both discussed earlier, are such poems. The initial shared treatment of scenery emphasizes the different second half, which in juxtaposition poems takes the form of topical references. In other words, pastoral poems tend to be devoid of topical subjects, although they are often informative about Tu Fu's personal life. (Both may be contrasted with the *ch'ing/ching* principle. Like pastoral poems but unlike juxtaposition poems, *ch'ing/ching* expects the response aroused to be an outcome of the contemplation of the landscape. Like juxtaposition poems, however, the response usually is not tranquil.)

The customary view of a contented Tu Fu may be amended by noting that the pastoral poems show Tu Fu not only contented but also controlled. By contrast, the disjunctive poems show that his hold on tranquillity is maintained with difficulty, faltering often even within the brief space of eight lines. To quote the pastoral lines of disjunctive poems alone, as often happens when his Thatched Hut period is discussed, is unnecessary, since so many genuinely pastoral poems are available. More important, the practice is misleading, for attention to the contrast between the two reveals the effort it cost Tu Fu to keep his little world intact.

An unexpected glimpse of such effort is revealed in an extreme form in the poem "Floating on the Stream" (106/7/6). The scenes of this twenty-four line narrative poem, in which Tu Fu takes a serene journey by boat from Ch'eng-tu to the Thatched Hut, are extraordinary in their lovingly concrete details. Yet after twenty-three lines in this vein, the twenty-fourth and final line poses a threat of war and negates the image developed at length of a peaceful country life. Nonetheless, it does not seem to be the poet's intention to provide twenty-three lines of pastoral scenes in order to nullify them in one last line. The poem begins with Tu Fu starting home to his village from Ch'eng-tu. Outside the city, the beauty of autumn near and far meets the poet's eyes (lines 5–8). In a shift to a scene reminiscent of European genre paintings, Tu Fu's gift for kindly observation shows us boys playing on the river bank, fishing, catching birds, and picking lotuses, mud everywhere:

> Children play on left and right banks,
> Each one with nets and snares, 10
>
> . . . . . .
>
> They set to scaling their catch right away,
> And don't bother to wash mud off the lotus roots. 14

As his village comes into sight, its welcoming appearance confirms the rightness of his return home:

> My village just so under rosy clouds,
> In each home, the hens already roosting. 16

The moon comes out and frost appears as he covers the last distance (lines 17–18). With lines 19–23, the poet arrives home, and wine is poured ("The cloudy brew has just been drawn," line 23). The reader might now expect a closure focusing on journey's end and arrival home. Instead, an entirely different possibility is opened up by the final line:

> Many are the drum sounds from the city to the east.

These reminders of war are borne on the air from Ch'eng-tu. Ch'iu Chao-ao comments that the drum sounds show that even on returning home, one can find no haven.[18] This is true, but more is involved: the sound of drums surely did not hold off until Tu Fu had arrived home and settled back. It is more as though he finally could not hold tight the circle of peace he had drawn around himself. Earlier in the poem, there

---

18. *Tu shih hsiang-chu* 9.770. P'u Ch'i-lung rejects Ch'iu's interpretation, feeling instead that the final line shows Tu Fu delighting in his removal from the concerns of the world (*Tu Tu hsin-chieh*, p. 91).

had been another break when the pleasant sights of boys fishing and picking lotuses rather surprisingly brought on moralistic reflections about the ways of the world:

> People go after what is rare and pretty,
> When one is lowly, things naturally go against one.[19]

A rather strong moral for such a pretty scene, it too intrudes into the recounting of simple country pleasures. Thus one sees that any contentment is hard won and chancily maintained. This is not unknown about Tu Fu, but to illustrate this truth in terms of strong poetic contrasts is another matter.

The development of a different poem, "Leaning on My Staff" (384/ 24/27), appears on the surface to be similar to that of "Floating on the Stream." That is, a final, anguished line breaks in upon descriptions of people and things that are particularly full of life. When taken together with the preceding line, however, this final line seems planned and the contrast intentional. The poem was written during the year Tu Fu spent away from the Thatched Hut to avoid warfare in the Ch'eng-tu area. In the poem, Tu Fu watches the bustle of a small county town: the day market is being cleared away, and boats are congregated on the river. That the day is especially beautiful is emphasized by seagulls and wild geese that are delighting in the water and sky. "Everything is full of life," the poet writes in line 7 – and in line 8, he writes, "Wretched, alone, I remember the years past." It does seem that the whole sense of rightness about the day has been built up to support line 7, which is then used to contrast with line 8.

One final poem is given here to show a variation on the theme of contentment and control in the Thatched Hut period. "On a Boat" (345/21/12) illustrates a reversal of the usual interruption of a peaceful scene by current, turbulent events. Instead, a longing for Ch'ang-an comes at the beginning, but a recovery is then made. The poem opens with homesickness:

> Long a guest in the Southern Capital, plowing southern fields,
> To look northward is painful as I sleep by a northern window.

When day comes, however, "painful" thoughts are quickly set aside, and Tu Fu decides to take his wife out on the boat. A pastoral poem then ensues, providing a pretty picture of the husband and wife in a boat, the children playing ("bathing") in the water, and the contented conclusion that "we don't need Hsieh family jade for our utensils." For Tu Fu, it is

19. Lines 15–16. It seems the reflection is caused by the way the boys move on to the next thing so quickly, discarding as they go.

an unusual recovery from a slide into melancholy. It seems that the entire poem is composed after the poet has already made a recovery in spirits. Note that the opening couplet, despite the melancholy contrast between home and exile, is playful in its wording, for "south" is used twice in the first line and is matched by "north" twice in the second line.

After Tu Fu's departure from his Thatched Hut near Ch'eng-tu, he next lived for two years in K'uei-chou (766–8). The great poems of Tu Fu's last years, centering on the K'uei-chou period but including as well the Hunan wanderings, make up an outstanding body of poems which has been frequently studied.[20] An oblique approach is taken here, which employs the concept of juxtaposition to examine one important motif: what Ch'ang-an came to symbolize in this period. Such an approach may both shed light on juxtaposition and make a contribution to the study of Tu Fu's late poems by analyzing some of their distinctive traits.

Exactly when or why Tu Fu left the relative security of his Thatched Hut is not clear,[21] nor is his destination known from his poetry. To depart by boat, however, had been long planned. Tu Fu had owned a boat for several years, and intermittently he mentioned plans to travel downriver, naming, however, a different destination each time. Certainly the route down the Yangtze presented more opportunities for changes in itinerary than if Tu Fu had retraced the overland route by which he had reached Ch'eng-tu. Tu Fu stopped in several river towns along the Yangtze before he settled in K'uei-chou in the spring of 766, nine or ten months after his departure from Ch'eng-tu. The decision to stop there was probably made because he had found a patron in the local governor. Tu Fu remained in K'uei-chou for two years, until the spring of 768.

K'uei-chou, in the Yangtze Gorges, was not any farther from the capital at Ch'ang-an than Ch'eng-tu had been. Indeed, K'uei-chou was closer, in that it lay on the river route from Ch'eng-tu to Ch'ang-an. This is the route that the poet had so happily visualized in "On Hearing of the Recovery of Ho-nan and Ho-pei by Imperial Troops" (763). He planned, he wrote then, to go down through Pa Gorge to Wu Gorge (that is, K'uei-chou), thence to Hsiang-yang and home again. Despite this hopeful

---

20. Most recently by David McGraw, *Du Fu's Laments from the South*.
21. Hung thinks it is "an open question" whether Tu Fu left Ch'eng-tu before or after his patron Yen Wu's death in the fourth month of 765 (*Tu Fu*, p. 216). He refutes the evidence on which the two T'ang histories base their statements that Tu Fu was still in Ch'eng-tu after Yen's death (*Notes*, p. 97), for they depend heavily on the fantastical anecdotes about Yen Wu and Tu Fu which Hung has rejected as fabrications. Hung, however, does not suggest why Tu Fu would have left if he had had a reliable patron in Yen Wu.

itinerary, Tu Fu's present removal to K'uei-chou seems to have brought to the fore a sense of geographic isolation from the capital. Perhaps it represented one more change in a life already made formless with uncertainties. Once in K'uei-chou, geography becomes a poignant symbol for Tu Fu's obsessions. He continued to plan a return to the Central Plains, but with the passage of years came the unavoidable knowledge that "at autumn equinox, this traveler is still here" 秋分客尚在 and that "every year, at the solstice, I am still a traveler" 年年至日常為客.[22]

Ch'ang-an acquired an antonym in K'uei-chou, in whose striking landscape the poet was held a spiritual prisoner. He was not insensible of the strange beauty of his surroundings, for, as he wrote, "It is lonely to be far from home, / But how rare to see such mountains and rivers."[23] Given the circumstances, however, the symbolic polarity is also a natural one, but the polarity itself is new in the K'uei-chou poetry, as are the ways it is manifested in the poems. The familiar unattainable goals of service to the state, peace and good administration, and memory of the past – all come to be focused on and symbolized by the capital at Ch'ang-an. "My native country in peace is always in my thoughts" 故國平居有所思, Tu Fu writes in "Autumn Meditations."[24] The opposite motifs, too, are focused upon Ch'ang-an: the still-unvanquished rebels, the still insubordinate generals, the still stumbling imperial advisers. Ch'ang-an and K'uei-chou, the unattainable and the present reality, each comes to depend on the other for definition. In this intricate intertwining, we seem to see that on some level the poet has accepted that a return to the Central Plains was unlikely. This is another example of the way in which a recurrent theme is, in the K'uei-chou period, treated in increasingly metaphoric and imagistic ways.

Geography had earlier been a part of Tu Fu's poems while he was in the Ch'eng-tu region. In particular, Sword Pass and the high mountain roads that separate the Szechuan basin from the Central Plains often figure in the poet's longing for a return. Thus from the Ch'eng-tu years, we find a line like "The long road here – a heavy heart grieves over Sword Pass" and from Kung-an, "Old gardens cut off by green mountains."[25] In K'uei-chou, the longing is also directed toward Ch'ang-an:

> Wu Gorge here outside Shu River,
> The Ch'in city by the North Star.[26]

22. Line 7 of "Late Clearing," 449/29/14, and line 1 of "Winter Solstice," 515/32/41.
23. "River Village in the Ninth Month," 500/31/52, lines 7–8.
24. "Autumn Meditations," (467/30/32), poem 4, line 8.
25. "An Old Country Man," 346/26/17, line 5. "Presented to the Deputy Administrator Yü Fifteenth," 536/34/21, line 20.
26. "The Ch'in city" refers to Ch'ang-an, anciently the site of the capital of the state of Ch'in. "Year after Year," 462/30/13, lines 5–6.

New in the K'uei-chou poems, however, is the poet's investment of significance in his location simply because it is half of a polarity. He needs that polarity, for K'uei-chou is the only grasp he now has on something whose other end is slipping away. "The way is obscured – Where lies the Three-Ch'in land?", he asks.[27] The set "Autumn Meditations" perhaps most famously employs this contrast as a basic pattern.

Sometimes the polarity is simply expressed. The poet is in one place, his thoughts in another. His gaze traces the line joining the two ends of the polarity and travels where he cannot:

> On a solitary K'uei-chou, the setting sun slants,
> I always turn to the north Star to gaze toward the capital.

Of the moon seen in Wu Gorge, he writes, "I think of it shining in West Ch'in."[28]

More complex are lines in which scenes from the past insistently rise up before the poet and disturb his present concentration:

> In Wu Gorge, I suddenly seem to be gazing at Mount Hua,
> In Shu River, I appear to see Yellow River.[29]

The overlay of inner and outer visions – Mount Hua superimposed on Wu Gorge, and the Yellow River on the Shu River – perfectly expresses Tu Fu's inability to put aside his longing for everything that is never to be again. The double vision, their inseparability imagistically so well evoked, is what makes the visionary author of the great K'uei-chou poems. The poet, weighted down by circumstances, has a soaring, space-traversing imagination. This magnificent achievement should be contrasted, on the one hand, with the abrupt displacement of present reality by the inner eye that we find in juxtaposition and, on the other hand, with the sharp and concrete clarity that we find in Tu Fu's poems of realism.

The polarity between Ch'ang-an and K'uei-chou finds many different expressions, for, as is common in Tu Fu's poetry, the same elements combine in more than one way. Of interest here is what can be learned from its occurrence in juxtaposition poems. We shall examine as an example the poem "Written on a Boat during the Small Cold Food Festival."[30] In this poem in seven-character regulated verse, written in the

27. Line 8 of "Winter Solstice," 515/32/41.
28. "Autumn Meditations," poem 2, 467/30/32B, lines 1–2, and "The Moon," poem 1, 431/28/13A, line 1.
29. "Taking in the Gorge Scenery," 448/29/10, lines 3–4.
30. 562/36/20. Small Cold Food Festival is the second (some say the third) of the three fireless (hence Cold Food) days of the festival. They come on the one hundred and fourth to sixth days after the winter solstice and are usually marked by family reunions and ancestor worship.

last year of Tu Fu's life, Ch'ang-an is again the antonym of his exile, now in T'an-chou. The mention of Ch'ang-an in the last line is only the last of several disjunctions in the poem.

Written on a Boat during the Small Cold Food Festival

A lovely morning, I force myself to drink a little, the food still cold,
By this table, I feel melancholy, wearing my hermit's cap,
With the spring water, the boat seems sitting in the sky,
In old age, flowers are seen as through a fog,
Flecks of grace, playful butterflies pass these parted curtains,
Curves of white, light gulls ride the rapid currents.
Clouds are white and mountains green, three thousand miles,
Heavy-hearted I look – straight north is Ch'ang-an.

Ch'ang-an is called into sudden existence, defined by a straight line from the poet's unswerving heart. His intent, arrowlike, finds the shortest distance to its goal. "Straight north," Tu Fu wrote earlier, in the fourth poem of "Autumn Meditations": "Straight north, beyond the passes, sounds of gongs and drums."

"Small Cold Food Festival" presents an interesting problem of poetic unity, for a number of reasons. The images of lines 3 and 4, which manage to be simultaneously clever and bold, seem to turn the poem toward phrasemaking, whereas the suddenness of line 8 seems wholly sincere. A complicating factor is that both sets of lines, the self-conscious and the sincere (lines 3–4 and 7–8), echo lines from the poet Shen Ch'üan-ch'i (d. ca. 713).[31] Tu Fu has a special feeling for Shen Ch'üan-ch'i: Tu Fu's grandfather, Tu Shen-yen, had moved in the same circles as Shen Ch'üan-ch'i and had exchanged a number of poems with him. Quotation is not unusual, of course, and quotation from a family connection is that much more interesting. The question is whether the marked difference in tone between these lines is bridged by their shared borrowing, and, if that is the case, whether the evident feeling of line 8 is compromised by its allusive link to a middle couplet so notably arch.

The poem seems fractured by its changing intentions. It begins with the type of circumstantial reality customary in the occasional poem: that

31. Huang T'ing-chien pointed out that line 3 is based on an image that Shen Ch'üan-ch'i was fond of. Shen wrote, "The boat seems sitting in the sky, / People seem walking in a mirror," and, pleased with his invention, he used it again: "The boat seems sitting in the sky, / Fish seem suspended in a mirror." The model for lines 7 and 8 is more problematic: many critics point out that the last line imitates one, also in a final position, in a poem addressed by Shen Ch'üan-ch'i to Tu Fu's grandfather, Tu Shen-yen. The line is not abrupt, but it is equally effective. This last Shen Ch'üan-ch'i poem is in *Ch'üan T'ang shih* 96.1043. The issue is laid out in Hu Tzu, *T'iao-hsi yü-yin shih-hua, ch'ien-chi,* 6.33.

is, the poet appears as himself, and we learn that it is Small Cold Food Day and that he is a semi-invalid, cosseting himself and a bit self-pitying. It ends with a return, on a higher level, to that circumstantiality: now his view is wider, he looks outward to the distant view of mountains and clouds, which leads his thoughts farther on to Ch'ang-an. It is clear that his worries are now not for himself alone. Quietly, implicitly, Tu Fu has brought his whole world into the poem. Between the opening and closing couplets lie four lines that describe the spring scene, reminiscent of the middle couplets of "Serpentine." The movement from what is near at hand, in the middle couplets, to a wider view in the final couplet is a progression that is commonly made in lyric poems, but the greater than normal disparity here leaves the reader with little guidance concerning, particularly, the final line. On the one hand, lines 3 and 4 are more consciously clever than usual – compare them to lines 5 and 6, for example – and on the other hand, line 8 is more striking than usual. The lifted, wider gaze of line 7 does prepare us for a larger perspective to come, especially in the wonderful shift in midline from visible mountains to mountains and clouds that are beyond one's sight, extending for "three thousand miles." Even so, line 8 represents an unexpected turn, for the poet's gaze changes from an open, steady look that takes in everything to a focused, unseeing gaze that has eliminated everything merely visible. After a number of changes of tone (indicating, it seems, changes of mind about the poem's purpose), in line 8 all ordinary concerns drop away, displaced by Ch'ang-an.

A similar unexpected shift to a wider view in the last line is found in another K'uei-chou poem, "Bound Chickens" (186/13/13), and makes an interesting comparison. In this famous poem, the subject close at hand provides another example of Tu Fu's genius for creating poetry out of the most trivial of household incidents. In "Bound Chickens," he simply changes his mind about selling some chickens. At the end of the poem, the shift to a wider gaze takes in the Yangtze River rather than distant Ch'ang-an, but the suddenness in the change of perspective is similar to that in "Small Cold Food Festival."

> The little slave has bound the chickens for the market,
> And the chickens, bound up, struggle and squawk,
> My family is tired of the chickens eating up ants,
> But forget that selling chickens off means having them cooked.
> Ants and chickens, to which is man more beholden?
> I have the slave untie their bindings,
> The respective merits of chickens and ants cannot be judged –
> My gaze pauses on the cold river, as I lean against our mountain building.

The poet is touched by the chickens' noisy struggle and, acting on his sympathy, extended Buddhistically to all creatures, he reprieves the chickens. Perhaps it is the sympathy of someone who chances to encounter one of the cruelties that is otherwise routinely carried out on his behalf. At any rate, he has them released.

The unusual in this poem should be distinguished from the unexpected. The first unusual element is, of course, the topic itself, whose humbleness has kept it from entering poetry until Tu Fu's open, unjudging attention rendered it visible. Unusual also is the extreme advantage taken of the leeway in old-style verse to repeat words. Notably, "chickens" is used six times in the eight lines, while other repetitions include "bind up" "bindings" (both *fu*), used three times, and "ants," also used three times. Clearly, verbal fun as well as plain narrative is present. The unexpected element – the final line – is more difficult to pin down. Tu Fu, having made an intervention, now searches for the principles that have led him to act as he did. He finds the knotty ethics of the human treatment of creatures to be insoluble, but he comes to the opposite conclusion from his family, with the difference that he has first considered the claims of both chickens and ants. The last line, then, may be read as an indirect response to his dilemma. As the Ming-dynasty critic Hung Mai puts it, "imagery reaches where discourse cannot."[32]

Toward the end of Tu Fu's life, after his departure from K'uei-chou, juxtaposition gives way to and then deteriorates into disorganization. Tu Fu had always employed swift, frequent changes in tone, even in the early years, but now many poems seem barely structured. From the early years, "Ballad of Mei-p'i Lake" (27/2/6), a poem that like "Song of Lo-yu Park" predates the Troubles, shows rapid, perplexing changes in language that cannot be explained away by the dramatic, changeable weather encountered on the poet's excursion to Mei-p'i Lake. The source of changeability is in the poet. Indeed, as Tu Fu notes in the poem's final line, "Always, such a plenitude of joys and sorrows" 向來哀樂何其多. With the prolongation of the An Lu-shan rebellion, the continuing uncertainty of life causes him to review recent events more and more frequently. Some of these reflections are far from systematic. "Sent to be Inscribed on the Thatched Hut by the River" (122/8/1), composed when he had fled from a local rebellion to Tzu-chou, seems jottings rather than a poem with a sequential development. Later still, in 766, we have the two poems "Living as a Sojourner" (151/11/9) and

32. Hung Mai, quoted in Ch'iu Chao-ao, *Tu shih hsiang-chu* 18.1566.

"Sojourn in the Thatched Hut" (151/11/10) written when illness detained him for some months in the river town of Yun-an (after which he settled in K'uei-chou). Each covers a number of topics, starting from the traveler's environs, moving on to the state of the empire, back to Tu Fu's own circumstances, and on to wider thoughts again. The shifts in moods and thought seem a direct reflection of what might have existed in life, quite unmediated by the exigencies of putting brush to paper.

These examples from earlier times notwithstanding, disorganization invades many more poems in the last two years of his life. In these years, nearly every plan for finding a patron failed, and local rebellions drove Tu Fu from place to place along the Hsiang River. Two years earlier, in K'uei-chou, a function of poetry that assumed importance was the use of poetry to record the daily chores of the poet's life, from raising chickens to supervising the laying of water pipes. In a way, the disintegrating poems of the Hu-nan years constitute a continuation of that function. Whereas the settled life of K'uei-chou produced warm portraits of a busy farm and family life, the dwindling hopes along the Hsiang River pass directly into incoherence. The concept of juxtaposition is not really adequate to describe how, in the Hu-nan poems, topics are introduced and soon forgotten, one after another.

A good sample of such poems, intermittent and spasmodic in movement, is found in William Hung's pages on Tu Fu's last years. In his translations, Hung tries to smooth out some of the jerkiness, but the poems' disjunctions remain quite apparent. "My Feelings" (two poems), "Living on the water, I express my feelings, presented to you gentlemen," and "Entering Heng-chou" are three of several poems of this kind that Hung translates.[33] A brief description of each will amplify my point. "My Feelings," two poems written in Heng-chou in 769 scarcely a year before his death, show the poet ill in Heng-chou and unsure of his plans. Especially in the forty-line second poem, he veers from thought to thought, each thought scarcely sketched out, the whole a portrait of an exhausted mind. "Now old," Tu Fu wrote in another poem from this period, "I cannot fend off worries" 身老不禁愁.[34] "Living on the water" is a strange poem, reciting, to presumably uninterested recipients ("you gentlemen"), each of Tu Fu's various travails and then gratuitously listing his rather uncomplimentary reasons for not paying a personal call on the gentlemen. The poem, which is, inter alia, a begging poem,

33. The translations are found in Hung, *Tu Fu*, as follows: second poem of "My Feelings" (239/15/24), p. 267; "Living on the water, I express my feelings, presented to you gentlemen" (528/34/2), p. 268 (Hung's title is "Staying in the Boat: Presented to the Gentlemen of the City"); and "Entering Heng-chou" (250/16/15), pp. 274–5.
34. "On Departing for Home in Late Autumn," 552/36/4, line 4.

hardly seems designed to obtain from comparative strangers the assistance desired. Contrast this with earlier poems soliciting help, poems that, written under happier circumstances in Ch'eng-tu, seem better attuned to the benefactor's psychology.[35] The third example, "Entering Heng-chou," like "Journey North," is made up of several topics connected by a journey undertaken in trying conditions. Like that poem, the sections are not illogical in themselves, but they belong together only because Tu Fu has determined they should. "Entering Heng-chou" too begins with a survey of the general situation facing the empire. Tu Fu then details the specific local rebellion which has sent him and his family fleeing again. Then he is carried away, for sixteen lines, by the thought that a Prefect Yang of his acquaintance is the very person to organize a force against the rebels. A final sixteen lines sketch an excited and scarcely realistic picture of what he expects life to be like at his destination, under a cousin's patronage. (In the event, no poem survives to indicate that this journey was completed and the cousin found.)

Given the pathos of the final years, it is suitable that juxtaposition, or, to be more exact, the disintegration of even the juxtaposition structure, should characterize the ending of Tu Fu's record of his life. "Thirty-six Rhymes Written on the Boat, in Bed with a Fever, and Presented to Friends and Relatives in Hu-nan" (556/36/12) is possibly his last poem.[36] It is, for this reason, and also because of its content, a sad poem to read. The poem is a restless, disorganized explanation of himself, his hopes, his present predicament, his recent past, his qualifications for office, his various actions; its ending dies out rather than closes. To the sympathetic reader it is extremely moving, but one wonders what the recipients made of it.

The discussion unfolded here under the heading of "Chronology" should not be taken for an attempt to set up a chronology for juxtaposition in Tu Fu's work, for this is not possible. What is possible is the identification of specific juxtaposition traits at the beginning and at the end of Tu Fu's writing life. At the beginning, we see from the example of "Song of Lo-yu Park" that juxtaposition predates the An Lu-shan rebellion, for it occurs without the characteristic content of later juxtaposition poems. At the end, poems from the last two years show an incoherence that takes juxtaposition many steps beyond its identifying trait of abruptness. This is the extent of chronological development that

35. See the poems listed in *Tu Fu nien-p'u*, p. 125, poems by which Tu Fu obtained numerous plantings as well as funds and utensils.
36. Ch'iu Chao-ao's *Tu shih hsiang-chu*, which is chronologically ordered to the extent possible, places this poem in the final position in the entire collection (23.2091). P'u Ch'i-lung concurs (*Tu Tu hsin-chieh*, p. 816), and this is Hung's view as well (*Tu Fu*, p. 278).

is reliably traceable. In the great middle time span, juxtaposition seems to show no correlation with time. This is not surprising when we remember that most of the categories into which Tu Fu's poems are classified are difficult to trace in terms of development over time. (The single major exception is seven-character regulated verse, whose development is soundly established.) Juxtaposition's usefulness lies in its relation to a given other characteristic. The connection with chronology is established indirectly, in that the characteristic may in turn be one commonly associated with particular periods of Tu Fu's life. For the Thatched Hut period, juxtaposition acted as a foil to the pastoral poems. For K'uei-chou and the last two years of wanderings in Hu-nan, it acted as a foil to the finished symmetry of regulated verse.

Even when chronology is not specifically at issue, juxtaposition can usefully function as a foil to alert us to slight changes in authorial moods. It is in this spirit that I conclude this section with an example of a poem that just manages to avoid juxtaposition. In this poem, Tu Fu, as he frequently does, falls into sweeping worries and despair after no very great stimulus. This time, however, other events intervene, and a sequence that might have resulted in juxtaposition is averted. I am thinking of the famous poem "Drunk, I fell from horseback; some friends came to see me, bringing wine" (215/14/2). This poem begins with another bravura show of Tu Fu's command of physical comedy and his disarming ability to make himself a figure of fun. The boisterous poem captures well the momentary return of youthful spirits to an old man as Tu Fu tells how, after getting drunk at a party, he commandeers a horse and careers down a sheer path outside White Emperor City. The horse, given his head, rises to the challenge and picks up speed, and so the rider's fall ends this adventure. Tu Fu's brief fling with bravado brings a rueful reflection: "In life, impulses mostly bring on disgrace" (line 16). "Disgrace" is used lightly, and the tone strikes just the right note of sheepishness.

Tu Fu must add more, however. The next couplet prolongs the lessons of the escapade:

> . . . lying in bed, I worried and despaired,
> What with old age and other vexations.   18

It seems that Tu Fu cannot help it; deeper self-reproach is ever ready to slip in. As he was to write in his last poem, "My high spirits disappeared even as I shook off gloom / Worries rushed in, their flow unchecked."[37] In the poem here, control returns with the next line, through the agency

37. "Thirty-six Lines Written on the Boat," 566/36/12, lines 19–20.

of friends rather than himself. Just as Tu Fu, lying in bed, begins to fret in earnest, friends turn up. Now he tells the story on himself, for everyone's entertainment, his friends drag him off for a consolatory drinking party, and all end up pleasantly inebriated. The low spirits of the quoted couplet is thus subordinated to a jolly visit. Indeed, the momentary break in good spirits would be easy to overlook were it only in this poem. Yet we might note that even in a poem that begins and ends ebulliently, the control is not perfect. The suspicion that, with Tu Fu, low spirits show themselves everywhere and in every period of his life is provided with poetic proof.

Mechanism

Juxtaposition was earlier defined by its end result, its poetic characteristics. Here let us briefly reconsider the mechanism of juxtaposition in terms of its originator, the poet. The pattern by which the poet's personality and changes in mood result in juxtaposition is a recurring one. A poem begins in the usual way, occasioned by a scene or by an event observed; thoughts of family or the state or memories of the past intrude without transition; this is sometimes followed by a turn to a third subject such as the poet himself (his failure to be of use, his declining health). This familiar pattern accounts for the most instances of juxtaposition. Tu Fu himself lays out clearly the basic relationship between poetry and memory in the poem "The First Day of Spring" (419/27/24) written in K'uei-chou in 768.

> A spring day, and a spring dish with delicate fresh greens,
> I suddenly recall the two capitals in their prosperous days,
> White jade dishes of illustrious families made the circuit,
> Food was handed on, fine greens delivered by fragile hands.
> How can the chilly river at Wu Gorge please the eye?
> This traveler, far from Tu-ling, cannot conquer his grief,
> I do not yet know where home is to be,
> I call my son to get paper for a poem.

The steps that take the poet from observation to memory to self-absorption are plainly sketched for us. The scene before Tu Fu is here observed in synecdoche in the fresh greens eaten on the first day of spring, New Year's Day. They cause him to recollect the past, when, in the homes of great families, the first day of spring was observed with due elaborateness. Unusually, in this poem both the act of remembering and the fact that the memory comes unbidden are stated ("suddenly I remembered"), thus removing the element of unexpectedness that identifies juxtaposition. Compared to the sumptuous past called to mind, Wu Gorge before the poet's eyes is but a cold and bleak present. It appears that no ceremony will mark this day in the gorges. Tu Fu names only his despair, and twice he evokes his rootless existence. In line 8, sorrow finds expression through writing. We see that the poet composes on the impulse of the moment, as a relief for his overwhelming feelings. Again, unusually, in calling for paper in the last line, the impulse and the decision to write are explicitly stated. P'u Ch'i-lung criticizes Tu Fu for the explicitness of his final line. A pity, he felt, that it took away from the skillful, building evocation of grief in the poem.[38] Tu Fu is occasionally explicit elsewhere. "So long as an old brush lies in that case," Tu Fu writes in the final couplet of another poem, "I will take it out when emotions surface."[39]

Solipsism

In one way or another, all of Tu Fu's poems project or presume his presence and voice. That voice, that presence, is a vital element of the reader's sense of the uniqueness of Tu Fu's achievement and, by securing the reader's identification with Tu Fu, it has formed a central element in the transmission of his high esteem. It is important, therefore, to examine his portrayal of himself more closely. As expected, the portrayal is complex. Rather than tracing that portrayal in all of its complexity, let us examine it by isolating a single aspect, the trait of solipsism. His tendency to refract all experience through himself, I shall suggest, is an essential trait of Tu Fu's and a source of both his magnificent strengths and mawkish weaknesses. Analysis of the solipsistic depiction of self permits us to identify discrepancies between poetic and personal elements in Tu Fu and allows another glimpse of the intersection between his responses to the world about him and his poetic methods.

Solipsism is a comparatively unappealing trait, and it may seem unfair to apply such a word to a poet with Tu Fu's experience of hardship. Certainly the word carries the unpleasant impression of a bystander's easy judgment. Solipsism must be admitted, however, to be an aspect of Tu Fu's portrayal of himself, even though it is but one aspect of a complex portrayal. It is a fact that solipsistic sentiments can be found in every period of his work, and that it is an especially constant note of the last years. I shall offer examples of its prevalence and explore a number

38. P'u Ch'i-lung, *Tu Tu hsin-chieh*, p. 663.
39. "Living as a Sojourner," 151/11/9, lines 39–40.

of different ways of understanding this recurrent feature. Ultimately, when solipsism's place in Tu Fu's poetry is understood, the harshness of the characterization will be softened.

Solipsism concerns more than a focus on the poet himself. Another face of obsession, it results from the emotion-laden tone with which a poem dwells entirely on the poet, shutting out everything else from focus. "Spring Prospect" is an early example. The poet's view, which has been grand and inclusive –

> The state has fallen, mountains and rivers endure,
> Spring in the city, grasses and woods grow thick

– by poem's end has closed down to "white hair" that

> Soon will not take even a hatpin.

In particular, solipsism emphasizes the poet as sufferer, beset by troubles and scarcely distinguishing between large and small. Small troubles may be found in Tu Fu's frequent portrayals of himself as beaten down by ill health:

> Old and sick, here in Wu Mountains,
> Long detained among Ch'u guests.

"Ill all the years of my life," Tu Fu writes. And on his son's birthday, he writes, "I am tired, the feast begun, / I lean against something, unable to sit up."[40] Yet large public issues leave the poet similarly beset:

> How may battle weapons be stilled?
> My bitter worry – is it not this alone?[41]

Even though Tu Fu says his concern is for others, not himself, yet often his Confucian altruism is solipsistically refracted through his own state of mind. When he asks a neighbor to allow a poor widow to glean dates from his trees, the poem he writes has become famous for its empathy. Characteristically observant, he notices not only the widow's desperation but also her fearfulness and timidity. Yet at the end, when he comes to the cause of the widow's plight, the Troubles, he speaks in terms of his own feelings rather than hers:

> And thinking of the horses of war, tears wet my chest.[42]

40. The poems are "Old and Sick," 412/26/42, lines 1–2; "Climbing to a Height," 411/26/39, line 6; and "Tsung-wu's Birthday," 486/31/1, line 10.
41. "Written in Late Spring on the Wall of a Newly Rented Thatched Hut in West Nang," 425/28/3, poem 1, lines 7–8.
42. "Again Presented to Mr. Wu," 434/28/25, line 8.

Since, in his works as a whole, Tu Fu's is the consciousness which draws together his recurrent themes, it is not surprising that solipsism is one form that the unifying consciousness should take.

At times the poet's extraordinary self-absorption can be useful, for the speaker's unwavering certainty about the importance of what he has to say can successfully sweep his readers into his sorrow-filled world. With no sense of incongruity, Tu Fu can begin a poem like "One Hundred Rhymes" – and the reader can follow him unprotestingly – with a complaint about his diabetes:

> Adrift, alone, another hundred miles,
> Three years already of diabetes.[43]

(This is followed intermittently by further references to his ill health and loss of strength.) To begin a major poetic epistle of two hundred lines on such a note of pathos is, in its way, admirably heroic.

We may understand solipsism as a special case of the continuity of all themes to Tu Fu. One of his many points of originality lies in his ability to join together the large and the small, the public and the personal. The skill in making the conjunction is poetic, but we may speculate that the tendency to do so was personal. The topics that to Tu Fu are interconnected constitute almost the whole of his life. Although, on the surface, second-guessing the court's military appointments might seem a far remove from morose complaints about having to stop drinking, the poems as a whole show that each topic in Tu Fu's work is ultimately joined to every other topic. His health is linked to his recurrent sense of failure, which is linked to his continued desire to be of use to his country, which is linked to the cluster of social and political concerns that underlie his compassion for others. He makes the conjunction himself: "Sighing over the times – my medicine has little effect" 歎時藥力薄.[44] In a sense the interconnectedness is not surprising, for in accumulating experience through a lifetime, a person might well come to see everything as a reminder of something else. Yet, because knowing when to break off such interconnections is also a matter of experience and judgment, perspective is perhaps the most important quality that is missing when solipsism occurs. Tu Fu often does retain perspective, as is evident in his sense of humor, but when he loses perspective solipsism results.

A man repeatedly disappointed even before the An Lu-shan rebellion, Tu Fu endured until the end of his life year after year of false hopes and

---

43. Lines 3–4 of "One Hundred Rhymes Expressing My Feelings on an Autumn Day in K'uei Prefecture," 436/29/3.
44. "Matching Prefect Yüan's 'Ch'ung-ling hsing,'" 154/11/15, line 5.

only temporary security. "Everything is enveloped in war" 萬事干戈裏, he wrote in 764.[45] It is therefore not surprising that his own hardships, his family's well-being, the suffering of the common people, policy recommendations, reminiscence, homesickness, longing for the emperor, fate, and the universe all should present themselves to him with equal importance. Yet to treat them all as equivalent in importance reflects an inability to distinguish among categories of importance.

Tu Fu repeatedly demonstrates that to him all subjects are continuous. We might take again the example of illness. His many references to his illnesses are sometimes just the complaints of an old man, but at other times they form a link to the greater world, an infuriating reminder of how useless he is (never mind that even when well, he had never been called to serve). When Tu Fu treats a malady as just plain illness, he can write the wonderfully resigned poem "Deaf," in which an unsentimental account of his decline concludes with a wry example of it:

> Falling yellow – I am startled by the mountain trees
> And call to my son, asking about the north wind.

An earlier bout of illness is described in a similarly matter-of-fact manner:

> The autumn clearness has eased my breathing,
> Now I can comb my own hair.
> I hated always adjusting the amount of my medicine
> And hadn't had the courtyard swept.[46]

When his illness is linked to larger issues, sometimes pathos results, but other times a sense of tragic limitation is achieved. An example of pathos occurs in the poem "Leaving Kung-an at Dawn" (541/35/1). Written in the year before his death, when he and his family are taking leave of yet another temporary haven, the four lines of the first half bid a lingering farewell to the homely sights and sounds that have so recently become familiar: the watchman's strking of the hours, the neighbors' roosters. In the second half, a melancholy awareness of his merely transcient significance is well conveyed when Tu Fu imagines the shores of Kung-an after his boat's departure:

> Our boat – gone from here, into the vastness –
> Sailing on rivers and lakes with no clear aim.
> We will leave, and in a moment these will be but traces –

No reason to leave, nowhere to go, and no impression left behind – this detached knowledge is rendered with the artistic command of vast physi-

45. "Weary Night," 389/24/47, line 7.
46. "Deaf," 502/32/4, lines 7–8, and "Autumn Clearness," 452/29/23.

cal scale that typifies lyric poetry. It is followed, however, by an unexpected image, which forms the poem's final line:

> Only packages of medicine follow where I go.

The line evokes the poet's frailty by his dependence on medicine, but one cannot help also seeing the actual trail of litter – funny, sad, and incongruous.

When the linkage between illness and larger issues is more consistent, a tone of tragic resignation is achieved. Parallelism helps:

> Old and ill, I keep going south;
> My revered sovereigns – I turn to gaze north.[47]

Tu Fu's helplessness is expressed not only in the words "old and ill" but in the contrast between south and north: the requirements of survival take him in the opposite direction from the requirements of empire.

The joining together of personal and larger themes is a dangerous and difficult kind of continuity to maintain. It is not surprising, then, that in many of the regulated-verse poems cited earlier as examples of juxtaposition, we find personal and public concerns awkwardly placed adjacent to each other. In "Climbing to a Height" (411/26/39), the evocation of a landscape that embodies heroic forces is followed by plaintiveness:

> Hardships and sorrows have turned these temples to frost,
> I am disheartened to have had to stop drinking dark wine.

Solipsism both creates and accentuates juxtaposition, for a sentiment that is integrated into other concerns or other perspectives is less likely to appear solipsistic. Tu Fu's poems are nearly always dense with feeling, but some are overloaded with emotion, and these can now be seen to be both disjointed and solipsistic. The overwrought tone of the final sections of each of the "Eight Laments" constitutes a group of such examples.

The poet's solipsism and the poem's juxtaposition occur together. When the figure of the poet is poetically integrated, the focus on the poet does not strike the reader as self-centeredness. On the contrary, an outstanding feature of Tu Fu's work is that the vital connections of a poem are made by means of the figure of the poet rather than through, say, imagery (as in the poems of Li Shang-yin) or poetic voice (as in that of Wang Wei). "Thoughts while Traveling at Night" is such an example of the centrality of the poet. The first four lines present a night scene of some grandeur and melancholy:

47. "Journey South," 395/25/12, lines 5–6.

> Fine grasses and a light wind on the bank,
> A tall mast, a solitary boat in the night,
> Stars hang down over a vast level plain,
> The moon undulates in the flow of the great River.

The next four focus on the poet, a change that initially causes them to seem juxtaposed and solipsistic:

> Has my name become known through literature?
> My office is resigned due to illness and old age.
> Drifting, drifting, what am I like?
> A gull between heaven and earth.

The presence of the poet is felt differently in the first half from the second half, but it seems to me that this very shift is the essence of the poem's success. The poet appears to be absent from the calm description of lines 1 through 4, but he is not. It is his eye that takes in the grassy bank (in line 1), that withdraws to observe the boat carrying him (in line 2), that looks out onto the vast starry plains (in line 3), and that finally looks near at hand again, into the moon-reflecting waters around him (in line 4). Quietly, intimately, the focus of attention changes in each line, although always at ground level. In the second half of the poem, anguish and desperation break in, unmistakably calling attention to the poet's presence. His strong feelings culminate in a comparison of himself to a gull flying between heaven and earth. The breathtaking beauty of the image has often been noted. Here I will comment only that normally Tu Fu's poems do not have this final resolution but instead leave the reader with his despair.

By convention, endings often bring the poem's focus back to the poet, especially in the case of poems in regulated verse. Although this pattern serves to heighten and refocus the poem, it also provides a great opportunity for solipsism. Accordingly, in endings we can find many examples of lines that dwell entirely on the poet's own predicament. Especially in the late poems, the self-absorption of the ill-used and the labile tears of the convalescent frequently break through in the endings. It is as though the control which guides the aesthetics and development of a poem weakens when the last chance for direct expression is about to slip by. A poem especially worth noting in this connection is "Overnight in Rooms by the River" (487/31/4). The rooms of the title are available to officials, and Tu Fu occasionally stayed there when away from his farms in West Nang and East Nang. This place, overlooking the river, seems to have been conducive to writing, for several of Tu Fu's poems are set there. This poem is in regulated verse with five-syllable lines:

> Dusk light stretches along the mountain path,
> This tall apartment is by the water gate.
> Thin clouds linger by the cliffs,
> A solitary moon tosses in the waves.
> Storks and cranes fly in line silently,
> Jackals and wolves howl in seeking their prey.
> Unable to sleep for thinking of the wars,
> Helpless to set to rights the universe.

"Helpless to set to rights the universe": the last line is more out of scale than usual. The desire, the willingness to take on individual responsibility, is noble, but how out of scale, how risible the final line would be if the reader's identification with Tu Fu were not so intense. The disjunction of the final line is somewhat counterweighted by the parallelism of all four couplets, but compare this with the sentiment of the final line of another poem written in this K'uei-chou river apartment. In that poem, the final line reads, "With a hundred worries, I stand by the veranda"[48] – still the same obsession, but the intensity is lowered to a less abrupt level.

Dwelling on the past is another aspect of Tu Fu's solipsism. Absorption in the past shares with solipsism the qualities of engrossment and distortion. Even before the Troubles, the past had been important to Tu Fu: long poems that recapitulate the events of the recent past are notable in his work well before 756. One of his earliest surviving poems, "Twenty-two Rhymes Presented to Assistant Secretary of the Left, Wei Chi" (1/1/1), dated 748 or 749, devotes half of its lines to a rehearsal of the poet's past in the process of reminding the secretary of his availability for a post. With the Troubles, Tu Fu's recollection of the past becomes involuntary: "Year after year of events from the k'ai-yuan era / Stand clearly right before my eyes."[49] Tu Fu's themes are recurrent, engrossing, and ultimately distorting, and the theme of the past is no exception. A sympathetic reader might say that the hold that the past has over Tu Fu is a measure of the misery of the present and the hopelessness about the future. The exclusion of reality is brought to a solipsistic extreme in "Remembering the Past," poem 2 (116/8/14), where the poet's longing for Ch'ang-an brings about a strongly drawn, patently untrue picture of the past. The nightmare of the present was true enough:

> Could one have imagined a time when a bolt of silk was ten thousand cash,
> And if you had fields for planting, they would be running with blood?

48. "Rainy View from the Western Apartment," 492/31/22, line 8.
49. "Year after Year," 462/30/13, lines 1–2.

But the idyll of the past was clearly fantasy:

> The peasants' life rivaled in happiness that of court officials.
>
> . . . .
>
> Men plowed, women raised silkworms, all were happy.[50]

More than exaggeration is involved. To write thus shows that, contrary to his usual gift for accuracy, Tu Fu consulted only his desires, not his memories, and surely not his experience.

Tu Fu's frequent focus on himself is likely a consequence of using himself as the example of human suffering caused by the Troubles. This is confirmed by the structural interchangeability of Tu Fu's twin concerns of state and self. Each is as likely as the other to appear as the juxtaposed element in a disjoint poem. P'u Ch'i-lung makes a similar observation:

A poem may originally be about himself, and then suddenly in the middle it is about affairs of state, or else the situation at court will crop up at the end. Is this muddled and unstructured? Not in the case of Tu Fu. . . . [These two poems show that] for Tu Fu, lament for the state equals lament for the self.[51]

The truth and the absurdity of this equation give us a sense of the delicate line Tu Fu must walk. Conversely, that he is often not interested in preserving the balance tells us much about both his attitude toward himself and his attitude toward poetry. When Tu Fu is completely subjective, he is not free from a lachrymose self-pity. At the same time, he seems peculiarly indifferent to the sorry picture of himself that he is presenting. That self-centered figure refuses to fade into the omniscient poetic voice, meditating on all before him, that is familiar from the acclaimed poems such as "Autumn Meditations." Rather, it often appears that neither aesthetics nor amour propre is foremost with Tu Fu. In poetic terms, all *are* brought before Tu Fu with equal importance.

When the poet so frankly and so repeatedly places himself, one way or another, at the center of almost every poem, reader identification is a necessary first step in order to empathize with his approach. Collections of remarks on poetry echo with the voices of readers who both identified with the pathos of Tu Fu's situation and admired the obduracy of his dedication. It seems that whatever one's initial stance, in the end the constant reader of Tu Fu is brought to acknowledge the essential need for admiration and identification in order to read his poems.

50. "Remembering the Past," poem 2, 116/8/4B, lines 13–14 and lines 2 and 8.
51. P'u Ch'i-lung, in *Tu Tu hsin-chieh*, under the prefatory material "Tu Fu t'i-kang," pp. 62–3. The two poems P'u refers to are "Hating to Part" (349/21/27) and "After a lengthy stay in K'uei Prefecture, I leave White Emperor City by boat" (523/33/10).

As Tu Fu wrote, seeking to explain himself to his sons, "In my unsettled life, I have seen many changes, / And things of sorrow deepened with the years."[52]

Coda

To conclude the discussion of juxtaposition, let us consider what it can contribute to our understanding of Tu Fu's views on his own writing. Tu Fu often commented on what writing meant to him, sometimes lightly, sometimes seriously, and sometimes with a tone which is hard to pin down precisely. Naturally, the lines and couplets in which he made his comments are much studied, usually with the relevant lines singled out for examination. In taking up the topic anew at this point, I hope that the restoration of context, particularly structural context, will add insights to those derived from an examination of the lines alone. I shall analyze here "Incidentally Penned" (476/30/44), which is, at forty-four lines, the longest expression of Tu Fu's views on writing.

"Incidentally Penned," probably written in 767, is famous for the much-quoted opening passage of twenty lines in which Tu Fu explains his view of the development of poetry and names the writers whom he admires and has taken as his models. There is much that is suggestive in this compressed account of twenty lines. Besides naming names and plumbing for a Confucian lineage, Tu Fu conveys his sense of how a tradition is developed and transmitted. Naturally, so much information issuing directly, if cryptically, from the greatest poet of tradition has attracted much attention. Here I would like to subsume this famous passage into a consideration of the poem as a whole, the twenty lines of the first part together with the remaining twenty-four lines of the poem. The second, slightly longer, section is concerned with the poet's situation in K'uei-chou and does not represent an obvious sequel to the discussion of the poetic tradition. Here is a translation of the twenty-four lines of this second section:

> It stems from feeling, a solace in my driftings,
> As, ensnared by illness, I am displaced again and again,
> In serving the state, I am ashamed of my plans,
> In my flights perched for the moment on a branch.   24
> This dust and sand are bordered by wasps and scorpions
> This River gorge aswirl with serpents and crocodiles.[53]

52. "Another Poem Shown to My Two Sons," 423/27/38, lines 3–4.
53. All four unpleasant creatures are common symbols for elements in the political world. The poet means that there has been no respite from troubles and unrest (*Chiu-chia*).

Desolate – the sage-kings T'ang and Yü are ever distant,
And the fierce rivalries of Ch'u and Han cease not.   28
A wise court, but still the bandits and rebels,
Among alien customs, ever more a noisy chatter.
Buried are the Morning Star swords,
Dark are the dragons in overcast, rainy lakes.   32
The two capitals have set up military headquarters,
And from ten thousand homes, army flags fly.
In the south, remnants of a bronze pillar;[54]
Blown eastward, all flee from the Yueh-ch'ih.[55]   36
Here the crows and magpies bring no letters,
Strange are the wrathful cries of bear.
Farming interrupts when inspiration comes,
A poor household, we learn from the natives.   40
Among mountains of the past lies White Tower Peak,
In autumn waters, the memory of Imperial Lake;
I dare not demand great lines of myself,
When worries come, I sing of separation.   44

The organization of these twenty-four lines deserves separate consideration before we analyze the poem as a whole. Let us consider first those elements that are familiar from earlier analyses of other poems. There is the familiar pairing of Ch'ang-an with K'uei-chou, in lines 29 and 30, here as parallel situations: both the court and the poet are forced to accept alien surroundings. There is also the familiar way in which unshakable memories of Ch'ang-an are rendered through overlaid images, in lines 41 and 42. (Both White Tower Peak and Imperial Lake of these lines had figured in poems from happier days.[56]) Finally, the large middle portion, lines 27 throught 36, is vintage Tu Fu. In these ten lines, he again frets about the current state of events and goes over familiar elements: the elusiveness of peace (such as had existed during Antiquity with T'ang Yao and Yü Shun), and the unceasing contentions for the empire (as had prevailed between Ch'u and Han) (lines 27–8); Ch'ang-an's political compromises and K'uei-chou's personal makeshifts (lines 29–30); talents unemployed by the court (lines 31–2, swords and dragons standing in for great men); the current disposition of forces in

54. A bronze pillar was set up by General Ma Yuan of the Later Han dynasty to commemorate his victories in the south. Its deterioration betokens the loss of imperial control in the south.
55. Yueh-ch'ih, Han-dynasty enemies, here stand in for T'ang enemies, probably Tibetans. A difficult line, primarily because "east wind" seems to lack a specific referent.
56. Of the former, Tu Fu wrote, "Upside down is the image of White Tower Peak" ("Southwest Terrace at Mei-p'i Lake," 28/2/7, line 10), and of the latter, he wrote, "Thin clouds over Ts'ui-wei Temple, / The sky is clear over Imperial Lake" ("Another Visit to General He," 285/18/20B, lines 5–6).

the empire (lines 33–4); and the continual flareups of rebellion in the south and west (lines 35–6).

It is both before and after this middle portion that Tu Fu directly explains the role of his poetry in his life (lines 21–2 and 39–44). The two explanations differ in emphasis and in length. In the first, a couplet, he says that poetry is a solace, especially now that he finds himself always useless and rootless. In the second, six lines that close the poem, Tu Fu says that the time he needs for farming and other tasks and his recurrent memories of the past have together curbed his ambition. Now, rather than seek outstanding lines, which he had famously declared elsewhere as an ambition, he takes as his subject what is most constant in his life, separation.

What is the internal organization of these twenty-four lines? The intervention of a lengthy survey of contemporary events between two accounts of poetry's place in Tu Fu's life can be seen as a softened version of juxtaposition and provides a similar access to information about the poet. In lines 27 through 36 he again explains (to himself?) the larger circumstances whose incidental result has been to reduce the role of poetry in his life. It is a digression in that it is not required by anything in the poem but rather by the poet's own need to once again conduct a review. At the same time, the digression is not inconsistent with Tu Fu's method of writing. He is constantly taking stock of his situation, and the restatement of all his concerns in connection with the present topic is characteristic. The digression itself illustrates that he cannot put aside his concerns for long. Poetry has become personal and contingent, a "solace," whereas it might have been more, had external events not intervened.

Now let us consider the poem as a whole. As mentioned earlier, the twenty-four lines of the second part do not represent an obvious sequel to the first twenty lines of the poem, which take a lofty overview of the course of poetry. In addition to the digression within the second part, the poem is also disjoint between its two parts. It seems that poetry is the main subject of the poem. Tu Fu begins with it; in what might be seen as a second beginning, he comes back to it (line 21); and he ends with it. Yet the poem seems curiously diffuse. One problem is its tone. Why is the first section on poetry so abstract and the next so personal? A lengthy section of incidental, reflective lines is prefaced by a ringing and magisterial survey of poetry: how is the reader to make the transition? Another problem is the logic. What is the connection between the lofty overview of poetry and the more stopgap role that Tu Fu says he now assigns to poetry in his life? William Hung suggests that the reason is "his modest estimate of his own place"[57] in the poetic tradition. Tu Fu is indeed modest in this poem, but does that account for the discrepancy? After all, he opened by stating that even though literature transcended the limits of an individual's lifetime, an individual had the vital role of endowing it with value: "Literature is a thing of the ages / Whose successes and failures the attentive heart knows" (lines 1–2).

In answering these questions, we may begin from the poem's title. "Incidentally Penned" is a casual title indeed, and, as Hung notes, "rather colorless" for a poem that gives a "comprehensive view of the history of poetry in China."[58] If we suppose, however, that the title expressed exactly the author's mood, then we may shift our sense of the poem to accommodate that hint. Since the title indicates a collection of possibly unordered thoughts, we may immediately acknowledge that the poem's structure and content are unconstrained by poetic or aesthetic conventions. Its eclectic subject matter and lengthy disquisition seem to show that what the poet wants or needs to say has been the strongest guide to the contents. More specifically, we might consider the second part the focus of the poem and adjust the first part to it in some manner. After all, the title especially suits the second part, whose twenty-four lines wander from one subject to another. If we see this part as kept within the frame of the poem by the title, then paradoxically it is the more striking and more structurally coherent first part that requires justification.

What does poetry mean to Tu Fu? Typically with him, the answer is compounded of elements he has made peculiarly his own. Although Tu Fu says that he has scaled down his ambitions, his attitude to writing is still not a simple one. Twenty lines of poetic tradition are offset by twenty-four lines of what poetry comes down to in an individual case. Furthermore, despite a body of work of extraordinary variety, Tu Fu here confines himself to poetry as a "solace." Even while he declares that many things must now come before poetry, Tu Fu demonstrates that poetry is ever-present by his lingering consideration of it. The second part of the poem amounts to a renunciation of the tradition for which he has just sketched a history, and also a renunciation of the poetic craft which he elsewhere proudly brandished ("I dare not demand great lines of myself," line 43). The poetic tradition is segregated in the first twenty lines, while the untidy nature of an individual life is sketched point by point in the second part. A stronger connection than adjacency is not implied.

57. Hung, *Tu Fu*, p. 241.
58. Ibid. The poem is translated on pages 248–9, under the title "Just a Note."

It does not, however, seem fanciful to see in this adjacency an analogue to Tu Fu's general poetic approach. The complex, somewhat inconsistent, role in the poetic tradition that he locates for himself in the structural arrangement of this poem is reflected in his poetic works as a whole. On the one hand, the many masterly poems in his collection have more than earned him a place within the tradition so authoritatively delineated in the first part of "Incidentally Penned." Yet, in spite of his expressed veneration for this tradition, he set out in his own direction and wrote many poems that defied existing classifications. To take a general example of his innovations, in the juxtaposition poems he wrote many poems whose structure and aesthetics even now do not lie wholly within articulated conventions. In the poem here, "Incidentally Penned," this contradiction is manifested in a first part that states his desire to emulate the spirit of great predecessors and a second part that chooses an independence masked by its framing sentiments of regret.

Tu Fu wrote so much that one wonders about the compelling forces that lay behind his writing. Yet he delivered no comprehensive statement. In what he did say, as here, he tended to confine his reasons to a personal level – poetry as "solace," as a means of relief "when worries come" – while ascribing the principles to tradition. In a sense, not only his poetry but his whole life was conducted in silent adjacency to established traditions. As his writings were to the literary world, so were his ambitions to the affairs of state: they made no contemporary impression. In his poetry, as in his avowals of concern for the state, he persisted despite the apparent irrelevance of his efforts.

In "Incidentally Penned," as in the other poems analyzed in this chapter, the unacknowledged contradiction between tradition and invention contributes to the diverse richness of Tu Fu's poetry and to the difficulty of generalizing about it in poetic terms. Against the somewhat fissured nature of the poetic oeuvre, the figure of the poet, by reason of its constancy, takes on increased importance. The impassioned conjunction of moral temper and human content that is Tu Fu's unique contribution is manifested in multiple ways in the poetry but embodied with clarity in the figure of the poet. Thus, whereas the poetry is difficult to summarize, the figure of the poet is not. Its great explanatory power, instigated by the poetry and augmented by the poetry's reception, has brought upon it the function of unifying his work. This is yet another manifestation of the dual cultural and poetic legacies of Tu Fu.

Conclusion:
Sincerity reconsidered

The idea that "sincerity" is an essential quality of the lyric poem is a staple of traditional literary criticism which predates the time of Tu Fu. As used in the appreciation of Tu Fu, where sincerity is stressed as one of the excellencies of his poetry, the concept may be thought to have acquired a new theoretical importance. From being an essential quality of worthwhile poetry, sincerity evolved into a standard by which worthwhile poetry may be recognized. Applied with equal frequency to both his personal character and his poetry, it has extended its influence further into Tu Fu criticism by becoming the rationale for holding Tu Fu to be unique. "Sincerity" is the quality that has especially seemed to literary critics to justify his claim to uniqueness. The identification of sincerity as the salient characteristic of his character and his poems both reinforces and is reinforced by Tu Fu's position at the pinnacle of the poetic tradition. In this concluding chapter, we shall explore the dynamics of appreciation whereby sincerity both summarizes the traditional characterization of Tu Fu's poetry and has also placed that poetry beyond literary evaluation.

In seeking to avoid conflating appreciation of the poet with appreciating of his work, I have made distinctions between the poet and the poetry by devising neutral equivalents for traditional critical terms. Tradition, however, has favored their conflation. The dominance of critical terms which conjoin the person and work reflects a very long tradition of ad hominem interpretations of his poetry that dates back to the Sung dynasty. This brief concluding chapter examines the useful conflation of poet and writing in a central tenet of traditional interpretation, that of sincerity.

Tu Fu himself repeatedly emphasizes that his writing is almost compelled from him by the force of his feelings. Certainly the vehemence with which his feelings frequently burst out testifies to a fundamental lack of artifice. In reexamining the critical tradition of sincerity as a standard of excellence in the poetry, I shall briefly consider three points: the historical role assigned to the idea of sincerity; its identification with Tu Fu and his work; and its connection with the tenet that Tu Fu is unique.

Before considering these points, however, we should notice that in the traditional criticism two different arguments have been used, apparently interchangeably, to demonstrate that Tu Fu writes sincerely and that his poetry speaks sincerely. Only one of these strikes us as logical today. I can illustrate these arguments in the following two sentences. (Notice that the second sentence uses the same ideas as the first, but with their order reversed.)

Tu Fu's poems very often touch upon contemporary events, and thus we know that all his life he was concerned about his country.

All his life Tu Fu was concerned about his country, and thus his poems very often touch upon contemporary events.

In the first statement, the conclusion that Tu Fu was concerned about his country is derived from evidence accumulated from details in the poems. To be sure, such evidence is not difficult to compile. After all, its plenitude is the reason Tu Fu's sincerity, his love of country, and his poems are such clichés of criticism. Nonetheless, though evidence is easy to come by, one must note the methodology: the statement makes a deduction from the poetry to the person. His poetry being our only primary source of information about Tu Fu's life, this is a procedure whose logic critics today would largely still support. (Objections have indeed been raised, on epistemological grounds, to the use of this approach. Deconstructionists, for example, assert the inherent unknowability of work, poet, or person, thus invalidating any chain of connection among them, but it may be doubted that such fundamental uncertainty obtains in the case of Chinese lyric poetry.)

The second statement, by contrast, is less easy to regard as reasonable. To begin by assuming that we know what kind of person Tu Fu is, when in fact our only information comes from the poems, and then to use this knowledge to explain the poems: this cannot but strike one as circular reasoning. Even within the context of Chinese lyric poetry, which we know, from anecdotes as well as from theory, has traditionally been regarded as an undisguised expression of the self – even within this context, the logic is circular. Yet, in general, remarks on Tu Fu have treated the two lines of reasoning as interchangeable. This fact is in itself informative about traditional attitudes toward the poet.

The second, less logical, sentence is quoted from the "General Rules" which introduce Yang Lun's edition of Tu Fu's poetry.[1] The first sentence is simply my reversal of Yang Lun's. There is, of course, the possibility that Yang Lun's arrangement of clauses is simply a case of careless phrasing. But if so, carelessness is possible because no real difference is perceived between the two ideas. In traditional criticism of Tu Fu, the second statement is made at least as often as the first. To understand Tu Fu criticism, it is important to recognize that many critics have found it unnecessary to make any distinction between the proposition that poems reveal the person and the proposition that the person explains the poems. Even contemporary critics express these sentiments and the same circular logic. This comment, written in 1985, is not exceptional: "Poetry comes out of the person. There was first the person of Tu Fu, and then there was the poetry of Tu Fu. [Conversely,] when reading the poetry of Tu Fu, the deepest intentions of Tu Fu may be discerned."[2]

In the critical comments that I shall quote in the following discussion, both lines of reasoning occur indiscriminately. The crucial difference between them having been noted here, I shall pass over this distinction in silence. (If still uncomfortable with these comments, today's readers will find that often a simple reversal of cause and effect will produce a process of deduction more suited to our modern sense of logic.) The critical sources that I quote do not use a uniform term for the concept I call "sincerity." Various terms are used, such as *ch'eng* (誠), *hsin* as an adverb (心 "from the heart"), and *hsueh* as an adverb (血, as in "[written] with blood"). "A tear in every word" (一字一淚) is another frequently used phrase.

The first point of discussion concerns the historical role assigned to the idea of sincerity. It is a large topic, and early invocations of sincerity in Chinese literary criticism are considered here only in order to emphasize that an ancient theme has been applied to the criticism of Tu Fu. For its early manifestations, Confucius and Mencius are most often quoted, necessarily with the original contexts of the statements somewhat altered. Confucius's remarks pertain to words in general rather than specifically to poetry. For example, he said, "The man of perfect virtue [*jen*] is cautious and slow in his speech."[3] With this comment, Confucius is answering once again his disciples' repeated questions on how to recognize the then-novel quality of *jen*. The correspondence that he

---

1. "General Rules," item 3, *Tu shih ching-ch'üan*, p. 11.
2. Ch'en Wei, *Tu Fu shih-hsueh t'an wei*, p. 42.
3. *Lün-yu* 12.3; translation by James Legge, *Confucius*, pp. 251–2.

finds between inward worth and outward manifestation is a direct one. Since "speech" can embrace literary expression, the authority of Confucius can be invoked concerning this fundamental tenet of literary criticism. In a similar vein, Mencius mentions literature as one of the ways by which one may know a man: "Once we chant his poetry and read his books – is it possible not to know his person?"[4] Poetry, it seems, provides a means by which one may judge a person. This utilitarian view of poetry reflects the concern of both Confucius and Mencius with the connection between the interior life and its outward manifestation. Poetry is (merely) a vehicle. Worthwhile poetry indicates a worthwhile man.

In the first century B.C., the "Great Preface" to the *Classic of Poetry* extended this thought in several ways. Its famous definition of poetry included the all-important attribute of directness or lack of artifice. "In the heart, it is intention," the Preface stated, "Expressed in words, it is poetry." Its description of how one gets from intention to poetry is one of unimpeded progression: as feelings gather force, their outward expression moves from words to sighs to chanting (poetry) to dance.

The "Great Preface" also established early on the content of what is thus expressed with so little impediment. Unsurprisingly, the content is not freely chosen from what lies in the heart but instead emphasizes affairs of state. In its bold definition of poetry – "In the heart, it is intentions; expressed in words, it is poetry" – the word "intentions" (*chih* 志) comes from the world of manly ambitions and public life. In this manner, well before the appearance of lyric poetry, the cultural bias was established that Tu Fu's iconic status was later to exploit so fully. In a later section of the "Great Preface," the assumption is made again that personal sentiment relates to one's public role rather than one's private life: "When the affairs of a state are tied to the feelings of a person – then the type of poetry known as *feng* results." In fact, *feng* poems, which make up the first section of the anthology *The Classic of Poetry*, are the only poems in the classic whose intentions are *not* obviously or predominantly public, for it contains many love poems and poems on seasonal folk rituals. In characterizing *feng* poems as an outcome of the speaker's concern about the state, therefore, the "Great Preface" makes an early appropriation of all poetry for the state. An early link is thus declared between direct expression and the poet's concern about the state.

Since in practice poetic expression was immediately encumbered by considerations of effectiveness and artistry, subsequent theorists of poetry have had to reconcile the contradiction between poetry's sup-

4. *Mencius* 5B.8.

posedly spontaneous production and their awareness of the actuality of composition. Aesthetic goals, too, may require extensive revision and may work against the prior claim of sincere expression. The competing influences then require balancing by theorists. Despite such turns away from the concept of unimpeded expression, theories of poetry retained their predisposition to reserve an important role for directness of expression. Anecdotes showed the same inclination and often emphasized a poem's instantaneous composition. Even anecdotes about a poet revising a poem or a line highlighted the inspired revision that came in a flash. Theorists sometimes debated the source of creation or debated its precise manifestation, but that it was essential was not doubted. "Poetry is the sound of the heart, it may not emerge against the heart; even less, it cannot emerge against the heart" is an often-quoted Ch'ing-dynasty statement[5] that could have been made in almost any century.

Even from this brief discussion, it is evident that comments in Tu Fu criticism concerning sincerity draw upon certain long-standing expectations of poetry. In this sense, the attribution of sincerity to a poet is hardly exclusive to Tu Fu criticism. What is new is the unanimity and frequency with which it is applied to him. This brings us to our second point, namely that the traditional identification of the work with the author's character is consolidated, in Tu Fu's case, to achieve a total identification between the poet and his work. As noted earlier, whether critics begin their remarks with the poet or with the poetry seems mostly a matter of chance. The total and inseparable identity of poet and poetry has had consequences that have permeated nearly all aspects of Tu Fu criticism. The quotations that follow show the critics' frequently expressed conviction of the absolute sincerity of Tu Fu's poems and his personal character.

One manifestation of this conviction is the insistence that the direct expression of feeling is to be found in every line of Tu Fu's. A preface, dated 1225, to the *Chiu-chia* edition of Tu Fu states, "The loyalty of his heart and the righteousness in his breast shone forth in lines and verse."[6] The Ch'ing editor Yang Lun writes, "Not a line does not flow out of genuine feeling."[7] Another common thesis holds that the main source of Tu Fu's greatness is his sincerity. Tu Fu's poetry "greatly surpasses others precisely in its sincerity and in its factualness," writes the Sung Buddhist monk Hui-hung.[8] The best literature, Hui-hung holds, is an unpremeditated overflow of feeling. In a sense he is saying that the best

5. Yeh Hsieh, *Yuan shih.*
6. Preface to *Chiu-chia chi-chu Tu shih*, p. 1.
7. Yang Lun, "General Rules," *Tu shih ching-ch'üan*, p. 14.
8. In *Leng-chai yeh-hua* 3.1. Quoted in Yang Sung-nien, *Chung-kuo ku-tien wen-hsueh*, p. 129.

literature surpasses literature, for he names single examples written by men who are known for accomplishments other than literature: Chu-ke Liang's "Memorial on the Army Setting Out," Liu Ling's "Hymn on the Virtues of Wine," and Li Ling-po's "Declaring My Feelings." (The exception is T'ao Ch'ien, but Hui-hung singles out his "Return," which epitomizes his unbending character, rather than other pieces.) In this company Hui-hung places Tu Fu's complete oeuvre. He is surely conceiving of the poems as a totality, bound together by Tu Fu's personal sincerity.

As one might expect, Tu Fu's sincerity is linked by critics to his concern with social and political issues. P'u Ch'i-lung makes this explicit: "Whenever the poems touch upon people – the sovereign and officials, father and son, brothers, husband and wife, friends – then it all rushes out with heartfelt sincerity."[9] Yang Lun writes similarly: "His loyalty and sincerity came from his innate nature."[10] Shan Fu writes, "His poetry all comes from the sincerity of his love for country."[11] We should note that there are consequences for literary interpretation, for such a stance allows moral significance to permeate everything. Yang Lun demonstrates this type of reasoning: "Thus even a moment such as climbing up to a height and reflecting there, or a minor description of things and events – all these moments have their significance – they are not just written for the writing."[12] Readers of the poetry have embraced this view wholeheartedly, making it difficult to choose any other approach.

Certain poems are often named in this context, especially "Journey North" and "Five Hundred Words." "In the past people had no deliberate intention to compose literary works. They found expression in works only when something had occurred. Thus 'Journey North' straightforwardly records a journey. . . . Its style resembles someone writing a letter home."[13] And, "the most important thing about poetry is that it issues from the innermost heart. 'Five Hundred Words' and 'Journey North' are poems issuing from the innermost heart."[14] Great poetry is brought into existence by the strength of the poet's feelings. Chao I finds this to be true of much of Tu Fu's work, not just of a few frequently cited examples. "Tu Fu," he writes, "was beset with worries all his life, and he used poetry to go on from day to day."[15]

The identification of sincerity with Tu Fu is eminently reasonable. At

9. *Tu Tu hsin-chieh*, Preface, p. 6.
10. *Tu shih ching-ch'üan*, Preface, p. 8.
11. Shan Fu, "Preface," *Tu Fu yü-te*, p. 2.
12. *Tu Tu hsin-chieh*, Preface, p. 6.
13. Ch'iang Yu-an (ca. 1091–1157), *T'ang-tzu hsi-wen lu*, in *Li-tai shih-hua*, 1:447.
14. Wu Ch'iao, *Wei-lu shih-hua* 2.10b–11a.
15. Chao I, *Ou-pei shih-hua* 2.15.

most one might find a point repeated too often or overstated. What needs to be noticed, however, is that precisely because this identification is so strenuously made, it is not innocent of practical consequences. In particular, the important question of poetic evaluation tends to be translated to a moral plane. The process begins by placing Tu Fu in a class by himself, for the extraordinary sincerity emphasized by critics creates for him a unique status. As a corollary, it is widely accepted that ordinary standards do not apply to Tu Fu. This is the third point to be discussed.

Such an attitude, unproblematic for the traditional critic, who was first of all a reader, is more tricky for a modern critic. If a separate standard is to be applied to Tu Fu, he is in effect removed from literary-critical evaluation. Moreover, the separate standard tends to be primarily moral, with literary achievements treated as a necessary complement. Consequently, many issues that would ordinarily be considered important poetic questions are ignored, for the argument is that "ordinarily" does not apply to Tu Fu, and that "important" poetic issues are subordinated when he is the poet in question. When this standard is explicitly applied, it is at least clear; when implicitly and unconsciously accepted, however, as is most often the case, the modern critic is left with little of the needed guidance from tradition.

The Ch'ing-dynasty editor of the poetry, P'u Ch'i-lung, makes explicit his categorical exemption of Tu Fu from literary failings. In his brief list of rules for reading Tu Fu, he includes a significant pointer on this score: "In reading Tu Fu, one has to be patient with awkward lines, hasty lines, extreme lines, blunt lines, unworked lines, clumsy lines – but they do not matter."[16] Earlier Hu Ying-lin had made the same point. He gave examples of lines from Tu Fu that were successively "too clumsy," "too rough," "too plain," and "too daring," but then concludes that "for Tu Fu, this is permissible, but Tu Fu may not be imitated in this."[17] Ch'iu Chao-ao, another great Ch'ing-era editor of the poems, makes a lengthier argument on the same point. As noted earlier,[18] his entire preface is rhetorically structured as an objection to Yuan Chen's and Han Yü's comments on Tu Fu. Their remarks consisted of praise, of course, and very high praise at that, but Ch'iu Chao-ao still objects to them, because "in what Yuan Chen and Han Yü say, no distinction is made between Tu Fu and other poets." That is, Han Yü and Yuan Chen are applying standards to Tu Fu (standards that, incidentally, he passed with flying colors) which can be legitimately applied to other poets. These standards, it turns out,

16. "Pointers in Reading Tu Fu" (Tu Tu t'i-kang), in *Tu Tu hsin-chieh*, p. 63.
17. *Shih sou, nei-pien*, 5.92.
18. See "Tu Fu and the Tradition of Tu Fu" in Chapter 1.

are poetic ones. Ch'iu Chao-ao, however, insists on a separate standard for Tu Fu. Ordinary poetic questions should not arise in Tu Fu criticism. "In discussing the poetry of other people, one may make comparisons as to the skillfullness of diction and line. But Tu Fu's poetry is an exception." Ch'iu Chao-ao prefers instead the pure accolades bestowed by Sung and Ming literati, "poet-historian" and "poet-sage" respectively.[19]

When it comes to the evaluation of particular poems, a critic often exempts a poem from ordinary criticism by appealing to the fact that the author is Tu Fu. Here comments concerning the set of poems "Eight Laments" may be taken as typical of the dynamics at work in practical criticism of Tu Fu's poems. Consisting of lengthy, rambling poems, "Eight Laments" has some obvious faults, but the defense of these poems has been at least as vigorous as the critical remarks. One defense is made by Wang Ssu-shih, who refutes Yeh Shih-lin's criticism that the fifth poem (on Li Yung), eighty lines in length, is repetitious: "This is true if we are discussing poetry. But he seems unaware that with Tu Fu, we cannot employ the same terms."[20] Wang Ssu-shih particularly has in mind the lines in which Tu Fu laments Li Yung's death, which he does several times in the course of the poem. The repeated laments are justified, Wang says, because Tu Fu felt so keenly the pitiful nature of that death. This is a curious argument to make, when the repetitions in fact are easily justified poetically as segment markers: each occurs at the end of a segment within the poem. Wang prefers to make the point that Tu Fu is a person of such strong and deep feelings that aesthetics can be ignored.

A different type of argument is made by Lu Shih-ch'ueh. He wrote, "It is true that in 'Eight Laments' the poems' excessiveness and their extensiveness are both faults, but the greatness of the spirit of poetry resides in 'Eight Laments.'"[21] Lu too excuses the problems in "Eight Laments." He argues, however, that the flaws are not important compared with the poems' greatness. Unlike Wang Ssu-shih, Lu Shih-ch'ueh balances the poetic faults against the overall poetic achievement; he appeals only indirectly to the identity of the author as an ameliorating factor.

Many theses in Tu Fu criticism pass for evaluation and discussion which are in fact variants upon the idea of uniqueness. For example, the popular thesis, often elaborated, that Tu Fu is a poet-historian or a poet-sage is basically an assertion of uniqueness, since each of these categories contains only one member: Tu Fu. In theory, the concept of

19. Preface, *Tu shih hsiang-chu.*
20. Wang Ssu-shih, *Tu i* 7.237.
21. Quoted in *Yü-hsuan T'ang Sung shih-ch'un.*

sincerity makes any poet a unique individual, and any poem can be imitated only to a limited degree. In practice, Tu Fu is regarded as inimitable for a special reason. His sincerity, especially as evidenced in his political and social concern, is tied to the unique historical occurrence of the An Lu-shan rebellion and to his unique witness of it in verse. We find that commentaries repeatedly emphasize historical veracity as the source of Tu Fu's effectiveness. Typically a commentator will write, "The situation is genuine, the language heartrending: if it were not actually so, could there be such a moving line?" And, "What he said was only the truth."[22]

The reasoning seems to be that since it is impossible for any later poet to write of the Troubles in this way, Tu Fu could not be imitated. Such a logically simple view is difficult to counter. On the contrary, it is usually enthusiastically embraced. A common exaggeration takes the form of the statement "Tu Fu alone can do this" and compares other attempts unfavorably with his. Or it will be stated rhetorically that "his poems are not easy to imitate – indeed they cannot be imitated."[23] An often-quoted opinion was expressed by Ch'en Shih-tao, who remarked "Merely not to fail [in imitating Tu Fu] is a mark of skill."[24] A similar view was expressed by the Ch'ing-dynasty critic Wu Ch'iao, who compared the attempts of Han Yü and Huang T'ing-chien unfavorably to their model. They erred, he felt, simply by making the decision to imitate Tu Fu. It should have been apparent, he reasoned, that the record of events which his poems represent was achievable only once, and by Tu Fu. "Tu Fu alone can do this," was his conclusion.[25] It was, presumably, also his starting premise. "Poetry comes out of the person," Wu continued, amplifying his point. "It is because there is the person Tu Fu that there is his poetry."[26]

The critical dismissal of what is, after all, an act of homage by Han Yü and Huang T'ing-chien can be contrasted with the phenomenon of widespread reader identification with Tu Fu. Paradoxically, although imitation of him by other poets was held to be impossible, personal identification with him by the reader was almost required. Many comments about Tu Fu were made in a tone of possessiveness, behind which lies a sense of identification. Perhaps identification is possible because it is granted to oneself, whereas imitation is something detected in another.

22. Wang Ssu-shin, *Tu i* 1.16 and 1.36. Wang's remarks are made of Tu Fu's plaint in "Song of Lo-yu Park" that he has no home to return to, and of his description in "Five Hundred Words" of Emperor Hsuan-tsung's extravagance.
23. Wang Ssu-shih, New Preface, *Tu i.*
24. *Hou-shan shih-hua,* in *Li-tai shih hua,* p. 304.
25. In *Wei-lu shih-hua* 2.10b–11a.
26. Ibid.

The concept of sincerity in traditional Tu Fu criticism conflates two entities, the poet and the poetry, that are already largely overlapping. Through the dynamics of its application, the person and the poetry of Tu Fu have become intricately linked. The multiplicity of the interconnections has, paradoxically, made them invisible and unquestioned. By tracing the different ways in which the poetry and the person are intertwined and by analyzing the many processes that have been at work in the literary criticism of Tu Fu, we can begin to see why his reputation has become so monolithic. Understanding its evolution, it becomes possible to analyze and appreciate his poetry in spite of its formidable estimation and to accept and endorse that estimation wholeheartedly.

Tu Fu died in his fifty-eighth year, disappointed in his hopes for office and unable to provide for his family. His life, darkened by practical difficulties in his final years, had been unsettled and far from distinguished. He likely had no objective reason to believe that his name would survive beyond the memory of his descendants. As it happened, he achieved a renown beyond that of any other literary figure. His name came to stand as the epitome of Chinese literature, and together with Li Po, he defined the golden era of T'ang literature. His personal qualities and the events of his time fused to create the figure of a man who was an unparalleled poet, a loyal subject, a staunch friend, and a devoted husband and father. Ironically, the many disappointments of his life perhaps engendered a closer empathy than unbroken successes would have. Repeatedly, readers spoke of him as a poet who "struggled from day to day," as one for whom "the feelings of that very day leaped upon the page."[27]

Like his predecessors, Tu Fu was committed to the expressive depiction of the visible world, in which human action was conceived to be ineluctably connected with the affairs of state. In his poems, he brought this depiction to a more brilliant and more brilliantly varied level. In addition, he introduced into his poetry the human drama of the life of an individual committed to a Confucian mode of thought. This novel step both raised the visibility of the human factors and personalized the Confucianism that could not be separated from his understanding of the world. The melding of personal traits and public concerns induced in readers a deep identification with one who seemed the embodiment of individual conscience molded in the Confucian tradition.

Appreciation for Tu Fu's work shaped, and was shaped by, the energy that infused the culture of the scholar-official world in the eleventh

27. The first description is by Chao I, *Ou-pei shih-hua* 2.15, the second by Chang Yuan, *Tu shih hui-ts'ui*, Preface, 2b.

century. The extraordinary continuity of that world view and its disposition to value the past, in which Tu Fu occupied so prominent a position, collaborated for a millennium to preserve a stable audience for his poetry. The appearance today, however, of a differently based and differently educated elite serves to raise the question of pertinence, and raises it in a profound way. For the first time since his eleventh-century ascendancy, justification for paying attention to Tu Fu has had to be made anew. What significance will be assigned to his achievements, and to the culture for which he is emblematic is an important issue whose existence is only now becoming clear. At the least, our era has its own questions, as well as a different range of disciplines and contexts on which to draw in formulating answers. This volume represents one attempt to reconsider Tu Fu in circumstances far different from those in which he lived and wrote. That the interpretation of his person and his poetry can so closely concur with tradition, albeit from a different perspective, is an indication that our intellectual world remains somehow continuous with the past. That Tu Fu is able to speak so clearly across the formidable barrier of time represents the most optimistic evidence for his continued survival, testimony to the authenticity of his genius and the infinite humanness of its product, his poetry.

Selected editions of the works of Tu Fu

Chang Yuan 張遠. *Tu shih hui-ts'ui* 杜詩會粹. 24 *chüan*. 1688.

Ch'ien Ch'ien-i 錢謙益 (1582–1664). *Ch'ien chu Tu shih* 錢注杜詩. 20 *chüan*. 1667; rpt., Shanghai: Ku-chi, 1979.

Chin Sheng-t'an 金聖歎. *Ts'ai-tzu Tu shih chieh* 才子杜詩解. 1659; rpt. Honan: Ku-chi, 1986.

Chiu-chia chi-chu Tu shih 九家集注杜詩. 36 *chüan*. 1181; rpt., Harvard-Yenching Institute Sinological Index Series, Suppl. 14. 3 vols. Peiping: Harvard-Yenching, 1940.

Ch'iu Chao-ao 仇兆鰲. *Tu shih hsiang-chu* 杜詩詳註. 28 *chüan*. 1703; rpt., Peking: Chung-hua, 1979.

Chu Ho-ling 朱鶴齡. *Chi-chu Tu kung-pu chi* 輯注杜工部集. Ca. 1667.

Huang Sheng 黃生. *Tu kung-pu shih shuo* 杜工部詩説. 1696.

P'u Ch'i-lung 浦起龍. *Tu Tu hsin-chieh* 讀杜心解. 1724; rpt., Peking: Chung-hua, 1961.

Shan Fu 單復. *Tu Fu yü-te* 杜甫愚得. 1434; rpt., *Tu shih ts'ung-k'an*, 2nd series, no. 11. 3 vols. Taipei: Ta-t'ung, 1974.

Shih Hung-pao 施鴻保. *Tu Tu shih-shuo* 讀杜詩説. 1890; rpt., Hong Kong: Chung-hua, 1964.

Wang Ssu-shih 王嗣奭. *Tui* 杜臆. 1870; rpt., Peking: Chung-hua, 1963.

Wu Chien-ssu 吳見思. *Tu shih lun-wen* 杜詩論文. 1672; rpt., *Tu shih ts'ung-k'an*, 3rd series, no. 27. 4 vols. Taipei: Ta-t'ung, 1974.

Yang Lun 楊倫. *Tu shih ching-ch'üan* 杜詩鏡銓. 20 *chüan*. 1791; rpt., Peking: Chung-hua, 1962.

Works cited

Allen, Joseph R. *In the Voice of Others: Chinese Music Bureau Poetry*. Michigan Monographs in Chinese Studies, no. 63. Ann Arbor: University of Michigan Center for Chinese Studies Publications, 1992.

Birrell, Anne. *Popular Songs and Ballads of Han China*. London: Unwin, 1988.

Chang Chieh 張戒. *Sui-han t'ang shih-hua* 歲寒堂詩話. 2 chüan. In *Li-tai shih-hua hsu-pien*.

Chang Chih-lieh 張志烈. "Chien tu i hsing tsai – t'an Su Shih te p'ing Tu yü hsueh Tu'' 簡牘儀刑在 – 談蘇軾的評杜與學杜. *Ts'ao-t'ang* 2 (1981), 38–43.

Chang, Kang-i Sun. *The Evolution of Chinese "Tz'u" Poetry: From Late T'ang to Northern Sung*. Princeton: Princeton University Press, 1980.

Chao I 趙翼 (1727–1814). *Ou-pei shih-hua* 甌北詩言. Peking: Jen-min, 1963.

Ch'en Ch'ang-chü 陳昌渠. "Pai-nien chien ts'un-mo, lao-luo wu an fang – shuo 'Pa ai shih'" 百年間存歿牢落吾安放 – 説八哀詩. *Ts'ao-t'ang* 草堂 8 (1984), 74–83.

Ch'en Hang 陳沆. *Shih pi hsing chien* 詩比興箋. Preface, 1854. Rpt., Hong Kong: Chung-hua, 1965.

Ch'en Shih-tao 陳師道 (1053–1102). *Hou-shan shih-chu* 後山詩注. Ssu-pu ts'ung-k'an edition.

Hou-shan shih-hua 後山詩話. In *Li-tai shih-hua*.

Ch'en Tzu-lung 陳子龍. *Ch'en Tzu-lung shih chi* 陳子龍詩集. Shanghai: Ku-chi,1983.

Ch'en Wei 陳偉. *Tu Fu shih-hsueh t'an-wei* 杜甫詩學探微. Taipei: Wen-shih-che,1985.

Ch'en Wen-hua 陳文華. *"Pu fei chiang-he wan ku liu" – Tu Fu shih shang hsi* 不癈江河萬古流 – 杜甫詩賞析. Taipei: Wei-wen tu-shu kung-szu, 1978.

Tu Fu chuan-chi T'ang Sung tzu-liao k'ao-pien 杜甫傳記唐宋資料考辨. Taipei: Wen-shih-che, 1987.

Ch'en Yao-chi 陳瑤璣. *Tu kung-pu sheng-p'ing chi ch'i shih-hsueh yuan-yuan he t'e-chih* 杜工部生平及其詩學淵源和特質. Taipei: Hung-tao wen-hua, 1980.

Ch'en Yi-hsin 陳貽焮. *Tu Fu p'ing-chuan* 杜甫評傳. 3 vols. Shanghai: Ku-chi, 1988.

Cheng Ch'ing-tu 陳慶篤, Chiao Yü-yin 焦裕銀, Chang Chung-kang 張忠綱, and Feng Chien-kuo 馮建國. *Tu-chi shu-mu t'i-yao* 杜集書目提要. Chinan: Ch'i-Lu shu-she, 1986.

Cheng Te-k'un. "A Report of a Trip of Archaeological and Historical Investigation in the Provinces of Hopei, Honan and Shantung, 1931." *Yenching Journal of Chinese Studies*, Suppl. 1 (1932), 89–90.

Cherniack, Susan. "Three Great Poems by Tu Fu." Ph.D. thesis, Yale University, 1989.

Ch'i He-hui 祁和暉. " 'Mao-wu wei ch'iu-feng suo p'o ko' hsin t'an" 茅屋為秋風所破歌新探. *Ts'ao-t'ang* 2 (1981), 44–50.

Chiang Fan 蔣凡. "*Ho yueh ying-ling chi* yü Tu Fu" 河嶽英靈集與杜甫. *Ts'ao-t'ang* 5 (1983), 49–53.

Chiang K'uei 姜夔. *Pai-shih shih-shuo* 白石詩説. In *Li-tai shih-hua*.

Ch'iang Yu-an 強幼安. *T'ang-tzu hsi-wen lu* 唐子西文錄. In *Li-tai shih-hua*.

Chien En-ting 簡恩定. *Ch'ing-ch'u Tu-shih-hsueh yen-chiu* 清初杜詩學研究. Taipei: Wen-shih-che, 1986.

Chien Ming-yung 簡明勇. *Tu Fu shih yen-chiu* 杜甫詩研究. Taipei: Hsueh-hai, 1984.

Ch'ieh-chung chi 篋中集. In *T'ang-jen hsuan T'ang-shih*.

Ch'ien Ch'ien-i 錢謙益. *Ch'u-hsueh chi* 初學集. Ssu-pu ts'ung-k'an edition.

Ch'ien-lung Emperor (r. 1736–95). *Yü-hsuan T'ang Sung shih-ch'un* 御選唐宋詩醇. Shanghai: Hung-wen shu-chü, 1895.

Chin Ch'i-hua 金啟華. "Lun Tu Fu te ch'i-ku" 論杜甫的七古. *Ts'ao-t'ang* 2 (1981), 25–34.

Chiu T'ang shu 舊唐書 (Old T'ang History). Peking: Chung-hua, 1975.

Chou Shan 周杉. "Tu Fu's 'Eight Laments.' " Ph.D. thesis, Harvard University, 1984.

"Wen-hsueh sheng-yü te han-yi" 文學聲譽的涵義. *Chiu-chou hsueh-k'an* 九州學刊 3, 2 (1989), 53–66.

Chou Ts'ai-ch'üan 周采泉. *Tu chi shu lu* 杜集書錄. Shanghai: Ku-chi, 1986.

Chu I-tsun 朱彝尊. *P'u-shu-t'ing chi* 曝書亭集. Ssu-pu ts'ung-k'an edition.

Ch'üan T'ang shih 全唐詩. 1706. Peking: Chung-hua, 1960.

Ch'üan T'ang wen 全唐文. Neifu, 1814.

Davis, A. R. *Tu Fu*. New York: Twayne, 1971.

Egan, Ronald C. *The Literary Works of Ou-yang Hsiu (1007–72)*. Cambridge: Cambridge University Press, 1984.

"The Problem of the Repute of *Tz'u* during the Northern Sung." In *Voices in the Song Lyric in China*, edited by Pauline Yu, pp. 191–225. Berkeley: University of California Press, 1994.

Fang Yü 方瑜. *Chan i hua yü* 沾衣花雨. Taipei: Yuan-ching, 1982.

Tu Fu K'uei-chou shih hsi-lun 杜甫夔州詩析論. Taipei: Yu-shih, 1985.

Fu Keng-sheng 傅庚生. *Tu shih hsi-yi* 杜詩析疑. Shensi: Shensi jen-min, 1979.

Tu Fu shih-lun 杜甫詩論. Shanghai: Ku-chi, 1985.

Graham, A. C. *Poems of the Late T'ang*. Baltimore: Penguin Books, 1965.

van Gulik, Robert Hans. *The Gibbon in China: An Essay in Chinese Animal Lore*. Leiden: Brill, 1969.

Hawkes, David. *A Little Primer of Tu Fu*. Oxford: Oxford University Press, 1967.

Hinton, David. *The Selected Poems of Tu Fu*. New York: New Directions, 1989.

Hirose Tansō 廣賴淡窗. *Tansō shiwa* 淡窗詩話. In *Nihon shiwa sōsho* 日本詩話叢書. Vol. 4. Tokyo: Tōkyō bunkaidō, 1920.

Ho Shu-chen 何淑貞. *Tu Fu wu-yen chin-t'i-shih yü-fa yen-chiu* 杜甫五言近體詩語法研究. Taipei: Fu-chi wen-hua, 1983.

Ho-yueh ying-ling chi 河嶽英靈集. In *T'ang-jen hsuan T'ang shih*.

Hsiao Li-hua 蕭麗華. *Tu Fu: Ku-jin shih-shih ti-yi jen* 杜甫 – 古今詩史第一人. Taipei: Yu-shih, 1988.

Hsiao Ti-fei 蕭滌非. *Tu Fu yen-chiu* 杜甫研究. Rev. ed. Chi-nan: Ch'i-Lu shu-she, 1980.

Hsin T'ang shu 新唐書 (New T'ang History). Peking: Chung-hua, 1975.

Hsu Jen-fu 徐仁甫. *Tu shih chu-chieh shang-ch'ueh* 杜詩注解商榷. Peking: Chung-hua, 1979.

Hsu Tsung 許總. "Tu Fu 'i shih wei wen' lun" 杜甫以詩為文論. *Ts'ao-t'ang* 2 (1981), 19–25.

Hu Chen-heng 胡震亨 (1569–1644). *T'ang-yin kuei-ch'ien* 唐音癸籤.

Hu Ch'uan-an 胡傳安. *Shih-sheng Tu Fu tui hou-shih shih-jen te ying-hsiang* 詩聖杜甫對後世詩人的影響. Taipei: Yu-shih, 1985.

Hu Hsiao-shih 胡小石. "Tu Fu 'Pei-cheng' hsiao-chien" 杜甫北征小箋. In *Tu Fu yen-chiu lun-wen chi*, 3: 205–18.

Hu Shih 胡適. *Pai-hua wen-hsueh shih* 白話文學史. Preface, 1939. N.p.: Wen-kuang t'u-shu kung-ssu, n.d.

Hu Tzu 胡仔 (1082–1143). *T'iao-hsi yü-yin ts'ung-hua* 苕溪漁隱叢話. Peking: Jen-min, 1981.

Hu Ying-lin 胡應麟. *Shih-sou* 詩藪. Shanghai: Ku-chi, 1958.

Hua Wen-hsuan 華文軒, ed. *Tu Fu chüan* 杜甫卷. 3 vols. Peking: Chung-hua, 1982.

Huang Chih-ch'üan 黃犀荃. "Tu shih tsai Chung-kuo shih-shih shang te ti-wei" 杜詩在中國詩史上的地位. *Ts'ao-t'ang* 5 (1983), 1–6.

Hung, William. *Tu Fu: China's Greatest Poet*. Cambridge, Mass.: Harvard University Press, 1952.

A Supplementary Volume of Notes for "Tu Fu: China's Greatest Poet." Cambridge, Mass.: Harvard University Press, 1952.

Jao Tsung-i 饒宗頤. "Lun Tu Fu K'uei-chou shih" 論杜甫夔州詩. *Chūgoku bungaku hō* 中國文學報 17 (1962), 104–18.

"Tu Fu yü T'ang shih" 杜甫與唐詩. In Wu Hung-i 吳宏一 and Lü Cheng-hui 呂正惠, eds., *Chung-kuo ku-tien wen-hsueh lun-wen ching-hsuan ts'ung-k'an: shih-ke lei* 中國古典文學論文精選叢刊：詩歌類. Taipei: Yu-shih, 1980.

Kao Hsi-tseng 高熙曾. "Tu shih gei-yü Nan-Sung ai-kuo-shih-jen te ying-hsiang" 杜詩給於南宋愛國詩人的影響. In *Tu Fu yen-chiu lun-wen-chi*, 3: 76–84.

Ke Li-fang 葛立方. *Yun-yü yang-ch'iu* 韻語陽秋. In *Li-tai shih-hua*.

Ku yao-yen 古謠諺. Edited by Tu Wen-lan 杜文瀾 (1815–81). Peking: Chung-hua, 1958.

Ku Yen-wu 顧炎武 (1613–82). *Jih-chih lu* 日知錄. Ssu-pu pei-yao edition.

Kuo-hsiu chi 國秀集. In *T'ang-jen hsuan T'ang-shih.*

Kuo Shao-yü 郭紹虞. *Sung shih-hua chi-i* 宋詩話輯佚. 2 vols. Peking: Chung-hua, 1980.

Kuo Shih-hsin 郭世欣. "Ch'eng-tu ts'ao-t'ang i-chih k'ao" 成都草堂遺址考. *Ts'ao-t'ang* 1 (1981), 67–79.

Kuo Tseng-hsin 郭曾炘. *Tu Tu cha-chi* 讀杜劄記. Shanghai: Ku-chi, 1984.

Kurokawa Yōichi 黑川洋一. "Chū-Tō yori Hoku-Sōmatsu ni itaru To Ho no hakken ni tsuite" 中唐より北宋末に至る杜甫の発見について. *Shitennōji Joshi Daigaku kiyō* 四天王寺女子大學紀要 3 (1970), 81–112.

Li Ju-lun 李汝倫. *Tu-shih lun kao* 杜詩論稿. Canton: Kuang-tung jen-min, 1983.

Li-tai shih-hua 歷代詩話. Edited by He Wen-huan 何文煥. 1770. 2 vols. Peking: Chung-hua, 1981.

Li-tai shih-hua hsu-pien 歷代詩話續編. Edited by Ting Fu-pao 丁福保. 1915. 3 vols. Peking: Chung-hua, 1983.

Liang Ch'i-ch'ao 梁啟超. "Ch'ing-sheng Tu Fu" 情聖杜甫. In *Yin-ping shih he-chi*, 7:37–50. Peking: Chung-hua, 1989.

Liao Po-ang 廖柏昂. "Lun Tu shih te 'tun ts'uo'" 論杜詩的頓挫. *Ts'ao-t'ang* 6, 2 (1983).

Ling Tzu-liu 凌子鎏. *T'ang-shih hsuan-pen Tu Fu shih ts'ai-hsuan t'ung-chi* 唐詩選本杜甫詩採選統計. Hong Kong: Chu-hai shu-yuan, 1970.

Liu Chung-he 劉中和. *Tu shih yen-chiu* 杜詩研究. Taipei: Yi-chih shu-chü, 1985.

Liu Hsin-sheng 劉新生. "T'an T'ang-jen ch'ou-tseng Tu Fu shih" 談唐人酬贈杜甫詩. *Tu Fu yen-chiu hsueh-k'an* 杜甫研究學刊 2 (1988), 46–51.

Liu K'ai-yang 劉開楊. *T'ang shih t'ung-lun* 唐詩通論. Ch'eng-tu: Ssu-ch'uan jen-min, 1983.

Liu Pin 劉攽. *Chung-shan shih-hua* 中山詩話. In *Li-tai shih-hua.*

Lu Chih-hsuan 魯質軒. *Tu kung-pu shih-hua chi-chin* 杜工部詩話集錦. Taipei: Chung-hua, 1979.

Lü Cheng-hui 呂正惠. "Tu Fu yü jih-ch'ang sheng-huo" 杜甫與日常生活. In *T'ang-shih lun-wen hsuan-chi* 唐詩論文選集, pp. 287–98. Taipei: Ch'ang-an, 1985.

Lun yü 論語. Translated by James Legge, *Confucius.* In *The Chinese Classics.* 5 vols. Hong Kong: Hong Kong University Press, 1960.

Ma Ch'ung-ch'i 馬重奇. *Tu Fu ku-shih yun-tu* 杜甫古詩韻讀. Peking: Chung-kuo chan-wang, 1985.

McGraw, David R. *Du Fu's Laments from the South.* Honolulu: University of Hawaii Press, 1992.

McMullen, David. *State and Scholars in T'ang China.* Cambridge: Cambridge University Press, 1988.

Meng Ch'i 孟棨. *Pen-shih shih* 本事詩. Preface, 886. In *Li-tai shih-hua hsu-pien.*

Meng-tzu 孟子. Translated by James Legge, *The Works of Mencius.* In *The Chinese Classics.* 5 vols. Hong Kong: Hong Kong University Press, 1960.

Muir, Edwin. *Scottish Journey.* 1935. Rpt., London: Fontana, 1985.

Owen, Stephen. *The Great Age of Chinese Poetry: The High T'ang.* New Haven: Yale University Press, 1981.

Princeton Encyclopedia of Poetry and Poetics, edited by Alex Preminger, Frank J. Warnke, and O. B. Hardison, Jr. Princeton: Princeton University Press, 1975.

Rotours, Robert des. *Traité des examens.* Paris: Ernest Leroux, 1932.

   Traité des fonctionnaires et traité de l'armée. 2 vols. Leiden: Brill, 1947–8.

Ruskin, John. *The Literary Criticism of John Ruskin.* Edited by Harold Bloom. Garden City, N.Y.: Doubleday, 1965.

Shih Chih-ts'un 施蟄存. *T'ang shih pai-hua* 唐詩百話. Shanghai: Ku-chi, 1987.

Shih Jun-chang 施閏章. *Huo-chai shih-hua* 蠖齋詩話. 1 *chüan.* In Chao-tai ts'ung-shu, no. 62.

Sun Wang 孫望. *Yuan Tz'u-shan nien-p'u* 元次山年譜. Shanghai: Ku-tien, 1957.

Sung shih-hua chi-i. See Kuo Shao-yü.

Ta-T'ang liu-tien 大唐六典. 1724.

T'an Wen-hsing 譚文興. "Tu Fu wei-shemme miao-hsieh lao-tung jen-min te chi-k'u" 杜甫為什麼描寫勞動人民的疾苦. *Ts'ao-t'ang* 1 (1981), 63–6.

T'ang-jen hsuan T'ang shih 唐人選唐詩. Shanghai: Chung-hua, 1958.

Teng K'uei-ying 鄧魁英. "Shih 'shih-shih'" 釋詩史. *Ts'ao-t'ang,* 7 (1984), 6–15.

Ts'ai Ch'i 蔡啟. *Ts'ai K'uan-fu shih-hua* 蔡寬夫詩話. In *Sung shih-hua chi-i.*

Ts'ai tiao chi 才調集. In *T'ang-jen hsuan T'ang-shih.*

Ts'ao Mu-fan 曹暮樊. *Tu-shih tsa shuo* 杜詩雜說. Ch'eng-tu: Ssu-ch'uan jen-min, 1984.

Tseng Tsao-chuang 曾棗莊. "Lun T'ang-jen tui Tu shih te t'ai-tu" 論唐人對杜詩的態度. *Ts'ao-t'ang* 1,1 (1981), 54–62.

Tu Fu chüan. See Hua Wen-hsuan.

Tu Fu nien-pu 杜甫年譜. Edited by Ssu-ch'uan wen-shih yen-chiu-kuan. Ch'eng-tu: Ssu-ch'uan jen-min, 1981

Tu Fu yen-chiu lun-wen-chi 杜甫研究論文集. 3 vols. Peking: Chung-hua, 1963.

Wang Fu-chih 王夫之. *T'ang-shih p'ing-hsuan* 唐詩評選. In *Ch'uan-shan yi-shu* 船山遺書, 1840–2.

Wang Li-chi 王利器. "Chi Tu Fu yu hou yü Chiang-chin" 記杜甫有後於江津. *Ts'ao-t'ang* 2,2 (1981), 62–4.

Wang San-ch'ing 王三慶. "Tu Fu shih-yun k'ao" 杜甫詩韻考. M.A. thesis, Taiwan Normal University, 1973.

Wei Ch'ing-chih 魏慶之. *Shih-jen yü-hsieh* 詩人玉屑. Preface, 1244. Shanghai: Ku-chi, 1978.

Wen T'ien-hsiang 文天祥. *Wen-shan hsien-sheng ch'üan-chi* 文山先生全集. Shanghai: Shang-wu, 1934.

Wen-yuan ying-hua 文苑英華. 1567 edition. Rpt., Taipei: Hua-wen shu-chü, 1965.

Wu Ch'iao 吳喬. *Wei-lu shih-hua* 圍爐詩話. Taipei: Kuang-wen, 1973.

Wu Hung-i 吳宏一. *Ch'ing-tai shih-hsueh ch'u-t'an* 清代詩學初探. Taipei: Mu-t'ung, 1977.

Yang Sung-nien 楊松年. *Chung-kuo ku-tien wen-hsueh p'i-p'ing-lun chi* 中國古典文學批評論集. Hongkong: San-lien, 1987.

Yeh Chia-ying 葉嘉瑩. *Chia-ling t'an shih* 嘉陵談詩. Taipei, San-min, 1970.

Yeh Hsieh 葉燮. *Yuan shih* 原詩. 4 *chüan.* Wu-shih Shan-fang.

Yeh Meng-te 葉夢得. *Shih-lin shih-hua* 石林詩話. In *Li-tai shih-hua*.

Yen Yü 嚴羽. *Ts'ang-lang shih-hua* 滄浪詩話. Commentary by Kuo Shao-yü. Peking: Jen-min, 1961.

Yoshikawa Kōjiro. *An Introduction to Sung Poetry*. Translated by Burton Watson. Cambridge, Mass.: Harvard University Press, 1967.

"Tu Fu's Poetics and Poetry: Farewell Lecture at Kyoto University (1967)." Published in English in *Yoshikawa Kōjiro zenshū* 吉川辛次郎全集. 22 vols. Chikuma shobō, 1968–70.

Yu hsuan chi 又玄集. In *T'ang-jen hsuan T'ang-shih.*

Yü-t'ai hsin-yung 玉臺新詠. Compiled by Hsu Ling 徐陵 (507–83). 2 vols. Peking: Chung-hua, 1985.

Yueh-fu shih-chi 樂府詩集. Compiled by Kuo Mao-ch'ien 郭茂倩 (fl. 1084). Peking: Chung-hua, 1982.

Poems by Tu Fu

English titles

After a lengthy stay in K'uei Prefecture, I leave White Emperor City by boat in
spring of 768 and sail out of Ch'ü-t'ang Gorge: about to go to Chiang-ling, I
write a poem of forty rhymes while afloat. Ta-li san-nien ch'un Pai-ti ch'eng
fang-ch'uan ch'u Ch'ü-t'ang hsia chiu-chü K'uei-fu chiang shih Chiang-ling
p'iao-po yu shih ssu-shih yun.

Again Presented to Mr. Wu. Yu ch'eng Wu-lang.

Another Poem Shown to My Two Sons. Yu shih liang-er.

Another Visit to General He. Five poems. Ch'ung-kuo He-shih, wu shou.

Autumn Clearness. Ch'iu ch'ing.

Autumn Meditations. Eight poems. Ch'iu-hsing, pa-shou.

Autumn Wind. Ch'iu-feng

Ballad of Army Carts. Ping-ch'e hsing.

Ballad of Beauties. Li-jen hsing.

Ballad of Firewood Carriers. Fu-hsin hsing.

Ballad of Mei-p'i Lake. Mei-p'i hsing.

Ballad of an Old Cypress Ku-po hsing.

Ballad of One Hundred Accumulated Worries. Pai-yu chi hsing.

Ballad of P'eng-ya. P'eng-ya hsing.

Bound Chickens. Fu chi hsing.

Ch'eng-tu Prefecture. Ch'eng-tu fu.

Ch'iang Village. Three poems. Ch'iang ts'un, san-shou.

Climbing the City Wall of Tzu-chou on the Ninth of the Ninth. Chiu-jih teng
Tzu-chou ch'eng.

Climbing the Hill in the Back of the Garden. Shang hou-yuan shan-chiao.

Climbing to a Height. Teng kao.

Climbing to the Height behind Nang at Dusk. Wan teng Nang-shang t'ang.

Climbing Tz'u-en Temple with Other Gentlemen. T'ung chu-kung teng Tz'u-en-
ssu-t'a.

Climbing Yueh-yang Tower. Teng Yueh-yang lou.

Cold Food Festival. Han-shih.

Convalescing in the Garden on a Quiet Day, about to Plant Autumn Vegetables,

Lament by Serpentine River. Ai chiang-t'ou.

Lament for Ch'en-t'ao. Pei Ch'en-t'ao.

Lament for Ch'ing-pan. Pei Ch'ing-pan.

Late Clearing. Wan ch'ing.

Leaning on My Staff. Yi chang.

Leaving Kung-an at Dawn. Hsiao fa Kung-an.

Leaving the Imperial Chancellery Late. Wan-ch'u tsuo-yi.

Left as Farewell for Two Gentlemen of Chi-hsien yuan, Ts'ui Kuo-fu and Yü Hsui-lieh. Feng liu-tseng Chi-hsien yuan Ts'ui Yü er-hsueh-shih.

Living as a Sojourner. K'e-chü.

Living on the water, I express my feelings, presented to you gentlemen. Shui-su ch'ien-hsing feng-ch'eng ch'ün-kung.

Madman. K'uang-fu.

Matching Prefect Yuan's "Ch'ung-ling hsing." T'ung Yuan Shih-chun "Ch'ung-ling hsing."

The Moon. Three poems. Yueh, san-shou.

The Moon on the Hundred and Fifth Night. Yi-pai-wu-jih tui yueh.

Moonlit Night. Yueh-yeh.

A Morning Walk through Cold Rain to See the Garden and Woods. Han-yü chao-hsing shih yuan-lin.

Moving to Live in K'uei-chou. Yi-chü K'uei-chou-kuo.

My Feelings. Two poems. Yung-huai, er-shou.

Night at the Pavilion. Ke-yeh.

Northern Neighbor. Pei lin.

Now that it's autumn, my agent Chang Wang, who had gone to oversee the farmwork at East Village, reports harvest is near, and early this morning I sent the girl slave Ah Chi and the boy servant Ah Tuan to bring back news. Ch'iu hsing-kuan Chang Wang tu-ts'u Tung-chu hao-tao hsiang pi, ch'ing-ch'en ch'ien nü-nu Ah Chi shu-tzu Ah Tuan wang wen.

Observing Fishermen, a Song. Kuan ta-yü ke.

Observing Fishermen, Another Song. Yu kuan ta-yü ke.

The Official at Hsin-an. Hsin-an li.

The Official at Shih-hao. Shih-hao li.

Old and Sick. Lao ping.

An Old Country Man. Yeh-lao.

On a Boat. Chin t'ing.

On a winter's visit to the Taoist temple at Chin-hua Mountain, I find the ruins of the academy attended by the Late Reminder Lord Ch'en. Tung tao Chin-hua shan kuan yin te ku shih-yi Ch'en kung hsueh-t'ang yi-chi.

On Current Events. Chi shih.

On Cutting Trees. K'e-fa-mu.

On Departing for Home in Late Autumn, a Farewell to Friends and Relatives at Military Headquarters. Mu-ch'iu chiang kuei Ch'in liu-pieh Hu-nan mu-fu ch'in-yu.

On Hearing of the Recovery of Ho-nan and Ho-pei by Imperial Troops. Wen kuan-chün shou Ho-nan Ho-pei.

One Hundred Rhymes Expressing My Feelings on an Autumn Day in K'uei
   Prefecture. Presented to Cheng Shen, Director of the Imperial Library, and to
   Li Chih-fang, Adviser to the Heir Apparent. Ch'iu-jih K'uei fu yung-huai feng-
   chi Cheng chien Shen Li pin-k'e Chih-fang yi-pai-yun.
Orange Grove. Kan-lin.
Overnight at Hua-shih Garrison. Su Hua-shih shu.
Overnight in Rooms by the River. Su chiang-pien ke.
Overnight in Spring at the Imperial Chancellery. Ch'un su tso-sheng.
Parting from No One. Wu-chia pieh.
Parting of the Aged. Ch'ui-lao pieh.
Parting of the Newlyweds. Hsin-hun pieh.
The Pass at Lu-tzu. Sai Lu-tzu.
Piping Water. Yin-shui.
Presented to the Deputy Administrator Yü Fifteenth. Tseng Yü shih-wu ssu-ma.
Presented to the Recluse Wei Eighth. Tseng Wei-pa ch'u-shih.
Quitting Shu. Ch'ü shu.
Rain in the Village. Ts'un yü.
Rainy View from the Western Apartment. Hsi-ke yü-wang.
Relieving Pent-up Feelings. Ch'ien hsing.
Remembering the Past. Yi-hsi.
Retreating from Lang-chou to the Shu Mountains with My Wife and Children.
   Three poems. Tzu Lang-chou ling ch'i-tzu ch'ueh fu Shu-shan hsing, san shou.
Return. Kuei.
Return in Spring. Ch'un kuei.
The River Rises. Chiang chang.
A River Village. Chiang ts'un.
River Village in the Ninth Month. Chi-ch'iu chiang-ts'un.
Seeing off Prefect Lu of Ling-chou, Departing to Take up his Duties. Sung Ling-
   chou Lu Shih-chun fu-jen.
Seeing off Wei Feng, Departing for Lang-chou as Military Administrator. Sung
   Wei Feng shang Lang-chou lu-shih-ts'an-chün.
Seeking out Ts'ui Chi and Li Feng on the Last Day of the Month. Hui-jih hsun
   Ts'ui Chi Li Feng.
Sent to be Inscribed on the Thatched Hut by the River. Chi-t'i chiang-wai ts'ao-
   t'ang.
Serpentine. Two poems. Ch'ü chiang, er-shou.
Seven Songs, Composed in the Year 759 While Living Temporarily in T'ung-ku
   County. Ch'ien-yuan chung yü-chü T'ung-ku hsien tsuo ke, ch'i-shou.
Shown to the Native Servant Ah-Tuan. Shih liao-nu Ah-tuan.
Since Peace. Tzu p'ing.
Sojourn in the Thatched Hut. K'e t'ang.
Song at Year's End. Sui-yen hsing.
Song of Barley. Ta-mai.
Song of Boatmen. Tsui-neng hsing.
Song of Lo-yu Park. Lo-yu yuan ke.

Song of My Thatched Roof Torn by Autumn Winds. Mao-wu wei ch'iu-feng suo
  p'o ke.
Southern Neighbor. Nan lin.
Southwest Terrace at Mei-p'i Lake. Mei p'i hsi-nan t'ai.
Spring Prospect. Ch'un wang.
Spring Waters. Ch'un shui.
Stopped by Rain, Unable to Return to the Orange Grove in West Nang. Tsu-yü
  pu-te kuei Nang-hsi kan-lin.
T'ai-sui Day. T'ai-sui jih.
Taking in the Gorge Scenery. Hsia-chung lan wu.
Ten Rhymes for Lord Yen on His Return to Court. Feng-sung Yen kung ju-ch'ao
  shih-yun.
Thatched Hut. Ts'ao-t'ang.
Thirty-six Rhymes Written on the Boat, in Bed with a Fever, and Presented to
  Friends and Relatives in Hu-nan. Feng-ping chou-chung fu-chen shu-huai san-
  shih-liu-yun feng-ch'eng Hu-nan ch'in-yu.
Thoughts. Two poems. Hsieh-huai, er-shou.
Thoughts while Traveling at Night. Lü-yeh shu-huai.
Three Officials. (The Official at Hsin-an, at T'ung-kuan, and at Shih-hao.) San li.
Three Partings. (Parting of the Newlyweds, of the Aged, and from No One.) San
  pieh.
Tsung-wu's Birthday. Tsung-wu sheng-jih.
Twenty-two Rhymes Presented to Assistant Secretary of the Left, Wei Chi. Feng-
  tseng Wei tsuo-ch'eng-chang er-shih-er-yun.
Urging Tsung-wen to Put up the Chicken Coop. Ts'ui Tsung-wen shu chi-shan.
Voicing My Feelings. Ch'ien huai.
Voicing My Worries. Ch'ien ch'ou.
Wanderings of My Prime. Chuang yu.
Weary Night. Chüan-yeh.
White Emperor City. Pai-ti.
Winter Solstice. Hsiao-chih.
Word Recently Came. Chin wen.
Written in Late Spring on the Wall of a Newly Rented Thatched Hut in West
  Nang. Five poems. Mu-ch'un t'i Nang-hsi hsin-lin ts'ao-wu, wu-shou.
Written on a Boat during the Small Cold Food Festival. Hsiao-han-shih chou-
  chung tsuo.
Written to Match Secretary Chia Chih's "Morning Court at Ta-ming Palace."
  Feng-ho Chia Chih she-jen "Tsao chao Ta-ming kung."
Year after Year. Li-li.
Year's End. Sui-mu.

Chinese titles

The numbers refer to the page, *chüan*, and poem number of the *Chiu-chia*
edition, as printed and numbered for use in the Harvard-Yenching Concordance
to the poems of Tu Fu.

Ch'un-yeh hsi yü 春夜喜雨. Enjoying the Rain on a Spring Night. 370/23/5.

Ch'ung-kuo He-shih, wu-shou 重過何氏五首. Another Visit to General He. Five poems. 285/18/20.

Ch'ü chiang, er-shou 曲江二首. Serpentine. Two poems. 308/19/30.

Ch'ü chiang tui-chiu 曲江對酒. Drinking by Serpentine River. 308/19/31.

Ch'ü Shu 去蜀. Quitting Shu. 413/27/1.

Ch'ü shu-tzu chai ts'ang-er 驅豎子摘蒼耳. Getting the Boy Servant to Pick Dark Mushrooms. 161/11/26.

Chüan-yeh 倦夜. Weary Night. 389/24/47.

Chueh-chü, ssu-shou 絕句四首. Four Quatrains. 408/26/26 A–D.

Er lung 耳聾. Deaf. 502/27/1.

Fa T'ung-ku hsien 發同谷縣. Departure from T'ung-ku County. 96/6/17.

Fan chao 反照. Evening Sunlight. 433/28/22. (Seven-character regulated.)

Fan chao 反照. Evening Sunlight. 511/32/27. (Five-character regulated.)

Fan hsi 泛溪. Floating on the Stream. 106/7/6.

Feng-ho Chia Chih she-jen "Tsao chao Ta-ming kung" 奉和賈至舍人早朝大明宮. Written to Match Chia Chih's "Morning Court at Ta-ming Palace." 309/19/34.

Feng liu-tseng Chi-hsien yuan Ts'ui Yü er hsueh-shih 奉留贈集賢院崔于二學士. Left as Farewell for Two Gentlemen of Chi-hsien yuan, Ts'ui Kuo-fu and Yü Hsiu-lieh. 293/19/1.

Feng-ping chou-chung fu-chen shu-huai san-shih-liu-yun feng-ch'eng Hu-nan ch'in-yu 風疾舟中伏枕書懷三十六韻奉呈湖南親友. Thirty-six Rhymes Written on the Boat, in Bed with a Fever, and Presented to Friends and Relatives in Hu-nan. 556/36/12.

Feng-sung Yen kung ju-ch'ao shih-yun 奉送嚴公入朝十韻. Ten Rhymes for Lord Yen on His Return to Court. 374/23/17.

Feng-tseng Wei tsuo-ch'eng-chang er-shih-er-yun 奉贈韋左丞丈二十二韻. Twenty-two Rhymes Presented to Assistant Secretary of the Left, Wei Chi. 1/1/1.

Fu chi hsing 縛雞行. Bound Chickens. 186/13/13.

Fu-hsin hsing 負薪行. Ballad of Firewood Carriers. 186/13/14.

Han-yü chao-hsing shih yuan-lin 寒雨朝行視園樹. A Morning Walk through Cold Rain to See the Garden and Woods. 475/30/43.

Han shih 寒食. Cold Food Festival. 358/22/13.

Hen pieh 恨別. Hating to Part. 349/21/27.

Hsi-ke yü-wang 西閣雨望. Rainy View from the Western Apartment. 492/31/22.

Hsia-chung lan wu 峽中覽物. Taking in the Gorge Scenery. 448/29/10.

Hsia-jih hsiao-yuan san-ping chiang chung ch'iu-ts'ai tu-le keng-niu chien shu ch'u-mu 暇日小園散病將種秋菜督勒耕牛兼書觸目. Convalescing in the Garden on a Quiet Day, about to Plant Autumn Vegetables, Supervising the Plow Ox, and Writing of What Meets My Eye. 189/13/18.

Hsiao-chih 小至. Winter Solstice. 515/32/41.

Hsiao fa Kung-an 曉發公安. Leaving Kung-an at Dawn. 541/35/1.

Hsiao-han-shih chou-chung tsuo 小寒食舟中作. Written on a Boat during the Small Cold Food Festival. 562/36/20.

7/15.

Pei Ch'en-t'ao 悲陳陶. Lament for Ch'en-t'ao. 44/2/22.

Pei cheng 北征. Journey North. 47/3/3.

Pei Ch'ing-pan 悲青坂. Lament for Ch'ing-pan. 45/2/23.

Pei lin 北鄰. Northern Neighbor. 347/21/20.

P'eng-ya hsing 彭衙行. Ballad of P'eng-ya. 58/3/19.

Pin chin 賓至. A guest comes. 344/21/8.

Ping-ch'e hsing 兵車行. Ballad of Army Carts. 9/1/12.

Pu chien 不見. I Haven't Seen. 381/24/12.

Sai Lu-tzu 塞蘆子. The Pass at Lu-tzu. 57/3/18.

San ch'ou, er-shou 散愁二首. Dispelling Worries. Two poems. 410/26/36.

San li 三吏. Three Officials. (Hsin-an li, T'ung-kuan li, and Shih-hao li.) 53/3/9–11.

San pieh 三別. Three Partings. (Hsin-hun pieh, Ch'iu-lao pieh, and Wu-chia pieh.) 54/3/12–14.

Shang-ch'iu, 傷秋. Grieved by Autumn. 466/30/30.

Shang-ch'un, wu-shou 傷春五首. Grieved by Spring. Five poems. 424/28/23 A–E.

Shang hou-yuan shan-chiao 上後園山腳. Climbing the Hill in the Back of the Garden. 161/11/25.

Shih-hao li 石壕吏. The Official at Shih-hao. 54/3/11.

Shih liao-nu Ah-Tuan 示獠奴阿段. Shown to the Native Servant Ah-Tuan. 433/28/23.

Shu huai 述懷. Describing My Feelings. 46/3/1.

Shui-su ch'ien-hsing feng-ch'eng ch'ün-kung 水宿遣興奉呈羣公. Living on the water, I express my feelings, presented to you gentlemen. 528/34/2.

Su chiang-pien ke 宿江邊閣. Overnight in Rooms by the River. 487/31/4.

Su Hua-shih shu 宿花石戍. Overnight at Hua-shih Garrison. 246/16/9.

Sui-mu 歲暮. Year's End. 352/21/35.

Sui-yen hsing 歲晏行. Song at Year's End. 229/15/12.

Sung Ling-chou Lu shih-chun fu-jen 送陵州路使君赴任. Seeing off Prefect Lu of Ling-chou, Departing to Take up His Duties. 390/24/55.

Sung Wei Feng shang Lang-chou lu-shih ts'an-chün 送韋諷上閬州錄事參軍. Seeing off Wei Feng, Departing for Lang-chou as Military Administrator. 118/8/7.

Ta-li san-nien ch'un Pai-ti ch'eng fang-ch'uan ch'u Ch'ü-t'ang hsia chiu-chü K'uei-fu chiang shih Chiang-ling p'iao-po yu shih ssu-shih yun 大曆三年春白帝城放船出瞿塘峽久居夔府將適江陵漂泊有詩凡四十韻. After a lengthy stay in K'uei Prefecture, I leave White Emperor City by boat in spring of 768 and sail out of Ch'ü-t'ang Gorge: about to go to Chiang-ling, I write a poem of forty rhymes while afloat. 523/33/10.

Ta-mai hsing 大麥行. Song of Barley. 130/9/13.

T'ai-sui jih 太歲日. T'ai-sui Day. 519/33/1.

T'ang ch'eng 堂成. The Hut Completed. 344/21/10.

Teng kao 登高. Climbing to a Height. 411/26/39.

Teng lou 登樓. Climbing the Tower. 353/21/42.

Yi-chü K'uei-chou-kuo 移居夔州郭. Moving to Live in K'uei-chou. 420/27/27.

Yi-hsi 憶昔. Remembering the Past. Poem 2. 116/8/14B.

Yi-pai-wu-jih tui yueh 一百五日對月. The Moon on the Hundred and Fifth Night. 296/19/11.

Yin-shui 引水. Piping Water. 148/11/2.

Yu ch'eng Wu-lang 又呈吳郎. Again Presented to Mr. Wu. 434/28/25.

Yu kuan ta-yü ke 又觀打魚歌. Observing Fishermen, Another Song. 140/10/10.

Yu shih liang-er 又示兩兒. Another Poem Shown to My Two Sons. 423/27/38.

Yuan 園. The Garden. 43/28/15.

Yuan-jen sung kua 園人送瓜. A Gardener Makes a Present of Melons. 158/11/19.

Yueh, san-shou 月三首. The Moon. Three poems. 431/28/14.

Yueh-yeh 月夜. Moonlit Night. 295/19/6.

Yung-huai, er-shou 詠懷二首. My Feelings. Two poems. 239/15/24.

Index

[All poems are by Tu Fu unless otherwise indicated.]